FEMINIST ISSUES
in
LITERARY
SCHOLARSHIP

FEMINIST ISSUES
in
LITERARY
SCHOLARSHIP

Edited by
Shari Benstock

Indiana University Press
Bloomington & Indianapolis

Manufactured in the United States of America

Library of Congress Cataloging-in-Publication Data

Feminist issues in literary scholarship.
    Includes index.
    1. Feminist literary criticism.   I. Benstock, Shari, 1944–   .
PN98.W64F37   1987   801'.95'088042   85-45984
ISBN 0–253–32233–2
ISBN 0–253–20414–3 (pbk.)

1 2 3 4 5 91 90 89 88 87

ACKNOWLEDGMENTS

Ten of the essays included in this collection were originally published in volume 3 (1984–1985) of *Tulsa Studies in Women's Literature*—those by Auerbach and Baym (each in slightly altered forms), Benstock, Donovan, Gardiner, Marcus, Newton, Robinson, Showalter, and Treichler. The editorial assistance of Jan Calloway, Susan Hastings, Mary O'Toole, and Celia Patterson in the original publication of these essays is greatly appreciated. That volume won the Conference of Editors of Learned Journals award for best special issue of a scholarly journal at the 1985 Modern Language Association meeting in Chicago. Hortense J. Spillers's essay is reprinted from *Feminist Studies*, vol. 9, no. 2 (1983), 293–323, by permission of the publisher, Feminist Studies, Inc., c/o Women's Studies Program, University of Maryland, College Park, Maryland 20742. Susan Stanford Friedman's essay first appeared in Michael King, ed., *H.D.: Woman and Poet* (Orono, Maine: National Poetry Foundation, 1986) and is used with the permission of the National Poetry Foundation.

CONTENTS

FEMINIST ISSUES
in
LITERARY
SCHOLARSHIP

INTRODUCTION

Catharine R. Stimpson

Feminist literary criticism in the West, like women's writing in the West, begins with Sappho in the mid-seventh century B.C. In one paring of language, she writes:

> I took my lyre and said:
>
> Come now, my heavenly
> tortoise shell: become
> a speaking instrument[1]

Sappho's words dramatize a precondition for feminist criticism: the willingness to be aware of the meanings of the juncture, the crossing, of a woman and a literary act.

Despite the length of its lineage, feminist criticism did not become a force with a name until the mid-twentieth century A.D. One of its two major texts was *A Room of One's Own*, which Virginia Woolf issued in England in 1929; the second was *The Second Sex*, which Simone de Beauvoir published in France in 1949. Signifying the lack of a history that might have bonded women to each other was the brevity of *The Second Sex's* one-sentence response to the prior text: "*In A Room of One's Own* Virginia Woolf contrasts the meager and restricted life of an imaginary sister of Shakespeare with his life of learning and adventure."[2]

Woolf and de Beauvoir display contrasting rhetorics. Feminist critics now negotiate between them, although writers within colleges and universities are more apt to resemble de Beauvoir's regularities than Woolf's reconnoiterings. Passionately, yet ironically, Woolf plays with a story, a fiction, about her narrator's quest for a vision of "Women and Fiction." Magisterially, de Beauvoir offers a systematic analysis, derived from existential philosophy, of the facts about the totality of women's condition. If Woolf lets the imagination fly after truth, de Beauvoir deploys the instrument of reason to assemble it. Despite this, or because of this, Woolf's grasp of history, if narrower than de Beauvoir's, is often hardier.

Together, the women carve out three of the principles of feminist criticism.

First, we cannot understand history, politics, and culture until we recognize how influential the structures of gender and sexual difference have been. Second, men, as men, have controlled history, politics, culture. They have decided who will have power, and who will not; which realities will be be represented and taught, and which will not. In so doing, men have relegated women, as women, to the margins of culture, if not to silence and invisibility. Third, the study of such ideas is insufficient. We must also act, politically and culturally, in order to change history. Theory and practice must meet, engage each other, wed. Judith Newton's strong essay, "Making—and Remaking—History: Another Look at 'Patriarchy'," details such an imperative.

In her peroration, Woolf calls out for women to prepare and struggle for the birth of a Judith Shakespeare. ". . . I maintain that she would come if we worked for her, and that so to work, even in poverty and obscurity, is worth while."[3] Even more firmly, de Beauvoir concludes: "It is for man to establish the reign of liberty in the midst of the world of the given. To gain the supreme victory, it is necessary, for one thing, that by and through their natural differentiation men and women unequivocally affirm their brotherhood" (p 814).

Notably, even notoriously, de Beauvoir's language of "brotherhood" repeats the pattern she otherwise so greatly disdains: blowing up men's experience until it becomes all experience, a universal happening; ballooning towards "brotherhood" while jettisoning "sisterhood." Massive though it is, *The Second Sex* erases women from history. In contrast, *A Room of One's Own* helps to create an archaeology of women, a dig for the literary artifacts that women have deposited, at least in England. Without de Beauvoir, Woolf outlined a fourth founding axiom of feminist criticism: the need to seek out and then to codify texts women have produced. In the 1970s, Elaine Showalter was to name such a task "gynocritics."

In the same decade, feminist scholars in history, art history, film, anthropology, and folklore were graphing women's traditions, signifying practices, and activities. For women, if choked, have still spoken. For women, if on the borders of culture, have still smuggled messages past border sentries. Their sentences begin in resistance. So far, they have no end. Perhaps Judith, the imaginary Shakespeare girl whom Woolf so vividly pictures, is an elegiac fiction, but wise women, witches, healers, and the tellers of folk tales are not. Nor is Fanny Burney. Nor are the Brontë sisters. Nor is Virginia Woolf.

Moreover, Woolf asserts, material and psychological conditions help to determine women's creativity. Like men, women need time, space, financial security, education, support and validation from others, and stamina in order to write well. Their works are as much the result of a room of their own and £500 a year as of divine revelation; Oedipal snarls, snarlings, and sorrows; or the lavish, eruptive, unpaginated, both invaginated and polymorphic lexicography of female sexuality.

Such ideas form the matrix for much of the thinking in *Feminist Issues in Literary Scholarship*. In "Still Practice, A/Wrested Alphabet," an act of homage to Virginia Woolf, Jane Marcus calls for critics to accept the ". . . authority of the female text." Marcus must be read against Judith Kegan Gardiner's study of the ambivalence of one female creator, Doris Lessing, towards the mother, an authority in the female text and time. In "Toward a Women's Poetics," Josephine Donovan maps a spacious "woman-centered epistemology," ways of being in and of looking at the world that women share. Women's themes include a knowledge of oppression; the domestic and private sphere; the creation of objects for use rather than for exchange; such physiological processes as menstruation; child-bearing and rearing; and a path towards maturity that differs from that of males. Susan Stanford Friedman and Paula A. Treichler show specifically how being a woman can mark poems and stories.

However, very little innocence clings to that phrase, "being a woman". A danger in feminism, and in feminist criticism, is the false, ahistorical over-universalizing of "woman." Ironically, as discourse once absorbed and sponged up all women under the rubric of "man," so feminist discourse can absorb and sponge up all women under the rubric of "woman." Fortunately, some of the most intelligent writing in *Feminist Issues in Literary Scholarship*—that of Nina Auerbach, Lillian S. Robinson, Hortense J. Spillers, Elizabeth Fox-Genovese—is about differences among women. Robinson's angle of vision is acute:

> . . . the difference of gender is not the only one that subsists among writers or the people they write about. It may not always be the major one. Women differ from one another by race, by ethnicity, by sexual orientation, and by class. Each of these contributes its historic specificity to social conditions and to the destiny and consciousness of individual women.

Recognizing differences among women, then, demands taking on other jobs, which *Feminist Issues in Literary Scholarship* mentions, touchs, but confronts imperfectly. One is the exacting exploration, and, ultimately, evaluation, of the work of the many, many women who are more than women. In the United States, feminist critics have tended to use the four categories of difference that Robinson gives: race, ethnicity, sexual orientation (largely, but not always, lesbianism), and class. Immense and complex though these four are, the list is half-drawn, perhaps a quarter of what it might be. For religion matters; colonization matters; tribe matters; nationality matters; time matters.[4] Moreover, placing women's writing in such varying contexts means seeing not only that men oppress and repress women, but that men and women also share other oppressions and repressions. A politically conscious feminist criticism must attend to the culture that glues together, but that also seeps and explodes from, interlocking structures of dominance and submission. It must hear, describe, and place languages from the many cells in the dirty, cruel labyrinths of history's prisons. It must, as well, remember that palaces, gardens, homes, and guard-houses surround those prisons. Women's language spins out from them as well.

In the late 1960s, in the United States, several realities bred and sustained the intellectual movement that found its substance in these principles and problems. First, no matter how pervasive and perverse the discrimination against women, enough had become a part of the literary professions and dis-ciplines to form a critical mass in support of women's questions. Next, the rebirth of feminism, like the general activity of the 1960s, had provided such women with an analysis of the cultural order, of what ordered what and for what purposes, and with an energizing sense of group identity. Then, too, other critics in the United States were restlessly ready to respond to fresh methods.

By the late 1980s, feminist criticism inexorably had a past of its own. Many of its early participants, who were graduate students or young faculty members or unknown writers in the late 1960s, had established careers. A persuasive, often poignant, essay in this volume, "Women's Time, Women's Space," by Elaine Showalter, who has become among the most influential of the pioneers, designs an astrolabe with which to observe the positions within that history.[5] Since 1975, she suggests, many feminist critics have arrived there ". . . via psychoanalytic, poststructuralist, or deconstructionist theory, rather than via the women's movement and women's studies." Their family of origin is more apt to be that of criticism, especially theory, than that of feminism. They may also represent cohorts born after Showalter (and after me). Their reading lists, then, may have included Millett and Showalter as well as Woolf and de Beau-voir. Paradoxically, to cleave to the revisionary impulses of Millett and de Beauvoir, they have to alter the practices of feminist criticism itself.

Unsurprisingly, one of the arguments within *Feminist Issues in Literary Scholarship* is about theory. Directly, forcefully, Nina Baym, in the bluntly titled "The Madwoman and Her Languages: Why I Don't Do Feminist Literary Theory," warns against both the totalizing tendency of theory and against pow-erful theories within feminist criticism itself. More obliquely, Elizabeth Fox-Genovese asks why white, Western, male critics are moping about the death of the "subject" and of the "author" when feminist critics, "like critics of Afro-American and third world literature," are valorising new subjects, different authors. Among the texts to which Fox-Genovese alludes is a famous 1968 Roland Barthes essay, "The Death of the Author."[6] However, Barthes, in part, kills the author in order to give birth to a reader. His construction of the relationship of reader to text is not that of many feminist critics. Where he finds pleasure at play, they tend to see power plays; tensions among sets of values; demands for reading as a subversive intervention. Nevertheless, Barthes's theories, like those of reader response criticism, co-exist with a feminist interest in reading as well as writing, cultural judgments as well as cultural production. Feminist critics watch the woman with a book, as well as with a word processor, in hand.

The assassinating phrase, "Death of the author," is also shorthand for a class of positions that Shari Benstock boldly asks feminist criticism to address, then dress up or down. Brilliantly articulated by Alice A. Jardine in her book *Gynesis*,[7] they may be the genesis of a new feminist criticism. Adapting post-structural, post-modern theories that interrogate the "feminine" in our symbolic contracts, these stances doubt the viability of traditional Western notions of the self, be it female or male; of realism and the status of representational strategies; and of the granddaddy of them all, truth. What if "truth" were a shell game?

Calling its own premises and proto-canons into question, such a revisionary feminist criticism would honor both the more ironic, ludic Virginia Woolf and the radically innovative Gertrude Stein. It would follow Stein's injunction in *Tender Buttons*: "Act so that there is no use in a center."[8] Such a feminist criticism could not abandon its political commitments to writing history; to exposing the ways in which ideology, discourse, and culture have malformed different women; and to women's taking and overtaking of ideology, discourse, culture, and power. Abandonment would strip the feminism from feminist criticism. However, it might choose to ally these commitments to a theory that questions the very language in which we now articulate them. The possibility or impossibility, the probability or improbability, of such an alliance is now at issue in literary scholarship.

I commend these essays about speaking women and their instruments. Written out of an arduous, ardent past that I share, they ask about a future that I wish to join, but that I cannot blandly predict. The lyre of feminist criticism will have to bring that into being.

NOTES

1. Fragment 8, *Sappho; A New Translation* by Mary Barnard (Berkeley and Los Angeles: University of California Press, 1958), unpaginated.

2. *The Second Sex*, trans. and ed. by H. M. Parshley (New York: Vintage Book, 1974, original North American edition 1953), p. 120. de Beauvoir's next sentence dislocates Aphra Behn, for Woolf the first professional woman writer in English, from the 17th century and relocates her in the 18th.

3. Virginia Woolf, *A Room of One's Own* (New York: Harcourt, Brace and World, Harbinger Book, 1957), p. 118.

4. See, for example, Gayatri Chakravorty Spivak's extraordinary "Three Women's Texts and a Critique of Imperialism," *Critical Inquiry*, 12, 1 (Autumn 1985), 243–261. Spivak shows how *Jane Eyre*, so far a canonical text for feminist critics, inscribes the British Empire.

5. Other new histories are *Making A Difference: Feminist Literary Criticism*, ed. Gayle Greene and Coppélia Kahn (London and New York: Methuen and Co., 1985), and the harder-edged, more provocative Toril Moi, *Sexual/Textual Politics* (London and New York: Methuen and Co., 1985).

6. In *Image/Music/Text*, trans. Stephen Heath (New York: Hill and Wang, 1977), pp. 142–148.

7. Alice A. Jardine, *Gynesis: Configurations of Woman and Modernity* (Ithaca, N.Y.: Cornell University Press, 1985). Jardine uses "modernity" where I use postmodern.

8. Gertrude Stein, *Look At Me Now and Here I Am: Writings and Lectures 1909–1945*, ed. by Patricia Meyerowitz (Baltimore: Penguin Books, 1971), p. 196.

BEYOND THE REACHES OF FEMINIST CRITICISM
A Letter from Paris

Shari Benstock

> If "woman" . . . designates that which subverts
> the Subject, Representation, and Truth, it is
> because "she" does so in the history of
> Western thought.[1]

The complacent Paris summer that Janet Flanner so often described in the pages of *The New Yorker* is strangely contradictory this year (1984): the weather is unpredictable, the government in crisis over an educational issue, the streets crowded with rich Americans and dispirited unemployed French youth. For the first time in this city, I feel squeezed in an uncomfortable cultural gap. My afternoon walk to the Bibliothèque Jacques Doucet takes me past the *galerie des femmes*, the women's bookshop on the rue de Seine where a photographic exhibit celebrates *l'année Colette* and the publication of the first volumes of the Pleiade edition of her collected works. The gallery walls situate Sidonie Gabrielle Colette against dark, nineteenth-century interiors while the chrome, glass, and mirrored decor of the bookshop refracts an almost blinding twentieth-century light. Free-standing shelves group white paperbound texts according to discipline—psychoanalysis, philosophy, politics, history, literature, gynecology, child care—and the book spines proclaim the latest works of Hélène Cixous, Julia Kristeva, Luce Irigaray, Monique Wittig. A huge poster of the late Clarisse Lispector dominates the front window while a single copy of Michel Foucault's *Histoire de la Folie* (a text almost impossible to find in Paris in the weeks following his death) is precariously lodged next to a collection of photographs: *La Bourgogne de Colette*. The uneasy relation these various writers bear to each other troubles me; the experience of this particular bookshop is disorienting.

Later, seated near a window in the library, I read the unpublished autobiography of Natalie Clifford Barney, whose house on the rue Jacob was a meeting place for French and American literati for almost sixty years. What was her relationship to the modernist literary movement that found its stimulus in Paris and how did the women who visited her home—Djuna Barnes, Gertrude Stein, H.D., Sylvia Beach, and Adrienne Monnier—contribute to the modernist enterprise? Glancing at a copy of Monnier's short-lived literary journal, *Le Navire d'Argent*, its pages weathered and musty smelling, I wonder about the style of these women and the decor of those two famous bookshops on the rue de l'Odéon—*La Maison des Amis des Livres* and Shakespeare and Company. Was it only a question of color scheme that distinguished their seedy comfort from the disconcerting modernity of the *galerie des femmes?* Which of these shops is the more modern, not to say modernist? Is the situation of the young woman dressed by Agnes B. and making out the Visa tickets on the rue de Seine significantly different from that of the two women who poured tea on the rue de l'Odéon at this hour of the afternoon? Are these women separated from each other by the short space of sixty years or do they speak their feminism and serve their literary movements in a different language? And would that language be French or English?

For Gertrude Stein, it was immensely important to live in a country in which English was not the lingua franca; for Natalie Barney it was immensely important to live in a country in which she could speak and write in French. And among the many important issues in feminist literary scholarship, not the least significant is a question of the languages we speak. This *décalage linguistique* exists in both time and space, and its effects have often been remarked—in the 1920s as well as in the 1980s. The Anglo-American expatriate community between the world wars occupied a small area on the Left Bank of the river Seine and established its literary territory on the linguistic ground of English. The French, meanwhile, continued to speak their own language and write their own literature, only the rarest and bravest of them venturing onto the American soil of 12, rue de l'Odéon or 20, rue Jacob. The literary balance of power in Paris between the wars was held by those who wrote in English; the critical balance of power in the 1980s seems to be held by those who write in French. And for Anglo-American feminist literary critics, the current tension between the languages of critical practice and of their literary subjects is particularly acute. It translates into discussions on the pages of feminist literary journals as a dialectic between theory and practice, between feminist literary critics in departments of English and those in departments of French or Comparative Literature, between those who define feminist critical practice as that which commits itself to literary texts written by women and to critical approaches that "construct a female framework for the analysis of woman's literature" ("Gynesis," 55) and those who feel that restricting ourselves to women's literature and to feminist theories developed by women is another means of "ghettoizing" women's creative powers.[2] The methodological debate is, therefore, cultural, and it defines itself along generic, linguistic, and national lines.

Perhaps the Paris culture that seems contradictory to me is the product of my misperception of it, the result of unnecessary worrying over questions of "theory" and "practice" and the effort to live simultaneously in French and English. If, at the Bibliothèque Jacques Doucet, I raise my eyes from Adrienne Monnier's essays on women and reading, I clearly see the inscription on the western facade of the Panthéon: *Aux Grands Hommes La Patrie Reconnaissante.* This inscription seems to countersign the reality of a monolithic culture in which egalitarianism extends only to men. Those women whose books line the shelves of the *galerie des femmes* are admittedly "in the best French tradition . . . direct disciples of those men" ("Gynesis," 55)—that is, the great men of France whose theories of psychoanalysis and philosophy structure current critical practice in both America and France. Those women serve in some sense as a "screen" through which male practice and male prerogatives operate to deny us not only a literature of our own but a literary practice of our own. If some of these men align themselves and their theoretical practice with *les marginaux* in western culture, we suspect it is only to secure for themselves a firmer grip on the center of theoretical discourse. As a French woman friend said to me at dinner, speaking of President Mitterrand's difficulties in solving the problems among the disadvantaged in French society, "It's a good question, who is marginal in France today—no one will admit to sharing *any* of the advantages extended by *la société française.* Those advantages always seem to belong to someone else. Only the burdens are carried by the individual to whom one is speaking at a given moment."

Perhaps, then, the western facade of the Panthéon is not as smooth as it appears. It situates itself on the original burial place of Saint Geneviève, patron saint of Paris. The building was used first as a church, now as a burial place for distinguished men. If we were to dig deep enough among the ruins that support the present building—the Roman ruins that the architect Soufflot feared might cause the collapse of his building design—would we find the female culture that supports this monument to male culture? When we found Saint Geneviève among the ruins, what could she tell us? And how—that is, in what language—would we speak to her? My search for her will begin against the facade of another seemingly monolithic institution of contemporary culture— modernism—precisely because it seems to me that modernism found more than mere setting in the Paris of the 1920s. It also discovered a subtle affinity between its literary goals and the French cultural imperative. As well, the critical method that elucidated the modernist project, that explained the works of James Joyce, T. S. Eliot, and Ezra Pound, has duplicated both the aesthetic and cultural values imbedded in the work of these men. In order to present this smooth facade of patriarchal values, modernism found it necessary—as have many literary movements before it—to hide all that was antithetical to its undertaking, all that was marginal in the culture it examined. And we know precisely who is to be found buried among the foundations of this gigantic edifice, whose works—diverse and rich—support the very columns on which modernism is constructed. We will find, among others, women. And not just the Virginia Woolfs and Gertrude Steins, acknowledged in their own time as exemplary writers. We will find all the others—Nancy Cunard, Caresse Crosby, Mina Loy, and Winifred Ellerman among them—who cooperated in this endeavor. What is frightening about such a critical venture is the very proximity of these women to us: women whose actions were well known to every major male modernist sixty years ago are almost beyond recall now. If it is difficult to rediscover women of our own century, how overwhelming the task of finding Geneviève, born in 422 A.D.

The project I suggest is related to, but importantly different from, the one outlined several years ago by Elaine Showalter, and subtly different too from the one initially undertaken by *Tulsa Studies in Women's Literature*:

> Before we can even begin to ask how the literature of women would be different and special, we need to reconstruct its past, to rediscover the scores of women novelists, poets and dramatists whose work has been obscured by time, and to establish the continuity of the female tradition from decade to decade, rather than from Great Woman to Great Woman. As we recreate the chain of writers in this tradition, the patterns of influence and response from one generation to the next, we can also begin to challenge the periodicity of orthodox literary history, and its enshrined canons of achievement.[3]

An "enshrined canon of achievement," modernism has already come under the critical scrutiny of postmodernist literary theory, one of whose founding claims is the "putting into question" of founding claims. The postmodernist worm has turned—against the very institution that gave it birth—to undermine the orthodoxy and institutionalization of modernism as a literary enterprise. To resurrect those lost women writers, publishers, booksellers, memoirists, and *salonières* is the first move in a critical project that might very well bring down the temple in which modernism has been enshrined. The question left unanswered, however, is how we go about resurrecting those buried behind the modernist facade, for surely the techniques we use to rediscover these women will influence the nature of our findings. And once we have rediscovered these women, what will we do with them—how will we treat their lives and works? Will we argue that their works be added to the canon, their names included on the list of authors graduate students preparing for doctoral examinations must memorize? Or will we set up an alternative canon, a hierarchy of women authors, placing Virginia Woolf (perhaps) at the top, Gertrude Stein in second place, Edith Sitwell in third? Will we find other ways of assessing the value of these individual contributions, avoiding the rank ordering of writers that itself seems one of the most unfortunate aspects of the patriarchal literary critical enterprise? Can we define a modernist aesthetic and poetic exclusive to women writers of the twentieth century? Will we divide the modernist canon between those works signed by males and those by females? Will we discover that women modernists suffered from an "anxiety of authorship" of the kind described by Sandra M. Gilbert and Susan Gubar for nineteenth-century women writers? Were those women writers embarked on creating a "literature of their own"? Can the theoretical models already established for discussing American and English women writers of the nineteenth century be applied to these twentieth-century women writers? And how do we assess, then, the contributions of those women and men who did not themselves write, but who contributed in other important ways to modernism?

Gertrude Stein, of course, would be furious at being grouped with these women writers—or any other set of women writers. Thoroughly aware of the risks of womanhood—its powerlessness and enforced isolation—Stein took on the powers of manhood by doing what no other female modernist dared do: she claimed the center for herself, toppling James Joyce from his elegant, but precarious, perch on the throne. What gall such an action required! And how galling that critical acclaim and book sales continued to suggest that Joyce, not Stein, held court among the expatriates. Not having successfully convinced the locals that she was the center of modernist activity, Stein next redefined the literary project that was hers, claiming that her methods had nothing in common with the outmoded literary forms practiced by others. For her, Joyce was old-fashioned and Hemingway "smelled of the nineteenth century." Stein was at one with the twentieth century, her work was "where the twentieth century was." Ironically, the isolation Stein feared as a woman writer found a correlative of sorts in the very *gloire* she sought: to be alone at the top, the one and only, the center of an activity that she herself defined. Nor did her daring claims for the centrality in the literary canon spare her the painful isolation of her Paris life: it is one of many pernicious expatriate myths that Gertrude Stein controlled a powerful Left Bank salon from which she dictated literary aesthetics. Gertrude Stein's Paris existence was, mostly, a separate one: like the James Joyce who so troubled her thoughts, she spent her time alone, writing. She was quite correct in redefining modernism in her own terms, however, and in separating her practice from that of others (notably Joyce). Her writing project differed from modernist "experimentalism" in every conceivable way. The discovery of Gertrude Stein and her work has been a recent one, but one predicted by Stein herself, who always argued that really original artists are so in advance of their time that they cannot be understood by their contemporaries: to be so would mean they inhabited the past. And it is post-modernist literary theory that has provided the tools for the discovery of Stein's work. By maintaining her separatism, she created the myth that she was at the center of a literary period whose borders were, in reality, sealed against her. Perhaps this separatism allowed her to create a literature very much of her own. This literature required, however, a methodology of its own—and it is precisely that methodology that is at issue: where to place Gertrude Stein and her work.

Obviously, our feminist project is not to recreate the orthodox forms that have traditionally excluded women, that divided a Gertrude Stein from her own womanhood, that forced her to deny for many years the wellspring of her creativity (what Adrienne Rich would call "the Lesbian in her"[4]). But in discovering our pantheon are we building a Panthéon? Are we duplicating the implicit patriarchal values that have insured our own burial in the march of literary history, as Gertrude Stein duplicated a heterosexual power structure in her relationship with Alice Toklas? Do we want the women writers we discover to join the canon of male writers or do we want a separate canon, and if we want a separate literary canon and a separate critical practice—*our own*— how will these differ from the "enshrined canons of achievement" around which course descriptions, dissertations, scholarly journals, and academic careers construct themselves? Do we claim the center for ourselves (taking up the modernist project) or do we redefine the limits of authority by which the center constitutes itself (taking up the post-modernist project)? Or do we, like Gertrude Stein, try to do both? Certainly the reconstruction of women's literary past implies that such questions be asked at the moment of rediscovery, that they not be deferred until a later moment in our feminist history. And such questions poise themselves—and in so doing poise us—on that awkward border between modernism and post-modernism, between practice and theory. As feminist critics we participate in a *modernity* that is discomforting. We both welcome and fear the literary discoveries we invite because these discoveries inevitably unsettle the very foundations of our feminism.

Having just rediscovered Gertrude Stein, for instance, where do we put her? (The more important question, where does Gertrude Stein put *us*, is the ultimate concern of this essay.) Do we make her a marginal modernist or a thoroughgoing post-modernist, a woman whose genius was well in advance of her male compatriots? We might begin by reviewing the characteristics that mark modernism as a literary movement. The following description of the cultural condition that produced modernism is taken from Susan Stanford Friedman's work on H.D.:

> The starting point of modernism is the crisis of belief that pervades twentieth-century western culture: loss of faith, experience of fragmentation and disinte-

gration, and shattering of cultural symbols and norms. At the center of this crisis were the new technologies and methodologies of science, the epistemology of logical positivism, and the relativism of functionalist thought—in short, major aspects of the philosophical perspectives that Freud embodied. The rationalism of science and philosophy attacked the validity of traditional religious and artistic symbols while the growing technology of the industrialized world produced the catastrophes of war on the one hand and the atomization of human beings on the other. Art produced after the First World War recorded the emotional aspect of this crisis; despair, hopelessness, paralysis, angst, and a sense of meaninglessness, chaos, and fragmentation of material reality. In a variety of ways suited to their own religious, literary, mythological, occult, political, or existentialist perspectives, they emerged from the paralysis of absolute despair to an active search for meaning. The search for order and pattern began in its own negation, in the overwhelming sense of disorder and fragmentation caused by the modern materialist world. The artist as seer would attempt to create what the culture could no longer produce: symbol and meaning in the dimension of art, brought into being through the agency of language, the Word or Logos of the twentieth century.[5]

This description situates modernism historically as a post-World War I phenomenon, grounds its psychology in reaction to despair, and describes its pursuit as "an active search for meaning . . . through the agency of language, the Word or Logos." Fixing the modernist "moment" as post-war, this description renders troublesome discussions of modernist texts that preceded the First World War (the early work of H. D., Joyce, Eliot, and Pound, and eliminates from discussion those who did not survive the war years (Guillaume Apollinaire, for instance). What this analysis of modernism's defining features does not mention—but which is evident in all of Friedman's work on H. D.—is the set of masculine claims and heterosexual values embedded in the work of modernism. (Thus Marcel Proust is excluded because his artistic subject was homosexuality, and several writers, women and men alike, are overlooked because their work in no way demonstrates the despair and crisis of faith that the war presumably produced. Notable in this group is Gertrude Stein.) Nonetheless, there are several modernist practitioners who clearly fit Friedman's working definition: T. S. Eliot (*The Waste Land*), Ezra Pound (*Hugh Selwyn Mauberley*), Franz Kafka (*The Castle*), Wyndham Lewis (*Tarr*); included as well would be the various literary movements incorporated under the modernist logo: vorticism, futurism, Dadaism, surrealism. Such a definition pitches the tent of modernism on the ashes of burned-out rationalism and positivism.

Nothing is mentioned here of the ironic tone that marks this literary method, but irony has often been seen as the hallmark of modernist writing, the tool used to recast the impotence of despair into aggressive literary production. The "despair, hopelessness, paralysis, angst, sense of meaninglessness, chaos, and fragmentation of material reality produced by the collapse of traditional values" cited by Friedman became grist for the ironic mode. Irony, like various other literary techniques and experimental narrative modes, served as a mask to disguise the very traditional values—a belief in order and meaning—against which this writing set itself. A description of modernism that fixes its origins in a crisis of belief and despair at the "shattering of cultural symbols and norms" also eliminates, by definition, the acknowledged father of modernism, James Joyce, and, among others such as Wallace Stevens and e. e. cummings, at least six important women modernists: Edith Sitwell, H.D., Virginia Woolf, Djuna Barnes, Marianne Moore, and Mina Loy. The work of these writers does not situate itself in *reaction to* a collapse in cultural values, taking as its defense the ironic mode, but rather exposes the continuing hegemony of traditional material and patriarchal values. Unfortunately, the First World War had not made the world safe for democracy, but neither had it blown sky high the values that had supported western culture. When the air cleared from the smoke bombs, the old order quickly re-established itself. Alienated by this world, unwilling (and unable) to share its values, some of these writers turned away from the modern world, creating an interior landscape in which language recorded the psyche. In place of traditional material values, literature turned its attention to the ways in which the mind perceived the external world and recorded its impressions. Various modernists were interested in cultural symbols and norms as subjects under analysis, writing a literature that exposed the operations of these cultural norms as they were present *in* language. The ironic defense mechanism, the need for which exposed an attachment to the very culture whose loss it announced, was replaced by the mask of objectivity: the writer did not react, but rather perceived.

Of course, such descriptions of modernist operations are deceptive, if not actually deceiving. It would be virtually impossible to derive a definition of modernism—or any other literary movement—that included all whose work shared some of the defining characteristics without exposing important differences among those listed. Some definitions of modernism emphasize the role the war played in creating a new literary sensibility (Paul Fussell, *The Great War and Modern Memory*), another emphasizes the work of psychoanalysis (Leon Edel, *The Psychological Novel*), another the influence of individual writers (Hugh Kenner, *The Pound Era*). A complex literary phenomenon, modernism resists an all-inclusive description that either catalogues component phenomena or stamps the movement by a single, recognizable characteristic. Or does it ? Gertrude Stein's work puts into relief the single shared assumption that would seem to support the modernist project: the commitment to the Logos, the Word.

Modernist writing focused on the "agency of language" as a vehicle of meaning. To whatever degree other defining characteristics of modernism operated in juxtaposition to each other, in contradiction to each other, in uneasy alignment with each other, the determined emphasis on the Word or Logos over-shadowed all other divergences among these writers. The one sacred belief common to them all seemed to be the indestructibility of the bond between the word and its meanings, between symbol and substance, between signifier and signified. Multiple linguistic experiments—juxtaposition of unlike words, typographical experimentation, translations of language into the dreamworld of the night or the idiolect of the mad—only reinforced the linguistic claims on meaning. The word was the one thing in this modern world that remained sacred: it survived wars, resisted the claims of materialist culture, masked despair and exposed cultural hypocrisy. The word held within it the possibilities of restructuring and rewriting the world. The writer would succeed where God had failed. Indeed, "the artist as seer would attempt to create what the culture could no longer produce: symbol and meaning in the dimension of art, brought into being through the agency of language" (Friedman, 97–98). The discovery, however, that language could join symbol and meaning, that the artist could forge again the bond between sign and substance that the modern world threat-ened to dislodge, that despair could never be total as long as language held the power to create meanings, was discovered well before the catastrophe of World War I. It was the founding premise of Imagism, where form and sub-stance were intimately and irrevocably joined through the image, through lan-guage. All the various experiments in the working of language, from Imagism through Surrealism, could only confirm what the modernists already knew in their secret hearts: that the power of language was a transformative one, one that could remake the perception of the world and against which the world—despite its wars and crises of belief, despite radical changes in cultural norms, and redefinitions of physical and psychic occurrences—would remain stable. Experiments in language only revealed surprising new ways that language could "mean," by which language ordered itself, through which language could invest an otherwise bankrupt modern society with sense. James Joyce discovered, early in the writing of *Finnegans Wake*, that he could do anything he wanted with language. He had learned the principles by which language worked, he had broken its "code," he had mastered its secret, he had harnessed its energy for his own creative vision.[6] He had realized his early dream of becoming an Author, a "God of creation," the absent center of a linguistic universe.

Perhaps Gertrude Stein was a slow learner, as her brother accused her, or perhaps she was just a silly woman whose midnight writings were a childish game to counter boredom. Whatever the reason, Gertrude Stein never dis-covered she could do anything she wanted with language; she never mastered the principles by which language worked; she never broke its code or harnessed its energy. She always stood resolutely outside the mystery of language, just as she stood outside the gate of modernism. For more than sixty years we have read failure of communication in Gertrude Stein's nonsense writing. Even those who wanted to read her—that is, to understand her, to break the "code"—discovered that in applying the age-old tools of literary exegesis they reaped only minimal results. Surely, there must be some gold among all this dross, sighed frustrated readers. Interest in Stein followed the track of her personal charisma (and its opposite: hatred of her egotism). Readers repeated Stein's "Rose is a rose is a rose" like one proclaimed Sitwell's "Jane, Jane, tall as a crane," as though they were jump-rope rhymes, and at the end of which they collapsed into gales of uncomprehending laughter and rolled in the grass, re-membering their childhoods. Gertrude Stein was an overgrown infant, de-manding, unpredictable, egocentric—in need of socialization and civilization. What pretense to assume she was the equal of James Joyce! He was elegant and slim, polite and European; she was slovenly and fat, imperious and stolid. In brief, she was everything Joyce was not—and that is precisely the point. When she called Joyce old-fashioned, she was not referring to his old-world manner, which clashed so obviously with her American brusqueness, she was referring to the literary values that inhabited his work: he still believed in the Word, in the power of the Logos, in the immutable and undeniable link between form and substance, between word and meaning. He may have abandoned Ireland and Catholicism, become an expatriate and a heretic, but he had not become an atheist: God no longer spoke through the rites and rituals of Ca-tholicism, but rather through the forms and images of language that Joyce himself controlled. He did not abandon God; he replaced Him. This action required an enforcement of the artistic ego well beyond any effort of Gertrude Stein to make herself the literary empress of the Left Bank. By comparison with Joyce, Stein's relationship to language was one of humorous humility: it outwitted her every time, and every time she loved being outwitted.

Why was Gertrude Stein not a modernist, not even a failed one? Because she never believed in the indestructible relation between the word and its meaning, and she was able to demonstrate in multiple ways the uncontrollable divergences of form and content, style and substance, signifier and signified. Rather than trying to control language's every movement, to discover the per-fect match of word and meaning through an image, metaphor, or symbol, Stein began by careful observation of linguistic nuance, submitting herself to the rhythms and sounds of language, listening carefully to the speech around her, allowing herself to be educated by language. She did what no other writer has had quite the courage to do: she relinquished her right as a writer to make language submit to her will; instead, she submitted her will to a linguistic power (and play) that she recognized. Her experiments with language began when she was at Radcliffe, and there is evidence in those early themes of the direction her linguistic studies would later take. The really concentrated effort to learn the language *of* language was taken up in Paris, in the dead of the night after Leo—who consistently mocked her literary efforts—was safely asleep, unable to taunt her. In these quiet hours, she submitted to language. Although such an experiment could be—and frequently has been—dismissed as an effort at "automatic" writing, a sort of linguistic Rorschach or, perhaps, a self-induced hypnotic state, the method demanded a concentrated effort, a resistance against the need for absolute control over the pen.[7] Stein was to use this method in writing *The Making of Americans*, a text that analyzed the minute differences in spoken phrases and circled around its subject in almost endless repetition and revision. More than any other of Stein's works, *The Making of Americans* has been considered an unreadable white elephant—an experiment interesting only in the abstract and certainly not in the reading experience. However, Stein had proved before completing this experiment that she could write perfectly "acceptable" and "readable" English in the stories comprising *Three Lives*. And this collection, because it is less radically experimental than her later writings, has been most frequently the subject of critical analysis—precisely because it is still possible in *Three Lives* to deduce "meaning" from the language: the fragile link between sign and substance remains intact.

Once the experiment in the rue de Fleurus apartment had begun, however, it could not easily be stopped, even though Stein admittedly paid a high price in continuing a venture so easily misunderstood. During the years when she worked at night, isolated from the larger literary community growing up around her, she was learning something about her methods from the visual arts by watching the practice of the cubists, who divorced painting from representation and broke the visual subject into its component lines and dimensions. Stein knew that her experiments with language were similar to Picasso's efforts in painting, but her experiments were unsatisfying to the literary community— Indeed, they quickly became the butt of jokes. In retrospect, it is fortunate that she did not fall under the influence of the men of this community—Ezra Pound, for instance, a man who insisted on the integrity of sign and sense, who demanded absolute control of the linguistic medium, who revered all that was sharp, concise, devoid of the extraneous, free of sentiment. He deplored her repetitious and parataxic efforts; he found her writing inane and egregiously stupid. In short, Pound agreed with Leo Stein.[8] The early word portraits that separated the subject from its linguistic rendition constituted the antithesis of the Imagist doctrine: the image rarely fit the subject it would "render"; the image—often clear enough—was arbitrary. Without the title, how would one know that a portrait was of Guillaume Apollinaire or Pablo Picasso? (But then, without the title, how would one know that the most famous Imagist poem of them all was about faces seen in a station of the metro?)

Picasso's portrait of Stein, completed during the year that she was finishing

Three Lives, shares something in artistic method with Stein's early work: portraiture is still maintained, the subject is recognizable, although slightly distorted, to suggest the effects of character. Stein's word portraits coincided with Picasso's cubist period and resisted characterization altogether. Later efforts, in particular *Tender Buttons*, seem at first an absolutely arbitrary and unthinking juxtaposition of words on the page. Only later were they seen to be an interrogation of the very method that produces "characterization" or a representational rendering. By this point in her writing, Stein was well on her way toward a quite thorough and comprehensive analysis of those linguistic properties that define what had heretofore constituted the "literary." The lectures of Stein's later period, the series of talks given in America in the 1930s, recalled the stages of this analysis, the lectures themselves constituting an effort on her part to make herself understood to those who found her project incomprehensible. Because she was a witty and charming lecturer, quite capable of disarming the most determined opponent, Stein succeeded in winning the affection of audiences who still had not the faintest idea of what she and her writing were all about. (Back home in Paris, James Joyce was fighting a similar rear guard action against Pound, among others, on the grounds that certain readers found *Finnegans Wake* incomprehensible and were beginning to suspect that the master was losing his mind.)

What Stein was to discover through the more than thirty years of her determined experiment—an experiment carried out rather scientifically, reminiscent of the regimen she had learned in the laboratories at Johns Hopkins University medical school—was that language, when given its free play, tended toward apparently arbitrary alignments of signifier and signified, alignments that often resulted in the comic. What the later deconstructionists were to conclude—to the initial amazement of their scholarly colleagues—was that language can never be confined to its contextual mooring (indeed, the very definition of "context" is put into question by this effort); language slips and slides away from intended meanings to arrive at thoroughly unexpected destinations. One might almost think that Gertrude Stein's literary practice and Jacques Derrida's critical approach were made for each other, if it were not for Derrida's still shy insistence that the unexpected directions language takes are not unexpected at all, that they follow a sinister logic that can be traced through deconstructive practice. In its narrowest conception, deconstruction might be seen to be just another form of modernist epistemology: the Word still reigns supreme. Deconstructionist investigations take place through language, but the logic of representation—the word's relation to meaning—is seen to be far more devious and contradictory than previously assumed. As Catherine Gallagher interprets Gerald Graff's assessment of deconstruction in *Literature Against Itself*, "Derrida . . . is not a radical, destructive innovator, a snake in the critical garden, but rather the logical extension of a long line of modernist thinkers who have been arguing since the turn of the century for the independence of language from a determining world of objects."[9] Stein's writing, then, gives evidence of this move toward independence. Her writing first revises the relation between word and the "determining world of objects" (in *The Making of Americans, Tender Buttons*, the word portraits) and later breaks entirely the assumed connection between word and world (*Patriarchal Poetry, Lucy Church Amiably, Four Saints in Three Acts*, and so on). In Graff's view (and in the view of many of Stein's critics), such a break between language and objective, external reality makes literature "irrelevant" (Gallagher, 41). Certainly Stein's most experimental writing was seen to be irrelevant for many years.

Stein's project, then, could be seen to be radically self-destructive: her writing put into question the determinacy of meaning in language, suggesting that if meaning were not determinant, then the opposite must be true. And her critics were quick to agree that Stein's writing was nonsensical gibberish. Readers require that language "make sense"—that is, that it "make sense of" the world it presumably describes. Stein's language disabused itself of such a responsibility, denying a responsibility to either reader or author. Stein's work seems to deny the social reality—the lynchpin of external reality—that grounds literary effort in the representational. If a poem like "Pink Melon Joy" or a "detective story" like *Blood on the Dining Room Floor* resists explications premised on the notion that language represents reality and that its meanings can be recovered in tracing the link between language and the outside world, then it must be that Gertrude Stein's most abstruse writing—if it is not entirely nonsensical and meaningless—is the expression of an enormous ego that consumes the external world: "Wise or silly or nothing at all, down everything goes on the page with an air of everything being equal, unimportant in itself, important because it happened to her and she was writing about it."[10] Katherine Anne Porter's complaint against Stein, like the arguments of many others who were irritated by Stein's apparent self-centeredness, directs itself to Stein's writing style, the perverse flatness of a literary landscape across which one can only see Gertrude Stein and nothing that is *not* Gertrude Stein. But this complaint masks other, more serious, charges against Stein—ones that cannot be expressed in the pages of *Harper's* magazine or between the covers of scholarly books. Stein's perverse style has intimate connections to her lesbianism, which is the motivating force for this private language, at odds with any accepted forms of meaning, a language exploring seemingly arbitrary and coincidental links between signifier and signified. Stein's style served as mask for her lesbian subject matter, an "envelope," a "tricky disguise of Nature," that hid her real self, the American Amazon:

> she was of the company of Amazons which nineteenth-century America produced among its many prodigies: not-men, not-women, answerable to no function in either sex, whose careers were carried on, and how successfully, in whatever

field they chose: they were educators, writers, editors, politicians, artists, world travelers, and international hostesses, who lived in public and by the public and played out their self-assumed, self-created roles in such masterly freedom as only a few early medieval queens had equaled. Freedom to them meant precisely freedom from men and their stuffy rules for women. They usurped with a high hand the traditional masculine privileges of movement, choice, and the use of direct, personal power. They were few in number and they were not only to be found in America, and Miss Stein belonged with them, no doubt of it, in spite of a certain temperamental passivity which was Oriental, not feminine ("Gertrude Stein," 522).

Porter's analysis of American lesbian practice reveals anger at its "high handed" freedom, its privilege, its use of power, its "usurpation" of the male prerogative, and—worst of all—its success. Stein has denied her sex in the secret heart of her lesbianism. Her writing has denied the claims of intelligibility enforced by patriarchal language by encoding lesbianism *as* its secret heart. Porter, of course, never makes the leap between her own commentary on Stein's life-*style* and her complaint against Stein's writing *style*—indeed she seems to have missed altogether the lesbian subject matter of Stein's writing—but it is not difficult for us to make the theoretical leap. (And Porter's complaints against Stein include not only a prejudice against lesbians but a prejudice against Jews as well, her "self-portrait" of Gertrude Stein being an abusively anti-Semitic tract.[11])

Against the claim by Porter and others that Stein's writing was "nonsense" and "gibberish" has been the recent counterclaim that Stein's language renders meaning if one is familiar with its essentially lesbian code. Once the code is broken, meaning spills out, showing the link between word and meaning to be the same as in all literary works—over-determined, multiply self-reinforcing.[12] It is to this aspect of Stein's work that much feminist criticism has directed its attention, producing lists of code words, interpretations of dramatic scenes in these works, analyses of the reasons necessitating the code, and explications of the intimate links between language and style, woman and her sexual expression. Feminist criticism has succeeded in reading "sexuality" into Stein's "textuality."[13] The coded nature of Stein's writing gives evidence of the necessary secrecy of such sexuality within the patriarchal system: for feminist critics, the sexuality of Stein's texts liberated their textuality (that is, changed their linguistic codes) but this textuality was read by the patriarchy as self-indulgence, as empty linguistic forms, as child's play, as (linguistic) perversion. The patriarchy did not recognize in this writing a sexual confession for the simple reason that the patriarchy is only capable of reading *heterosexual* confessions (of the kind written by Joyce and Lawrence, to name only two modernists who took up the form). Katherine Anne Porter could recognize Stein's lesbian behavior but could not recognize the lesbianism of her texts precisely because

Porter's reading was bounded by its patriarchal assumptions. Stein's position as an alienated, misunderstood writer was not only the product of her status as a *woman* writer in a highly patriarchal environment but of her status as a *lesbian woman* writer. Her writing constituted both the expression of the social (the lesbian writer writing against the dominant culture) and the negation of the social (Stein's language denied the claims of the patriarchy by writing a different language—what Catharine Stimpson calls Stein's "anti-language," one that the patriarchy can only read as nonsense). This reading of Stein s work argues that she was writing *lesbian* modernism: the Word, once its meanings are made available, is the agency through which symbol and meaning are joined, by means of which the culture is rewritten. Word and meaning maintain their predictable and indissoluble links once the reader knows the social code that releases meaning. And here the "social code" is lesbianism.

Such a reading of Stein's works, brilliantly practiced by several contemporary feminist critics, conforms nicely to the deconstructionist project in following the contradictory and sinister logic of a writing against the grain (of patriarchal society), a revelation of the difference on which all language meaning is premised.[14] From the point of view of a feminism grounded in social reality—a feminism concerned with the "sex of the author, narrative destinies, images of women and gender stereotypes" ("Gynesis," 56)—such readings celebrate Stein as a woman writer, tying her subject matter and literary methods intimately to the womanhood she so often tried to deny. Indeed, the peculiar logic of writing is inextricable from the tensions inherent in her self-image and in her desire to be a great writer. Her contorted language and its contradictory logic reflect perfectly internalized contortions and contradictions resulting from her place in the culture. Everything about Stein's psychology, her situation as a woman in twentieth-century society, her familial relationships, and educational experiences conspire to make her "readable" as a woman when read by women. Here deconstructive practice and pragmatic American feminism have joined forces to reclaim a writer previously considered irrelevant by male critics and problematic for feminist critics. Surely, this must be a most fortunate marriage of theory and practice. Such a reading seems to demonstrate the potential held out by a socially-grounded feminist theory of the kind called for by Elaine Showalter: "gynocritics begins at the point when we free ourselves from the linear absolutes of male literary history, stop trying to fit women between the lines of the male tradition, and focus instead on the newly visible world of female culture" ("Feminist Poetics," 28).

Or does it? Such a critical method holds out, it seems to me, important possibilities for reading Stein's biography, for discovering her situation not on the outside of a male literary enterprise but at the center of a female culture to which Stein herself could not admit her own membership. Despite her efforts to deny her womanhood and in spite of her efforts not only to participate in modernism but to outdo the male modernists whom she considered her only worthy opponents, she ended up creating a womanly environment for herself that allowed her creative tendencies, which rested in her lesbianism, to find expression. If we take off the male modernist blinders through which we have for so long tried to read Stein and put on the feminist critic's glasses, we read her meaning as the expression of lesbian love, her comic verse and engaging wordplay as the expression of her femininity, a femininity that no longer need be repressed. The problem here is not how such a critical methodology would see Stein but how it sees *language*, a problem that Stein spent many years pondering. The gynocritical approach works best when it examines the links between women writers and their works in literary periods in which language itself was not under inspection, when language itself was not a crucial issue for writers, when language was accepted—as it was until the advent of modernism—as a transparent window through which the perception of reality found expression. The woman writer seated herself at the window through which she perceived and recorded reality, seeing through the pane of glass which was itself the language of that expression. The writing situation is made more complex when the woman writer at the window—a Virginia Woolf or a Gertrude Stein or a Hilda Doolittle or a Djuna Barnes—does not see *through* the window to an external reality, but rather sees in language a palpable subject that is the "subject" of the literary undertaking. To state it differently, the writer's situation is made enormously more complex when language is seen to *construct* external reality rather than to describe (or mirror) a separate, immutable, constant external. And this difference in "seeing" that rewrites the language of "seeing" is precisely the modernist question posed by Woolf, Stein, Doolittle, and Barnes (a question not posed by Charlotte and Emily Brontë, George Eliot, or Jane Austen, however complex and intricate the language of their writings).[15] The ways in which these four women modernists saw language and thought about it differ radically from each other, differ as much from each other as they do from the ways T. S. Eliot, James Joyce, Ezra Pound, and e. e. cummings thought about language. No critique of these women's lives and works that does not pay particular attention to their interest in and experiments with *language* can hope to account, even partially, for their contributions as women writers. And when it comes to dealing with a woman writer whose literary project was to deny the social, to question the ways language and reality bore a relation to each other, to make language itself a reality under investigation, the problem becomes immensely more difficult. It calls for a theory beyond a female framework, beyond the social and cultural givens of time and place, beyond history as it is currently understood. It calls for a reinvestigation of the principles of language.

And it is precisely at this point, at the gap between language theory and critical practice, that Paris offers a distinctly different perspective. In Alice Jardine's description of the French inquiry:

> the notion of "Self"—so intrinsic to Anglo-American thought—becomes absurd. It is not something called the "Self" which speaks, but language, the unconscious, the textuality of the text. . . . The assurance of an author's sex within the whirl-pool of de-centering is problematized beyond recognition. The "policing of sexual identity" is henceforth seen as being complicitous with the appropriations of representation; gender (masculine, feminine) is separate from identity (female, male). The question of whether a "man" or "woman" wrote a text (a game feminists know well at the level of literary history) is nonsensical. . . . The feminist's initial incredulity faced with this complex "beyonding" of sexual identity is largely based on *common sense* (after all *someone* wrote it?!). But is it not that very *sense* ("common to all," i.e., humanism) that the feminist is attempting to undermine? On the other hand, when you problematize "Man" (as being at the foundation of Western notions of the Self) to the extent that French thought has, you're bound to find "Woman"—no matter who's speaking—and *that* most definitely concerns feminist criticism." ("Gynesis," 57)[16]

Under the Panthéon, dedicated *Aux Grands Hommes La Patrie Reconnaissante*, one finds the buried bones of St. Geneviève. Anglo-American feminism, which emphasizes the authority of woman's experience in history, which has focused carefully on the link between the signature of literary texts with a woman's name and the world that the literary text discloses, has divided the textual world according to lines of (biologic) sexual decidability—a rereading of male texts along feminist lines and a rereading and rediscovery of woman's texts along feminist lines.[17] And it is here, on the question of who writes and who signs a text, that the Anglo-Americans and French part company: the French argue that the notion of "woman" (as in "woman writer," "woman scholar") is not necessarily defined by anatomy. Stein, for instance, was bio-logically a female, but defined aspects of her gender as "male," a definition that was underwritten by many who knew her (not merely Katherine Anne Porter, but also Alice B. Toklas). As well, the socially constructed concepts of "gender" that have received marked attention in America become, from the French point of view, another effect of the patriarchal fiction that has con-structed western culture. (As Alice Jardine suggests, the fiction of western civilization is constructed as a historical narrative; French theorists are at-tempting to account for the "crisis-in-narrative which is modernity" ["Gynesis," 58]). Indeed, the relation of fiction as a product of culture and the reality of that culture constitute a crossroads at which various theoretical hypotheses regarding women and writing are at an impasse. One group of critics concen-trates, in Elaine Showalter's words, on defining women "as a distinct literary group," assuming the biologic determinant of the female as the grounding of

women's writing and reading; another group, following Hélène Cixous, concentrates on the definition of *écriture féminine*, a writing whose characteristics
are associated with the feminine as it has been societally defined, whether
practiced by males or females; a third group pushes beyond the biologic definitions that underlie social categories to eliminate the constructs of "feminine"
and "masculine"—that is, beyond humanism.[18]

The differences between these various descriptions of women in western
society rest in language, in the intricate relation between biologic determination
and social definition as they are articulated *in* language. Does the language of
definition construct reality or reflect it? Are "woman" and the "feminine" constructed by linguistic convention, or does woman and her language stand outside
of patriarchal linguistic modes? Elaine Showalter and Nina Baym warn us against
conventional definitions of woman, of chaining woman's writing (*écriture féminine*) to stereotypical notions of womanhood as the incoherent, the hysterical.
Writes Showalter, "we must protest now as in the nineteenth century against
the equation of the feminine with the irrational. But we must also recognize
that the questions we most need to ask go beyond those that science can answer"
("Feminist Poetics," 39). But Gertrude Stein's project was precisely a "scientific" interrogation of linguistic forms, of the patriarchal demands of grammar,
logic, and syntax to produce "sense," hers a scientific experiment that resulted
in a discovery of the nonsensical possibilities inherent in language. If we can
agree that this *was* Stein's project and that this was what she discovered (and
not all of us will agree to such a reading of her work), then is there some link
between Stein's discovery and her own womanhood, a womanhood that was so
problematic to her? Certainly, we can read the unhappy history of Stein's place
among modernist writers of the twentieth century, the extent to which she was
marginalized and her work trivialized so that her discovery located itself in the
presumably irrational and nonsensical. The history of Stein criticism is a history
that duplicates responses to woman's situation *in* history: she was accused of
having a "style" (allied to the odd clothes she wore?) and no substance; she was
fun, but she made no sense; she was entertaining, but not to be taken seriously;
she was a joke. And at the end of this (dirty) joke was a very serious patriarchal
question: had Gertrude Stein, as Katherine Anne Porter claimed, usurped
manhood? She looked like a man and talked like a man and if it were to turn
out that she wrote like a man, then perhaps what was at first seen to be *nonsense* could actually be seen to be an important critique of the place of language
in western culture. Perhaps, then, (s)he could be placed with Alfred Jarry,
Louis-Ferdinand Céline, Samuel Beckett or Flann O'Brien as pointing toward
the ridiculous, arbitrary, and comic in culture.

The history of Stein criticism has stayed squarely within the dialectical mode

of western culture (male/female, speech/writing, sense/nonsense), avoiding—
not seeing (precisely because the field of vision was limited to dialectical op-
posites)—the ways in which Stein's writing put into question that dialectic,
refusing the dialectical, representational, mimetic conceptions. Her writing
followed language to its farthest point, a zero-degree where language and external reality split forever from each other, a moment at which language constituted itself beyond observable reality. The result was that her "narratives"
were, to use Alice Jardine's term, "delegitimized" ("Gynesis," 60) precisely
because they relinquished the tenacious grip of mastery over the Word. Stein's
narratives broke the one bond that joined all the modernists—a belief in the
mastery of experience, the re-creation of reality, through mastery of the Word.
Stein had seen what no other modernist saw—that meaning always slides away
from the word no matter how tightly the author tries to control the directions
that meaning might take.

The question, then, is whether Stein's discovery was related to her biologically determined womanhood and the problematic social definition of her (in
part, a definition constructed by Stein herself) as a woman who wanted to be
a man. Anglo-American feminist critics of Stein would probably say "yes," that
her discovery was directly linked to her womanhood *because* her womanhood
was so problematic to her. The French—if they were to think of her at all as
they passed the blue plaque on the rue de Fleurus—would also say "yes," but
for different reasons. For Hélène Cixous, Stein's writing is an example of *écriture féminine* by its formal characteristics of openness and irrationality. Monique Wittig, taking a different stance, might argue that Stein's writing was
lesbian and political because it refused to metaphorize woman, because it celebrated woman's body, for instance, in ways significantly different from the
fetishistic attachment to her body that the patriarchy has historically displayed.
To date, however, Stein has not been discussed by French writers of any critical
persuasion. Her work has been recovered by Anglo-American feminist critics
who, however refreshing their sensitivity to Stein as a woman within a patriarchal framework, have continued to discuss her work within the confines of the
modernist project. That is, her work has been viewed as the product of her
historical situation; she has remained "contemporary" with her contemporaries.
Many have suggested that Stein was not accepted among her modernist colleagues, but no one has posited Stein's literary project as itself beyond the
confines of modernism. Thus, her work has been measured by modernist principles even when, for instance, the discovery of a lesbian subject matter suggests
that it traced a subversive seam within the modernist mantle, that it was distinctly different from the literary/historical movement it seemed to inhabit. If
we take Stein out of her modernist setting, release her writing from the critical

dictates of modernist thought, then the possibility is open to seeing her work as distinctly different from her contemporaries (a claim she continually made for it). Because Stein's literary discoveries ultimately result in a reconceptualization of the notion of author and text, of writer and subject, and, in particular, a renunciation of the western construction of ego, Stein seems to be one of our contemporaries.

The questions her work asks are very similar to those contradictory and thorny questions being posed by feminist literary theory both in America and in France. Oddly enough, this new reading of Stein writes an ironic afterword to that early Stein criticism that accused her of having an ego as big as the Ritz. In order to make the kind of linguistic discoveries I am claiming she did make, Gertrude Stein had to renounce ego. The discovery required a commitment to nonmastery of the language that the ego would never allow. Certainly a modernist with an ego the size of Ezra Pound's or James Joyce's would not allow it. Gertrude Stein took an enormous risk—the risk of making a fool of herself—in order to *resist* the patriarchal (modernist) claim to mastery. And it is that claim to mastery, the French might say, that characterizes our outmoded efforts to understand women's texts: we "master" these texts every time we try to make them conform to our construction of the patriarchal norm (even when we read them in opposition to that norm), every time we apply to them the hierarchical value system created by a patriarchal world, every time we reveal that we are still thinking and writing and producing literary criticism within the bounds of the dialectic, every time we take the language of these texts for granted. These actions are just other forms of phallocentric repression of the very "play" that Stein's writing, as an example, released in language.

To "rediscover" Stein is to problematize the critical methods we employ in that discovery; indeed, without problematizing those critical methods Stein would never have been rediscovered. (The method of discovery determines, in no small measure, just what is discovered, as Lillian Robinson has told us countless times.) Now that we see Stein's outline on the twentieth-century horizon—an outline that shapes itself somewhat differently now than it did even five years ago—we must consider how the landscape she will inhabit will be changed by her presence. The presence of Stein in the literary Paris of the 1920s and 1930s will certainly enforce a change in the way we see the modernism of that time and place—our definitions of it, our assumptions about its place in literary history, our notion of what it seemed to be doing. In describing the methods that led to Stein's literary discoveries, we will in fact be redefining the modernist enterprise, not merely trying to place Stein within its boundaries. We will make her our contemporary in this exercise, place her in advance of the modernist movement, not merely marginal to its central concerns. And our critical project will be immensely difficult, because it will require us to interrogate our critical method just as Stein interrogated her literary method. What is the feminist critic's relation to the language she uses? What are the principles on which her method is founded? Is language—the literary language of the woman writer whose work she examines and her own critical language—an "issue"? What is the relation between Stein's use of language, for instance, and the "reality of objects" that her language so often examined? What is the relation between Stein's sexual identity and the nature of her linguistic discoveries? Can we understand what Stein was about without being able to explicate her work, without insisting that it be "decoded," without reading with blinders— patriarchal or feminist? If Stein's writing pointed beyond the dialectic of male and female, is it possible to read her "as a feminist," to practice feminist criticism on her work as well as on her life? Is there a theory that can inform our critical practice? These questions continue to plague us precisely because we seem to have come to the realization that theory informs *all* critical practice, whether or not the theory is acknowledged. Is it now a question of "choosing" a theory, as one chooses a profession or a brand of computer or a literary speciality? Must we choose, that is, between gynocriticism, with its emphasis on the reality, validity, and authority of woman's experience, and gynesis, "the putting into discourse of 'woman' as that process beyond the Cartesian Subject, the Dialectics of Representation, or Man's truth"? Do we choose gynocritics to explicate Gertrude Stein's life and gynesis to examine her literary works?

I will resist here the effort to come to grips with these perplexing issues in feminist literary criticism. The texts that follow explore in various ways the implications of these questions, mapping out the space of woman's experience on the literary landscape, pausing before the gulf between those critics who choose "theory" and those who emphasize "practice," between those who suggest that women should look to themselves and their own experience for models of critical discourse and those who suggest that we should look beyond the male-female dichotomies. To a certain degree, this dialogue between theorists and practitioners suggests that there is "nothing new" among the issues raised by feminist critics—and this discovery may be precisely the point at this moment in our literary critical history. Answering Elaine Showalter's and Germaine Greer's call for a discovery and rediscovery of woman's literary heritage, we are not clear how to undertake such an excavation into the subterranean passages of the patriarchal pantheon or what to do with Geneviève once we find her. How will we know her? How will we speak to her? Where will we place her? Perhaps more importantly, how will her renewed presence in the modern moment change our perceptions of ourselves—as women, as writers, as literary critics—and how will her presence redefine our notions of the patriarchy that presumably buried her?

NOTES

1. Alice Jardine, "Gynesis," *Diacritics*, 12 (1982), 55. Further references are cited parenthetically in the text. See as well her recently published study, *Gynesis: Configurations of Woman and Modernity* (Ithaca, N.Y.: Cornell University Press, 1985), which extends this argument.

2. See Nina Auerbach's essay in this volume, "Engorging the Patriarchy."

3. Elaine Showalter, "Towards a Feminist Poetics" in *Women Writing and Writing About Women*, ed. Mary Jacobus (New York: Barnes and Noble, 1979), p. 35. Subsequent references are cited parenthetically in the text.

4. Adrienne Rich, "It is the Lesbian in Us . . . " in *On Lies, Secrets and Silence: Selected Prose, 1966–1978* (New York: Norton, 1979).

5. Susan Stanford Friedman, *Psyche Reborn: The Emergence of H.D.* (Bloomington: Indiana University Press, 1981), pp. 97–98.

6. Richard Ellmann, *James Joyce* (New York: Oxford University Press, 1982), p. 702.

7. The most extended version of this complaint with Stein has been articulated by B. L. Reid, *Art By Subtraction: A Dissenting Opinion of Gertrude Stein* (Norman: University of Oklahoma Press, 1958). Although the title of this work suggests that it is a minority view of Stein, in fact the principles of Reid's investigation inform much of earlier Stein criticism.

8. Leo Stein's views are recorded in his *Journey Into Self*, ed. Edmund Fuller (New York: Crown, 1950). Gertrude Stein's relationship with Ezra Pound was problematic in part because of his pronounced anti-Semitism and also because she found him to be, like her brother, "a village explainer"—a type that wearied her. James R. Mellow examines this relationship in *Charmed Circle: Gertrude Stein and Company* (New York: Holt, Rinehart and Winston, 1974).

9. Catherine Gallagher, "Re-covering the Social in Recent Literary Theory," *Diacritics*, 12 (1982), 41. Subsequent references are cited parenthetically in the text.

10. Katherine Anne Porter, "Gertrude Stein: A Self-Portrait," *Harper's*, 195 (December 1947), 521–22. Subsequent references are cited parenthetically in the text.

11. Catharine R. Stimpson notes that Porter "sneered" at Stein as "a handsome old Jewish patriarch who had backslid and shaved off his beard" (quoted from Porter's *The Days Before* [New York: Harcourt, Brace and Co., 1952], p. 43). See Stimpson's "The Somograms of Gertrude Stein," *Poetics Today*, 6, 1–2 (1985), 67–80. I treat this subject at length in my study of expatriate modernist women writers, *Women of the Left Bank: Paris, 1900–1940* (Austin: University of Texas Press, 1986).

12. Those who have worked to explicate Stein's sexual language include Richard Bridgman, *Gertrude Stein in Pieces* (New York: Oxford University Press, 1970); Linda Simon, *The Biography of Alice B. Toklas* (New York: Doubleday and Co., 1977); Catharine R. Stimpson, "The Mind, The Body, and Gertrude Stein," *Critical Inquiry*, 3 (Spring 1977), 489–506; Elizabeth Fifer, "Is Flesh Advisable? The Interior Theater of Gertrude Stein," *Signs*, 4 (Spring 1979), 472–83. Catharine Stimpson is currently at work on a book-length study of Stein that continues this effort.

13. For an interesting discussion of recent French theoretical writing that would illuminate two very different facets of the sexuality of Stein's writing, see Diane Griffin Crowder, "Amazons and Mothers? Monique Wittig, Hélène Cixous and Theories of Women's Writing" in *Contemporary Literature*, 24 (Summer 1983), 117–44. As I comment later in this essay, neither Wittig nor Cixous discusses Stein's writing directly, but the principles their theories outline invite interesting—and diametrically opposed—readings of the sexual content of her work.

14. Recent critics who have revised readings of Stein's language include Marianne DeKoven, *A Different Language: Gertrude Stein's Experimental Writing* (Madison: University of Wisconsin Press, 1983); Neil Schmitz *Of Huck and Alice: Humorous Writ-

ing in American Literature (Minneapolis: University of Minnesota Press, 1983); Cynthia Secor, "The Question of Gertrude Stein" in *American Novelists Revisited: Essays in Feminist Criticism* (Boston: G. K. Hall, 1982).

15. My point is not to suggest that earlier works were not linguistically complex but to suggest that self-conscious linguistic experimentation was part of the modernist enterprise and as such constituted a conscious break with the earlier tradition in poetry and fiction. The question of style and its relation to subject and to the linguistic medium in which the writer works became an important concern of modernist authors, turning on the issue of the representational commitment of literature to external reality. One might argue that for a Jane Austen, for instance, the language of the written text was as complexly nuanced as the external reality it attempted to recreate. Style was the means by which the writer achieved a "fit" between the reality observed and the reality recorded. Modernists abandon a commitment to the representational, and in doing so render problematic the relation between language and style, between language and external reality. For modernists, language is no longer merely the medium of expression but the very subject under observation.

16. For an interesting assessment of the issues raised here in connection with the practice of feminist criticism, see Peggy Kamuf, "Replacing Feminist Criticism," *Diacritics* 12 (Summer 1982), 42–47.

17. For a discussion of the stages through which feminist criticism has passed (and is passing), see Showalter, "Feminist Poetics."

18. A fourth possibility that fixes critical practice within a theoretical construct is outlined in Myra Jehlen's "Archimedes and the Paradox of Feminist Criticism," *Signs*, 6 (1981), 575–601. Jehlen calls for a criticism that "engage[s] the dominant intellectual systems directly and organically: locating a feminist terrestrial fulcrum" (577). Her suggestion seems to be that before we can get "beyond humanism" as writers, readers, and scholars, we must more fully understand the implications of humanism for the institutions that direct our writing, reading, and scholarly efforts. Jehlen's call is for a rereading of the historical situation in which writing takes place, a rereading that would ground itself in a comparatist criticism that "join[s] rather than avoid[s] the contradiction between ideological and appreciative criticism on the supposition that the crucial issues manifest themselves precisely at the points of contradiction" (600). Jehlen's effort shares in the practice outlined by Judith Newton's essay printed here, "Making—and Remaking—History: Another Look at 'Patriarchy.' "

WOMEN'S TIME, WOMEN'S SPACE
Writing the History of Feminist Criticism

Elaine Showalter

The history of literary criticism, according to Grant Webster's study, *The Republic of Letters*, obeys laws similar to those proposed by Thomas Kuhn for the structure of scientific revolutions. The paradigms or charters of successful critical revolutions make their way through predictable phases from the ideological period that produces them to the emergence of strong authority figures who dictate what will henceforth be "normal" criticism and who redefine the literary canon, and finally to their obsolescence in the face of new writers, new ideologies, and new generations. The career of the individual critic parallels the rise and fall of the critical charter, from apprenticeship to superannuation; and for those who are especially original, productive, and bold, it offers the chance to become what Webster calls a Man of Letters, whose lucrative activities are best defined by the list on Edmund Wilson's notorious postcard of what he would not do.[1]

Feminist criticism fits this model reasonably well in most respects. If we have not quite seen our heresy become orthodoxy, and if our Women of Letters are scattered all over the map rather than concentrated in major universities, yet we have done the profession some service and it knows it; for a young critical school we have had an extraordinary degree of impact on the way literature is taught and read. If, as Gerald Graff has reminded us, "academic professionalism may require radical critical innovation as a condition of its expansion" as a "necessary spur to industrial growth,"[2] feminist criticism is obviously the most effective stimulant of the professional economy, since it has not only made it necessary to re-read the canon, but has also opened up for critical exploitation the vast, almost inexhaustible raw materials of women's texts.

But in many details feminist criticism seems like an anomaly in the history of modern criticism, and not only because it is gender-marked. We do not derive our charter from a single authority or a body of sacred theoretical texts.

There is no Mother of Feminist Criticism, no fundamental work against which one can measure other feminisms. Feminist criticism has been rather a powerful movement than a unified theory, a community of women with a shared set of concerns but with a complex and resourceful variety of methodological practices and theoretical affiliations. In addition to having a broad social and intellectual base, feminist criticism is unusually wide in scope. It is not limited or even partial to a single national literature, genre, or century; it is interdisciplinary in theory and practice; it can handle Harlequin Books as well as *Paradise Lost*.

In writing the history of feminist criticism, we need to ask at the start therefore where it belongs in the republic of letters. Is feminist criticism a discourse of marginality, criticism in "a different voice" outside of modern criticism and motivated by other concerns? Is it rather, as some male theorists think, inside modern criticism, less a different phenomenon than a mutation of modernism, "a special-interest glamorization of mainstream discourse"?[3] Or is feminist criticism the women's space within modern criticism, the "maternal subtext" of patriarchal theory, the repository for the questions of literary value, social change, and personal experience that modern criticism has tried to banish or repress?[4] How would we have to rewrite the history of modern criticism and its meta-histories of dynastic struggle and change if feminist criticism were seen as part of it?

One way of writing the history of feminist criticism would be to situate it in women's time—that is, to emphasize its specificity by narrating its development in terms of the internal relationships, continuities, friendships, and institutions that shaped the thinking and the writing of the last fifteen years.

In some sense the experiences and achievements of women have already been tacitly relegated to women's time in being hidden from history, obscured, or written out of the historical record. And from the masculinist point of view, women's time, like Miller time or the children's hour, may merely represent the pause in the day's occupations when serious business is set aside for a lighter entertainment, *le repos des professeurs*. Theorists of feminist historiography, however, such as Gerda Lerner, Joan Kelly-Gadol, Nancy Cott, and Elizabeth Fox-Genovese, have recuperated the concept of women's time as an essential model for writing the history of women. As they have explained, the process of restoring women's past to the historical record "is more than finding data about women and fitting it into the empty spaces within patriarchal history."[5] It demands that we challenge the temporal categories that have been adopted by traditional—that is, men's—history. Events and periods that are important to the development of male ideas and institutions may be negligible or irrelevant to women, and the temporal grid of men's history may filter out women's experiences, values, and achievements.

If we look at most male-authored histories of modern criticism, we will find that its periodization and conceptualization not only exclude feminist criticism but in a curious way negate it; one of the most commonplace and irritating ploys of this kind of mainstream critical history, in fact, is to condemn the apolitical nature of modern criticism and to issue a ringing call for a worldly, secular, oppositional critical practice, ignoring all the while the socially-based feminist criticism going on for fifteen years right under the author's nose. Presumably for Frank Lentricchia, Gerald Graff, and Edward Said, feminist criticism takes place in a women's time that is outside modernity.

But the "politics of exclusion," in Gayatri Spivak's term, are perhaps less problematic than the "politics of inclusion," which squeeze feminist criticism into an androcentric frame, distorting and devaluing its meaning.[6] Having omitted any reference at all to feminist criticism in *The Republic of Letters*, for example, Grant Webster now proposes in a sequel that we accommodate it to his Kuhnian model of critical change as a subcategory of the erotic revolution of the 1960s, a phenomenon not of criticism but of the counter-culture, and linked with the aesthetics of pornography and gay coming-out.[7]

The periodization of modern critical history in terms of New Criticism, structuralism, and post-structuralism also has unfortunate consequences for the history of feminist criticism, as Jonathan Culler has recently pointed out. In *On Deconstruction*, he argues:

> in mapping contemporary criticism as a struggle between New Critics, structuralists, and then post-structuralists, one would find it hard to do justice to feminist criticism, which has had a greater effect on the literary canon than any other critical movement and which has arguably been one of the most powerful forces of renovation in contemporary criticism. Though numerous post-structuralists are feminists (and vice-versa), feminist criticism is not post-structuralist, especially if post-structuralism is defined in its opposition to structuralism. To discuss feminist criticism adequately, one would need a different framework where the notion of post-structuralism was a product rather than a given.[8]

Generally speaking, of course, mainstream critical history has coped with the relationship between feminist criticism and these other movements by ignoring it. Most histories would locate the shift from structuralism to poststructuralism in the late 1960s, in the space between Roland Barthes's *Introduction to the Structural Analysis of Narratives* (1966), which appealed to a general grammar of narrative, and his *S/Z* (1970), which emphasized the self-contained difference of each text and rejected the idea of a system of narrative description. And they would point to the Johns Hopkins Conference on "The Structuralist Controversy and the Sciences of Man" in 1966, when Jacques Derrida first spoke to an audience of "Over one hundred humanists and social scientists from the U.S. and eight other countries."[9] But in a history of feminist criticism the Hopkins conference would occupy a minor place if it appeared at all, not only because, so far as I can determine, no women were invited to attend it; but also because the ideologies of structuralism were not the ones that galvanized women into an awareness that the time had come to speak out.

Looking at the question from the other side, Terry Eagleton has attempted to resolve the gender gap in the history of modern criticism by arguing that post-structuralism grew out of structuralism precisely as a response to the political demands and personal issues raised by the women's movement, the feminist insistence that neither Marxist economics nor the sciences of the text could explain the deeply held ideologies of gender. In *Literary Theory*, Eagleton asserts that for deconstructive theory and practice, the most blatant influential, perdurable, and virulent of all the binary oppositions must be that of masculine and feminine.[10]

But feminists will be as startled by this news of their power as their structuralist brethren. Eagleton passes over the details of the gritty historical process by which structuralism *recognized* the relevance of feminist issues and adapted to them. From the enlightened perspective of Eagleton's current admirable pro-feminist stance, it may appear that all along there has been steady and welcome feminization of critical discourse, but feminists miss accounts of real confrontations between critical positions, such as the first feminist literary session at the Chicago MLA in 1970, or the presentation of the Marxist-Feminist Literature Collective, a small and short-lived English group whose members since have produced about ninety percent of the most important feminist criticism in Great Britain, at the Essex Conference on the Sociology of Literature in 1977. The abstractions of most official histories of criticism are too coarse to accommodate the false starts, the lucky breaks, the material pressures, the intellectual slog, or, least of all, the human drama that make up a living critical movement.

To do justice to the texture of this history, we need to begin by seeing feminist criticism from within and by defining its periodization within women's time instead of as a subset of standard critical time. The history of feminist criticism is more than a history of ideas or institutions; it takes in events on many levels of women's daily lives. But to limit ourselves to women's time would be equally misleading, since feminist criticism is also constituted by the histories of the academy, the discipline, and modern criticism itself. Insofar as feminist criticism is a kind of women's writing, it is a double-voiced discourse that is influenced by both the muted and the dominant cultures, that operates at the juncture of two traditions, and that has both a Mother and a Father Time. In the second phase of this history, therefore, we need to trace the effects of modern criticism and especially modern theory upon feminist criticism as it evolved. But in the final phase, we must ask for a synchronization of women's time and critical time, a history of modern criticism to which feminist criticism has been restored and thus a history with a different rhythm and shape.

Ideally, a history of feminist criticism would begin with interviews of pioneers in the field about how they became feminist critics. It would explain how Gilbert met Gubar, how Catharine Stimpson and Domna Stanton came to edit *Signs*, how the Bunting Institute became a critical community. It would include the voices of black and lesbian and Marxist feminist critics discussing the factors of race, sexuality, and class. In writing this essay, I did in fact speak to a number of feminist critics in the United States, England, and France, about their motives, influences, and careers; and their comments have guided me in constructing a historical outline. But space permits me to tell only one story; and it seems fair that it should be my own.

In 1968 I was a faculty wife with a small child trying to write what seemed to be a hopeless dissertation on the double critical standard applied to Victorian women novelists. The dissertation seemed doomed for several reasons. In the first place, by choosing to write on this unfashionable topic, I had labeled myself as a limited scholar with a narrow range of eccentric interests, like an ornithologist writing on Shelley; or worse, as a strident feminist to whom better-adjusted women professionals reacted, as Sandra Gilbert recalls in her own memoir of the period, "with a mixture of curiosity and scorn."[11] It was frightening to write a dissertation that seemed so different from the criticism I was reading in scholarly journals; there were very few precedents for what I wanted to say. And even if I finished it, I saw no professional future for myself. Two of the three colleges within commuting distance of my husband's job had told me that they did not hire women. After a disheartening period as the worst statistician ever employed by the Educational Testing Service, I had taken a part-time temporary instructorship teaching composition at Douglass, the women's college of Rutgers, a job I had been warned would never become regular. I had been living in Paris watching the police pull down the barricades of May 1968, and I had been part of the radical protest at the MLA that December, but I had not really connected the political turbulence of that extraordinary year with the questions I faced in my own work.

It was not until I joined the women's liberation movement in the spring of 1969 and began to teach a course on women and literature, that the personal became the critical, and that my passionate interest in women's writing began to define itself as feminist criticism. It was not isolation, discrimination, radical politics, the structuralist controversy, or an Oedipal rebellion against Cleanth Brooks that made women feminist critics, but the polemical force, activist commitment, powerful analysis, and sense of mutual endeavor that came out of the women's movement.

Something of the change in tone that distinguished feminist criticism from its pre-1968 precedents may be gathered by noting the ambivalence of purpose and the deprivation of political context that characterized the writing of even such major female precursors as Simone de Beauvoir, Queenie Leavis, and Mary Ellmann. Beauvoir, for example, refused to call *The Second Sex* a feminist work and would not acknowledge its ambitions to provide a systematic analysis of women's condition. Sartre, she insisted, was a philosopher, that is "somebody who truly builds a philosophical system"; she was only "someone who likes philosophy."[12] In England, Queenie Leavis's highly original essays on nineteenth-century women writers were produced in between the lines of F. R. Leavis's master *oeuvre*. After his death, Queenie Leavis admitted to an interviewer that she had actually written large parts of *The Great Tradition* and other books "without acknowledgment. I didn't mind at all. He was very grateful of course. I was more scholarly than he was, perhaps, because I like ferreting about in libraries. He didn't have time to go to libraries."[13] If F.R. was the literary critic who built the system, she was simply someone who liked books and had time to go to libraries. Even Mary Ellmann's brilliant study, *Thinking About Women*, published in 1968, which anticipated and influenced the feminist critique of the next five years, revealed in its unassuming and offhand title the rejection or abdication of critical authority that made the construction of a feminist poetics historically impossible outside of a women's movement.

And yet there is a paradox in our history. While feminist criticism could not have existed without the galvanizing ideology and power of the women's movement, the women's movement would not have occurred without a generation of women who liked books—graduate students, assistant professors, editors, writers, faculty wives, highly educated products of the academic expansion of the 1960s—whose avid, devoted, socially-reinforced identifications with fictional heroines were coming into conflict with the sexist realities they encountered everyday.

Feminism spoke to our lived experience with the fierce urgency of a religious revelation, a Great Awakening. Sandra Gilbert is one of a number of feminist critics who have compared its beginnings to a conversion process, noting that:

> most feminist critics speak . . . like people who must bear witness, people who must enact and express in their own lives and words the revisionary sense of transformation that seems inevitably to attend the apparently simple discovery that the experiences of women in and with literature are different from those of men.[14]

Coming at a historical moment when the profession of literary studies in general seemed most sterile, pointless, and insecure, when for every Man of Letters there were one hundred English professors wishing they had gone to law school, the freshness and exuberance of feminist criticism, the sense of being embarked

on a great intellectual journey, the conviction that what we were doing mattered
in the world, the discovery of women's networks, indeed of sisterhood, made
its early years as joyous as they were fruitful, and with Gissing's heroines of
the 1890s we might have exclaimed, "Thank Heaven we are women."

If in its origins feminist criticism derived more from feminism than from
criticism, we could argue that today the situation is reversed. Since 1975 a
second wave has included many women, especially in French and Comparative
Literature, who have come to feminist criticism via psychoanalytic, post-structuralist, or deconstructionist theory, rather than via the women's movement
and women's studies. Recently, several male theorists, especially those engaged
in Marxist or black critical theory, have begun to write seriously about feminist
criticism as well.[15] And more generally, even pioneering practitioners have
been driven to ask theoretical questions and to accept the modern idea that
there can be no practice without theory, even if theory is unformulated or
incomplete.

The post-structural feminist critics see continental theory as the most powerful means to understanding the production of sexual difference in language,
reading, and writing. They argue too that the categories of the woman reader,
women's culture, and the woman's text, while politically useful, are unexamined
and essentialist. From the perspective of some post-structuralist feminists the
first phase of feminist criticism may be dismissed as theoretically naive, an
American "flight towards empiricism" which assumes "an unbroken continuity
between 'life' and 'text.' "[16] Only theory, they insist, can provide adequate
answers to feminist questions and a position from which to discuss the whole
of literature and culture, rather than one within a ghetto of female experience.

For some pioneering feminist critics, on the other hand, the glittering critical
theories of Derrida, Althusser, and Lacan seem like golden apples thrown in
Atalanta's path to keep her from winning the race. In the adaptation of continental theory to feminist practice they see the dictatorship of the dominant,
the surrender of hard-won critical autonomy to a reigning language and style.
The post-structuralist feminist, some would argue, is a rhetorical double agent,
a little drummer girl who plays go-between in male critical quarrels.

In writing the history of feminist criticism, I want to avoid, however, such
a hostile polarization of French and American feminist discourse, arid theory
and crude empiricism, obscurantism or essentialism. In formulating or endorsing such hierarchical binary oppositions, we not only fall into the old dualistic traps, but genuinely misrepresent the much more complex and nuanced
reality of feminist critical practice. American feminist criticism is as theoretically
sophisticated as its continental sister, while the sheer brilliance and ambition
of post-structuralist feminist writing has made its presence in the academy
impossible for even the most unreconstructed critics to ignore. While feminist

critical work will proceed on both fronts, this does not mean that we are torn by dissension, but rather that we are enriched by dialectical possibilities.

Since 1975, feminist criticism has taken two theoretical directions, that of the Anglo-American focus on the specificity of women's writing I have called *gynocritics*, and that of the French exploration of the textual consequences and representations of sexual difference that Alice Jardine has named *gynesis*.[17] These ought not to be taken as oppositional or exclusive terms either; in fact they describe tendencies within feminist critical theory rather than absolute categories. As such, however, they represent different emphases and perceptions of the role of feminist inquiry. Gynocritics is, roughly speaking, historical in orientation; it looks at women's writing as it has actually occurred and tries to define its specific characteristics of language, genre, and literary influence, within a cultural network that includes variables of race, class, and nationality.

Gynesis rejects, however, the temporal dimension of women's experience, what Julia Kristeva calls *le temps des femmes*, and seeks instead to understand the space granted to the feminine in the symbolic contract. "When evoking the name and destiny of women," Kristeva writes, "one thinks more of the *space* generating and forming the human species than of *time*, becoming, or history."[18] The problematic of women's space has had practical meanings, of course, for Anglo-American feminist inquiry as well; in social anthropology, where women's social maps and spatial domains have been topics for analysis; in the creative arts where "women's space" has become a code word for a feminist *salon des refusés*; and in literary theory where female space is the alternative linguistic and imaginative place from which women can speak. Gynesis goes beyond these, however, to repossess as a field of inquiry all the space of the Other, the gaps, silences, and absences of discourse and representation, to which the feminine has traditionally been relegated. As Alice Jardine explains, "the space 'outside' of the conscious subject has always connoted the feminine in Western thought— and any movement into alterity is a movement into that female space."[19] This space is most productively studied via theories of philosophy and psychoanalysis. In the texts of gynesis, very little attention is paid to women writers; even the concept of *écriture féminine* developed by the most influential critic of this school, Hélène Cixous, describes the symbolically or metaphorically feminine attributes of avant-garde writing rather than writing by women. Finally, some of the most prominent French theorists of gynesis, including Kristeva, Cixous, and Sarah Kofman, reject the label of "feminist," or even regard themselves as anti-feminist, seeing feminism in its activist mode as a liberal anachronism, or as "the final hysterization of middle-class women."[20]

Another very striking aspect of gynesis is its dependence on male masters and male theoretical texts. Although virtually all American feminist critics of the first wave were trained by men (as far as I know, I am one of the few in this group to have had a woman dissertation director), their graduate training occurred in a wide range of universities, and none became a disciple of a particular male teacher. It might be said that like the women of the Amahagger tribe described by Rider Haggard in *She*, pioneering American feminist critics "never pay attention to or even acknowledge any man as their father, even when their male parentage is perfectly well known."[21]

In contrast, Lacan's Ecole Freudienne, and especially his seminar of 1972–1973 on "Femininity," played a central role in the development of gynesis, and Derrida has been an even more significant figure in its recent years. According to Stuart Schneiderman, Lacan's American disciple and client, the seminar called "Encore," "spoke to women in a way few psychoanalytic texts have ever done, and it exerted an important influence on French feminism."[22] In these teasing and gnomic lectures on feminine sexuality Lacan gave his fullest account of the symbolic construction of the feminine through language and representation and his most explicit attack on essentialist beliefs in the nature of Woman. "There is no such thing as *The* woman," he declared, "where the definite article stands for the universal."[23] Lacan's emphasis on the symbolic construction of sexual difference and his recasting of Freudian biologism in terms of language influenced a number of female theorists in several fields. By 1974, as Jane Gallop reports, Lacan had become the "ladies' man" of French feminism, the subject of a special issue of *L'Arc* with essays by Shoshana Felman, Catherine Clément, and Luce Irigaray, among others.[24] In 1974, too, Lacanian ideas were introduced to Anglo-American feminist thought by Juliet Mitchell in *Psychoanalysis and Feminism*; and recently Mitchell, along with Jacqueline Rose, translated Lacan's essays on feminine sexuality. Her readings of Freud and Lacan were further mediated for American feminists in two important reviews, the first by the structuralist anthropologist Sherry Ortner in *Feminist Studies*, and the second by Jane Gallop in the "Textual Politics" issue of *Diacritics* in 1976, which concluded with a call to feminist theory to "reexamine its ends in view of Lacanian psychoanalysis."[25]

The very strangeness and difficulty of Lacanian theory and of French feminist writing made it fascinating to many American feminists who began to encounter it in translations of Cixous, Kristeva, and Irigaray; in the review essays by Elaine Marks and Carolyn Burke published in the late 1970s in *Signs*; and in the collection *New French Feminisms*, edited by Marks and Isabelle de Courtivron, which appeared in 1980.[26]

That Lacan was a man who, as Schneiderman sadly concedes, "loved women, but loved them too well and too much," has now become the topic of a certain brand of high Parisian scandal, as in Philippe Sollers's *roman à clef, Femmes,* in which many of the leading women in French gynesic feminism play what one hopes are fantasy roles.[27] But well before these post-mortem revelations, Derridean accusations of phallocentrism had seriously diminished Lacan's power as a theoretical force in gynesis. One factor in Derrida's ascendancy to the maitre's throne has been his acclaimed regular trips to the United States to teach at Hopkins, Cornell, and Yale, whereas Lacan's American tour in 1975 was a near disaster. More importantly, post-structuralist feminists such as Gayatri Spivak have found in Derrida's critique of phallogocentrism and radical questioning of all discourse a " 'feminization' of the practice of philosophy," and they believe that deconstruction is "an ultimately political practice," despite the skepticism of other critics, such as Christopher Norris, about Derrida's "curious equation" involving women, sexuality, and writing.[28]

The interest in women's writing, on the other hand, that is crucial to gynocritics preceded theoretical formulations and came initially from the feminist critic's own experience as a writer and from her identification with the anxieties and conflicts women writers faced in patriarchal culture. While modern criticism in general is a dialogue among critics because few contemporary writers have commanded the critic's attention, feminist criticism is again very different. Not only did Adrienne Rich, Tillie Olsen, Grace Paley, Audre Lord, Anne Sexton, and Alice Walker command attention, they also shared the platforms at conferences and contributed to feminist journals. And gynocritics has been linked from the beginning with the enterprise of getting women into print. In the past decade, feminist publishing houses like the Feminist Press, éditions des femmes, and Virago Press, to name the top three in the U.S., France, and England, have among them brought out more than three hundred books.

But theoretical issues rapidly began to emerge from reading and research. The point at which the difference or specificity of women's writing was conceptualized as the focus of feminist criticism was, in my opinion, the single most important breakthrough in its history. While a critical paradigm alters as it evolves, in establishing itself it must make what Frye called an inductive leap, discovering a new object that can be charted by new laws. Although critics and writers had talked for centuries about women's writing, when feminist criticism set out to discover how it worked, to map the territory of the female imagination and the structures of the female plot, it was doing something completely new; it broke with previous ways of thinking about women's writing even if it had been dependent on them for its own development.[29]

One of these breaks was the rewriting of the literary history of women novelists in women's time, a deliberate strategic foregrounding of the continuities and inter-relations of a women's literary tradition. A second break was the hypothesis of nineteenth-century women's writing as a coded response to male images, influences, and texts, a form of protest against patriarchal literary authority. But the theoretical history of gynocritics developed in tempo with political changes in the women's movement and with the increasing power of women in the profession. When I wrote *A Literature of Their Own* in the early 1970s, I felt that it was crucial for my whole critical enterprise to construct a history with minimal dependence on, even minimal reference to, male authorities. When Gilbert and Gubar wrote *The Madwoman in the Attic* a few years later, they were freer to juxtapose feminist insights with masculine traditions and to make their own theory a feminist revision of Harold Bloom. Subsequently, developments in the fields of psychology, history, and anthropology about the construction of gender and sexual specificity have increased the theoretical complexity of gynocritical analyses that were never as innocent or unself-conscious as later arrivals have complained.

Since 1980, as feminist criticism in general has moved inexorably, book by book, back into standard critical time, its canon has undergone a parallel change. In the early 1970s, Kate Chopin's *The Awakening* was the most popular text in women's literature courses for reasons that were predominantly thematic. In the *Kate Chopin Newsletter*, now defunct, Emily Toth explained that Chopin raised "questions which are still being asked by women today."[30] One of the reasons *The Awakening* became the scripture of early feminist criticism was the resonance of "awakening" itself. Along with *Jane Eyre* and Toni Morrison's *The Bluest Eye*, Chopin's novel will be reprinted in full in the *Norton Anthology of Literature by Women* (1985), edited by Gilbert and Gubar, which will establish a feminist canon for the next generation.

But as the euphoria of awakening subsided and was replaced by a vision of the small, difficult changes and immense intellectual labors ahead, identification with Chopin and with women's condition shifted to less accessible and more problematic works. With Brontë, *Jane Eyre* gave way to *Villette*. With Eliot, *The Mill on the Floss*, beloved of Simone de Beauvoir, gave way first to *Middlemarch*, which posed the "woman question" in painfully relevant terms, and then to *Daniel Deronda*, beloved of no one, which seemed to be Eliot's most contradictory and divided study of women in patriarchal culture. In 1974, *Daniel Deronda* too was read in radical feminist circles as a guide to living, as Jane Alpert tells us in her autobiography *Growing Up Underground*. After four years as a political fugitive, Alpert was holed up in a room in Pittsfield, Massachusetts, deciding whether to surrender to the FBI:

> A bit of George Eliot's dialogue [she notes] kept echoing in my mind. "If you determine to face these hardships and still try," the composer Herr Klesmer says to the heroine, "you will have the dignity of a high purpose, even though you may have chosen unfortunately". . . . I decided—and George Elliot had as much to do with my choice as anyone else—that I was going to take the high road. I was going to turn myself in.[31]

It is wonderful that Alpert should have had these high-minded meditations in Pittsfield, the headquarters of the American Renaissance, yet typical that in her moment of crisis she should not have turned to Hawthorne or Melville (although her lover, born Samuel Grossman, had renamed himself Melville in honor of the author of *Moby Dick*) but to Eliot's stern moralism, making Pittsfield a place of as much allegorical resonance for an American feminist radical of the early 1970s as Middlemarch or St. Oggs had been for Eliot's heroines of the century before.

Since the late 1970s, though, feminist readings of *Daniel Deronda* show the impact of deconstruction, since the juxtaposition of the novel's two stories seems made to order for deconstructionist double-readings. The theories of Lacan and Foucault have also influenced readings such as Catherine Belsey's analysis of *Deronda* as "the history of an impossible resistance," in which "the text confers upon Gwendolen a kind of heroism in that she consistently resists her own hysterization, refuses to identify with her own sexuality."[32]

To note that the interests and vocabularies of feminism and post-structuralism have coincided in the choice of this text brings me back to my original question: What is the relationship between feminist criticism and modern criticism? If we think of the history of feminist criticsm as an anti-history of modern criticism, it will appear initially that modern theory has been a defensive reaction against the feminization of the profession. Northrop Frye has been the frankest in acknowledging the "dismal sexist symbology," which says that "the sciences, especially the physical sciences, are rugged, aggressive, out in the world doing things, and so symbolically male, whereas the literatures are narcissistic, intuitive, fanciful, staying at home and making the home more beautiful, but not doing anything serious and therefore symbolically female."[33] Frye's *Anatomy of Criticism* (1957) attempted to make the study of literature more serious and manly by structuring its principles scientifically like the laws of physics, biology, or mathematics.

When contemporary male theorists attempt to characterize the opposition against which their new paradigm asserts itself, they frequently resort to metaphors of the feminine. For Graff, the target of the New Criticism was the "genteel schoolmarm theory of literature."[34] Worse yet, as Eagleton scornfully remarks in *Criticism and Ideology*, traditional criticism is a "mere handmaiden to literature," a humble, quasi-domestic and undoubtedly ill-paid servant of the text.[35] Even when the metaphor appears to flatter women, as in Geoffrey Hartman's "Muse of Criticism," "more a governess than a muse, the stern daughter of books no longer read under trees and in the fields," in fact it implicitly excludes women from critical production, since it assumes that the critic will be a man.[36] Modern critical theory, however, has made strenuous efforts to get away from the feminine dependencies conjured up in the images of the schoolmarm, the governess, and the handmaiden, by joining forces with the tougher disciplines of linguistics, philosophy, and psychoanalysis.

Yet it is striking that within the past year or two, a number of distinguished literary theorists have begun to acknowledge that feminist criticism offers a paradigm for the kind of criticism they really want to do, that it seems to offer a way out of the labyrinth of indeterminacy, non-interference and self-referentiality post-structuralism has built for itself. For Terry Eagleton, for example, feminism is the closest we have come to a revolutionary critical practice that "challenges the separation of cultural criticism from cultural production."[37] For Barbara Hernnstein Smith, feminist criticism is the only approach centrally concerned with the issues of literary value and evaluation that have been banished from modern theoretical discourse.[38] Even Edward Said, in the single sentence that mentions feminist critics in his recent book, concedes that we have been the ones to open up the question of the political contexts of culture.[39]

This belated interest in feminist strategies, however, holds as many dangers as opportunities for our future. As Gayatri Spivak has warned, we must be wary of the "recuperation of the critical energies of feminism into the ruling ideology of Departments of English" and the possibility that this integration "might involve compromises . . . that might not let a feminism survive."[40] Insofar as the production of theory is now the business of modern criticism, there will be increased pressure on feminist criticism to accommodate itself more and more to the prevailing terminologies and systems, abandoning in the process the political priorities and the concerns for the personal that have made it so effective in the past.

As women have been the second sex, so the feminist critic has been historically the second reader, not only of dissertations but also of texts. But we are far from obsolescence; as critical movements go, we are not even in our prime, and feminist critics i. .y be the first readers yet before our charter gives way to the inevitable mutations of history. Perhaps modern criticism, instead of graciously taking us into its historical embrace, will learn some lessons about itself from our anomalous movement, and will begin to question the myths of its own immaculate conception in the realms of pure and universal thought. At that point too, the power of gender will cease to be the special intellectual property of feminist criticism, and will be seen as a crucial determinant in the history of all forms of reading and writing. It may well turn out that in the critical histories of the future, these years will not be remembered as the Age of Structuralism or the Age of Deconstruction, but as the Age of Feminism. Wouldn't it be a surprise if, without having realized it, we have all been living in women's time?

NOTES

1. Grant Webster, *The Republic of Letters: A History of Postwar American Literary Opinion* (Baltimore: Johns Hopkins University Press, 1979), p. 33.

2. Gerald Graff, *Literature Against Itself: Literary Ideas in Modern Society* (Chicago: University of Chicago Press, 1979), p. 95.

3. See Carol Gilligan, *In a Different Voice: Psychological Theory and Women's Development* (Cambridge, Mass.: Harvard University Press, 1982); and Gayatri Chakravorty Spivak, "The Politics of Interpretations," *Critical Inquiry*, 9 (September 1982), 274.

4. See Coppélia Kahn, "Excavating 'Those Dim Minoan Regions': Maternal Subtexts in Patriarchal Literature," *Diacritics*, 12 (1982), 32–41.

5. Gerda Lerner, *The Majority Finds Its Past: Placing Women in History* (New York: Oxford University Press, 1979), p. 174.

6. Spivak, 276.

7. Grant Webster, "American Literary Criticism: A Bibliographical Essay," *American Studies International* (Autumn 1981), pp. 18–20.

8. Jonathan Culler, On *Deconstruction* (Ithaca, N.Y.: Cornell University Press, 1983), p. 30.

9. See Frank Lentricchia, *After the New Criticism* (Chicago: University of Chicago Press, 1980), p. 157.

10. Terry Eagleton, *Literary Theory: An Introduction* (London: Basil Blackwell, 1983), pp. 148–50.

11. Sandra M. Gilbert, "Life Studies, or Speech After Long Silence," *College English*, 40 (April 1979), 849.

12. Margaret A. Simons and Jessica Benjamin, "Simone de Beauvoir: An Interview," *Feminist Studies*, 5 (Summer 1979), 338.

13. See P.J.M. Robertson, "Queen of Critics: The Achievement of Q. D. Leavis," *Novel*, 16 (Winter 1983), 141.

14. Gilbert, 850.

15. See for example Terry Eagleton, *Literary Theory*; Wayne Booth, "Freedom of Interpretation: Bakhtin and the Challenge of Feminist Criticism," *Critical Inquiry*, 9 (September 1982), 45–76; Jonathan Culler, On *Deconstruction*; and Henry Louis Gates, Introduction to *Our Nig* by Harriet Wilson (New York: Vintage, 1983).

16. Mary Jacobus, "Is There a Woman in This Text?" *New Literary History*, 14 (Autumn 1982), 138.

17. Alice Jardine, "Gynesis," *Diacritics*, 12 (Summer 1982), 54–65. See also Jardine, *Gynesis: Configurations of Woman and Modernity* (Ithaca, N.Y., and London: Cornell University Press, 1985).

18. Julia Kristeva, "Women's Time," *Signs*, 7 (Autumn 1981), 15.

19. Jardine, 59–60.

20. See Alice Jardine, "Introduction to Julia Kristeva's 'Women's Time,' " *Signs*, 7 (Autumn 1981), 11–12 and n. 12.

21. Rider Haggard, *She* (New York: Airmont, 1967), p. 76.

22. Stuart Schneiderman, *Jacques Lacan: The Death of an Intellectual Hero* (Cambridge, Mass.: Harvard University Press, 1983), p. 30. See also the testimony of a French feminist who was there: Catherine Clément, *The Lives and Legends of Jacques Lacan*, trans. Arthur Goldhammer (New York: Columbia University Press, 1983), pp. 61–67.

23. Jacques Lacan, "God and the Jouissance of Woman," in *Feminine Sexuality: Jacques Lacan and the école freudienne*, eds. Juliet Mitchell and Jacqueline Rose (New York: Norton, 1983), p. 144.

24. Jane Gallop, *The Daughter's Seduction: Feminism and Psychoanalysis* (Ithaca, N.Y.: Cornell University Press, 1972), chapter 3.

25. Sherry Ortner, "Oedipal Father, Mother's Brother and the Penis," *Feminist Studies*, 2 (1975), 176–82; and Jane Gallop, "The Ghost of Lacan, The Trace of Language," *Diacritics*, 5 (Winter 1975), 24.

26. Elaine Marks and Isabelle de Courtivron, eds., *New French Feminisms* (Amherst: University of Massachusetts Press, 1980).

27. Schneiderman, p. 30.

28. See Gayatri Spivak, "Displacement and the Discourse of Woman," in Mark Krupnik, ed., *Displacement: Derrida and After* (Bloomington and London: Indiana University Press, 1983), and Christopher Norris, *Deconstruction: Theory and Practice* (London: Methuen, 1982), p. 71.

29. In this paragraph I have adapted Juliet Mitchell's statement about the discovery of the unconscious in psychoanalysis, in *Psychoanalysis and Feminism* (New York: Pantheon, 1974), p. 322.

30. Emily Toth, "Why a *Kate Chopin Newsletter?*" *Kate Chopin Newsletter*, 1 (Spring 1975), 2.

31. Jane Alpert, *Growing Up Underground* (New York: Morrow, 1981), p. 355.

32. Catherine Belsey, "Re-reading the Great Tradition," in *Re-reading English*, ed. Peter Widdowson (New York and London: Methuen, 1982), pp. 132–33.

33. Northrop Frye, "Expanding Eyes," *Critical Inquiry*, 11 (1975), 201–02. I also discuss this passage in "Towards a Feminist Poetics," in *Women Writing and Writing About Women*, ed. Mary Jacobus, (New York: Barnes and Noble, 1979), pp. 37–38.

34. Graff, p. 5.

35. Terry Eagleton, *Criticism and Ideology* (London: NLB, 1976), p. 11.

36. Geoffrey Hartman, *Criticism in the Wilderness* (New Haven: Yale University Press, 1980), p. 175.

37. Terry Eagleton, *Walter Benjamin, or Towards a Revolutionary Criticism* (London: Verso Editions and NLB, 1981), p. 99.

38. Barbara Hernnstein Smith, "Contingencies of Value," *Critical Inquiry*, 10 (September 1983), 7.

39. Edward Said, *The World, the Text and the Critic*, (Cambridge, Mass.: Harvard University Press, 1983), p. 169.

40. Gayatri Spivak, "A Response to Annette Kolodny," unpublished essay, University of Texas, Austin. Thanks to Gayatri Spivak for sharing this work with me.

THE MADWOMAN
AND HER LANGUAGES
Why I Don't Do Feminist Literary Theory

Nina Baym

Perhaps the central issue in academic literary feminism right now is theory itself. "Early" academic literary feminism—if one may use this word for an enterprise only launched in the early 1970s—developed along two clear paths. First, a pragmatic, empirical attempt to look at women—in society or in texts— as images in literature, as authors, as readers; second, a visionary attempt to describe women's writing in a reconstructed future, an attempt in which description often merged with exhortation. Theory developed later, mainly in response to what Elaine Showalter has described as an androcentric "critical community increasingly theoretical in its interests and indifferent to women's writing."[1] In other words, feminist theory addresses an audience of prestigious male academics and attempts to win its respect. It succeeds, so far as I can see, only when it ignores or dimisses the earlier paths of feminist literary study as "naive" and grounds its own theories in those currently in vogue with the men who make theory: deconstruction, for example, or Marxism. These grounding theories manifest more than mere indifference to women's writing; they are irretrievably misogynist. As a result of building on misogynist foundations, feminist theorists mainly excoriate their deviating sisters.

Feminism has always been bifurcated by contention between pluralists and legalists. Pluralists anticipate the unexpected, encourage diversity; legalists locate the correct position and marshal women within the ranks. As for recent literary theory, it is deeply legalistic and judgmental. Infractions—the wrong theory, theoretical errors, or insouciant disregard for theoretical implications— are crimes. Pluralists "dance"; theorists "storm" or "march."[2] Literary theories—in striking contrast to scientific theories—are designed to constrain what may allowably be said or discovered. Such totalizing by feminist theorists reproduces *to the letter* the appropriation of women's experience by men, substituting only the appropriation and naming of that experience by a subset of women: themselves.[3] Such structural repetition undermines the feminist project.

It is easier to totalize when one restricts application of theories to texts already sanctioned by the academy. These restrictions, however, elide such difficult matters as the relation of the canon to standards of "literariness,"[4] or of gender to genre. There is nothing natural or universal about "creative writing." Women or men in western society undertaking to produce what they hope will be viewed as "serious" writing do so in complicated, culturally mediated ways. "Seriousness" as a criterion of literary merit, for one obvious example, implies a profound Victorian patriarchal didacticism, and is often used to denigrate the popular women's genres. Still, no matter how our standards change in future, to name a work as "literary" will always endow it with a degree of artifice, that must inevitably traverse and confuse any hypothesized necessary, immutable relation between "women writing" and "writing by women."

Present feminist theory encourages us, as a chief means of expanding the concept of the literary, to study private—hence presumably "natural"—writings of women. But even diaries and letters are written according to rules. And such "expansion" could well be understood rather as a contraction of the idea of writing, and an iteration of the stereotype of woman as a wholly private, purely expressive being. Such reinscription, indeed incarceration, of women in the private sphere seems to me an ominous countertrend in an era notable for the dramatic entry of women into hitherto all-male preserves of public activity: not to mime men but to save our own lives *from* men. More specific to literature, the trend involves rendering invisible the public forms in which women have long written and continue to write so well. We neglect the writings—as writings—of (for example) Hannah Arendt, Margaret Mead, Suzanne Langer, and Rachel Carson. Indeed, we neglect all "non-imaginative" discourse: feature writing, journalism, scientific works both professional and popular, philosophical essays, legal briefs, advertising. At the root of the neglect, simply, is the desire to maintain "difference," for all current theory requires sexual difference as its ground. The title of a special issue of the androcentric journal *Critical Inquiry*, "Writing and Sexual Difference," made this assumption clear, and it appropriated the feminist label for theories that necessarily assumed differences fully known. Differences abound; but what they are, how they are constituted, what they entail, and whether they must be constant, seem to me above all questions that a feminist might ask, questions that are least adequately answered. Today's feminist literary theory makes asking an act of empirical antitheory, and hence a heresy. It is finally more concerned to be theoretical than to be feminist. It speaks from the position of the *castrata*.

To accept woman as castrated is to evince a "hegemonic" mindset that recapitulates and hence capitulates to fear, dislike, and contempt of women. What will concern me in the rest of this essay are some foci of misogyny in present theory. I concentrate on four recurrent motifs, which I name: the madwoman; a female language; the father; the mother.

i. The Madwoman

The name comes from Sandra M. Gilbert and Susan Gubar's impressive and influential study of nineteenth-century British women writers, *The Madwoman in the Attic*.[5] Their book applies traditional close-reading and image study techniques to the texts of already-canonized nineteenth-century women writers, in search of a sign of the writers'—presumably shared—biographical situation as writers. It assumes, then, that a sign will be found, and finds it in the recurrent figure of the madwoman. Literary achievement for the nineteenth-century woman, they claim, was psychologically costly because it required defiance of the misogynist strictures and structures of Victorian patriarchy. Defiance had to be hidden; suppressed, it smoldered as a pure rage revealed in the furious madwoman who disrupts or ruptures so many women's texts. Gilbert and Gubar derived this theory of the woman writer from Harold Bloom's "anxiety of influence." That theory had created authorship as an exclusively male phenomenon, wherein would-be-powerful poet sons struggled to overthrow, while avowing loyalty to, already-powerful poet fathers. Possibly, its ulterior motive was to eliminate women from the canon; possibly, the hostile male tradition against which Gilbert and Gubar found their madwomen authors struggling in what they labelled an "anxiety of authorship" was, at least partly, hypostatized in the work they took as their starting point. Possibly, however, Bloom simply expressed traditional misogyny in contemporary terms.

Gilbert and Gubar modified Bloom in one important way. His approach was ahistorical, imposing a quasi-Freudian father and son conflict on literary history as a function of the ineluctable nature of the (male) poet's psyche. The "anxiety of authorship," however, is advanced as a historical concept, a fruitfully accurate description of the state of literature and attitudes toward it in a particular place at a particular time. But though advanced as a historical fact, the anxiety of authorship, except for Emily Dickinson, is demonstrated only by intra-textual evidence; thus *The Madwoman in the Attic* assumes the existence of the historical and literary situation which its textual readings require. Strikingly absent, too, from consideration of the historical moment in the analysis is the appearance among women of a realizable ambition to become professional writers. Traditionally hermeneutic, Gilbert and Gubar concentrate on a hidden message—female anxiety of authorship—while reading past the surface evidence that their studies provide for the arrival of the woman professional author.

The madwoman who names Gilbert and Gubar's book is the nonlingual Bertha Mason from *Jane Eyre*. Gilbert and Gubar read her as "Jane's truest and darkest double . . . the ferocious secret self Jane has been trying to repress" (360). Jane, then—though Gilbert and Gubar do not explicitly say this—must be a vision of woman as she might in future become, rather than any woman presently existing, since women presently existing contain the madwoman within their psyche. While seeing this figure as Jane's alter ego as well as Brontë's, Gilbert and Gubar find little redemptive about her, and considering the way she is described, this is no wonder. "In the deep shade, at the further end of the room, a figure ran backwards and forwards. What it was, whether beast or human being, one could not, at first sight, tell; it grovelled, seemingly, on all fours; it snatched and growled like some wild animal; but it was covered with clothing, and a quantity of dark, grizzled hair, wild as a mane, hid its head and face." Further on, Jane notes how "the clothed hyena rose up, and stood tall on its hind feet" (chapter 26).

I can't ignore the work Brontë has put into defining Bertha out of humanity. Not a scintilla of recognition of Bertha's likeness to herself disturbs Jane's consciousness, or fashions an ironic narrator discourse by which she might be corrected. The creature is wholly hateful, and no wonder: she has *stolen Jane's man.* Jane's rage against Rochester, one might say, is deflected to what a feminist might well see as an innocent victim. The woman rather than the man becomes her adversary; that woman's death is as necessary for Jane's liberation as is Rochester's blinding. How, then, do Gilbert and Gubar "read" a woman's death as a good thing for women? It seems to me that they have been so far convinced by Brontë's rhetoric as not to see Bertha as a woman. "She" is simply the figuration of anger, at once true and false—true to the situation of women in patriarchy, but since patriarchy is a false system, witness to its falseness. Her disappearance will simply mark the passing of a false order, not the passing of a female subject. Gilbert and Gubar are not, to be sure, entirely happy with the novel's denouement, suggesting that "Brontë was unable clearly to envision viable solutions to the problem of patriarchal oppression" (369), but they refer here to the unfortunate damage inflicted on Rochester. They do not doubt that Bertha's elimination from the fiction is a pure good.

ii. A Female Language

Among Charlotte Brontë's outrages on her madwoman is the denial of ability to speak; Bertha will never get to tell her own story (Jean Rhys corrected this in *Wide Sargasso Sea*). But, simultaneously influential with Gilbert and Gubar's work, French feminist literary theory appears to accept the figure of the madwoman as redemptive. She is taken to be not what women have regrettably been made by a contemptuous and oppressive culture, but what women either essentially are, or have fortunately been allowed to remain, in a society that brackets but cannot obliterate the innate disruptive, revolutionary force of the female. Since society is bad, this force is good. The madwoman, articulating "otherness," becomes the subject. But, so long silent, what will she say, and how will she say it? A theory of uniquely female language emerges. Descriptions and prescriptions result from a common procedure: features of the dominant language, masculine because dominant, are identified; opposite features are advanced as appropriate for women.

Christiane Makward, one of the important translators of and commentators on French feminism, describes the female language: "open, nonlinear, unfinished, fluid, exploded, fragmented, polysemic, attempting to speak the body i.e., the unconscious, involving silence, incorporating the simultaneity of life as opposed to or clearly different from pre-conceived, oriented, masterly or 'didactic' languages."[6] The women usually associated with this idea are Hélène Cixous and Luce Irigaray, both trained as psychoanalysts by Jacques Lacan, their world view marked with his patriarchism. While they sometimes attempt to write in the style they recommend, both agree that such a language has never existed before. It is not a language that socially marked "women" have used in the past because such socially marked women are not "true" women at all. A student of the nineteenth-century concept of true womanhood experiences an odd sense of time warp: application of the theory demonstrates, mainly, the absence of "woman" from "women's" writing. The theory is also applied by certain especially ingenious critics to discover the mandated language in canonical women's texts via deconstruction.[7] Deconstruction, however, is a procedure whose vocabulary, shared by non-feminists and men, yields identical results no matter whose texts it analyzes.

More often the theory is an agenda for the way women might or should write in future; to me it seems a guarantee of continued oppression. The most militant theorists do not use the language they call for; the theory incorporates wholly traditional notions of the feminine. Domna C. Stanton, another sponsor of French feminist theory in this country, writes, "recurring identification of the female in *écriture féminine* with madness, antireason, primitive darkness, mystery" represents a "revalorization of traditional 'feminine' stereotypes".[8] Makward, again, writes that "the theory of femininity is dangerously close to repeating in 'deconstructive' language the traditional assumptions." It is an essentialist definition making women "incapable of speaking as a woman; therefore, the most female course of action is to observe an hour of silence, or to scream. . . . Women are resigning themselves to silence, and to nonspeech. The speech of the other will then swallow them up, will speak *for* them."[9]

Actually, "women" are not resigning themselves to silence and nonspeech; we cannot afford to, and as we enter the public arena in increasing numbers we are not silent, and we do not (publicly) scream. Wishing to speak *to effect*, we use rational sequential discourse and, evidently, we use it well. Have we, then, chosen to become *men*? Before assenting, consider that this open, non-linear, exploded, fragmented, polysemic idea of our speech is congruent with the idea of the hopelessly irrational, disorganized, "weaker sex" desired by the masculine Other. The theory leads to a language that is intensely private, politically ineffectual, designed to fail. Women entering public life, whether as Supreme Court justices or organizers of tenant's unions, disprove the theory empirically, and, indeed, would follow it at their peril. They leave "advanced" theorists of women's literature far in the rear, expose their theory as an esoteric luxury. Of course, along with relegating "woman" to uselessness, the theory affirms belles-lettres as an elite pastime.

Feminists reacting to this theory maintain that nothing inherently bars us from the use of common speech, denying the argument that the "mother tongue" is really an alien, "father" tongue. In one essay, Hélène Cixous announces: "Too bad for [men] if they fall apart upon discovering that women aren't men, or that the mother doesn't have one. But isn't this fear convenient for them? Wouldn't the worst be, isn't the worst, in truth, that women aren't castrated?"[10] Cixous's identification of language with castration derives from the Lacanian reading of Freud's late version of the Oedipus complex, in which the threat of castration becomes the instrument of male socialization. Cixous's suggestion here is quite different from her assertions elsewhere that women really are castrated and hence, having nothing to lose, must remain unreconstructedly asocial.

In their recent essay, "Sexual Linguistics",[11] Gilbert and Gubar propose that twentieth-century women's writing has been shaped by our need to contend with the "intensified misogyny with which male writers greeted the entrance of women into the literary marketplace" (a belated greeting, by the way, since women have dominated the market since the mid-nineteenth century); this, along with men's anxiety over the loss of their own literary language, Latin, the father tongue (another tardy awareness, since men have used English as their primary literary language since the seventeenth century), forced women into fantasies of "alternative speech." Such fantasies have dominated women's writing since the turn of the century and consist in a subterranean celebration of the real state of affairs, which is that it is women, not men, who have the primary relation to language (the mother tongue). Thus, men and women's writing alike in this century represents sharply differentiated recognitions, however distorted, of the linguistic as well as biological primacy of the mother.

In this intriguing argument, it is now men not women who experience anxieties of authorship; women not men who own the language; nevertheless, Gilbert and Gubar can only see women's writings as compensatory and competitive fantasies. Men are ceded possession of the very language that is the woman's domain, women driven into a defensive posture. I would respond that if women are "really" primary in the essentialist way that Gilbert and Gubar describe them, then the historical phenomena described could not have happened; that it need not happen (history is always contingent, anyhow, not necessary); and finally, most crucially, that it did not happen so massively that we must identify the form of twentieth century women's writing with it.

As alternative linguistic fantasists, women are not distinguishable from male modernists (of course their content is different, but their language is not); and modernism is only one kind of feminine practice in the twentieth century. The idea of an alternative language is as much an apotheosis of the modernist creed as a residue of exclusion from modernism. Emily Dickinson (no longer the cowering recluse of *The Madwoman in the Attic*) appears in "Sexual Linguistics" as the great celebrant of maternal witchcraft; but while granting that she may be the strongest womanist poet in English, we cannot deny that she has been perceived by many excellent critics as a precursor of modernism in her private, expressive, self-communing verse. Virginia Woolf and Gertrude Stein, other prime instances in the new Gilbert and Gubar argument, are also as modernist as they are feminist. We can view modernism, in short, as the creation as much of women as men writers, a view which the gender-differentiating theory Gilbert and Gubar employ cannot encompass. My point would not be that there are no differences; but that when you start with a theory of difference, you can't see anything but. And when you start with a *misogynist* theory of difference, you are likely to force women into shapes that many may find unnatural or uncongenial. Such women also have voices. If they—we—are drowned out or denied, what has our theory accomplished except to divide woman from woman?

Another way of viewing modernism is not as something new in our century, but as the culmination of entrepreneurial, self-oriented individualism that, in the nineteenth century, was identified by many popular women writers as especially masculine, controlled by selfish and self-aggrandizing commercial motives, involving a will to power, a drive to omnipotence, and the like. Against such values, nineteenth-century women (at least in America) fashioned a "female" ethic—not of private, alternative musings, but of domestic responsibility and communal action apart from self. Nineteenth-century popular American women writers, including feminists, were vitally concerned to gain access to the public sphere in order to transform it by their social and domestic idealism; for this goal, none other than the language in use could possibly serve. Therefore, they availed themselves of it; nor did they have any doubt that it was "their" language as much as it was men's. Hence, we might identify a linguistic tradition of woman's writing precisely by its reappropriation of the mother tongue, its emergence from privatism with an implicit claim that this powerful language is ours as much as it is men's.

And yet again, Elizabeth Hampstead's excellent work, *Read This Only to Yourself: The Private Writings of Midwestern Women*,[12] shows that nineteenth-century working-class women, unaffected by pretensions to "literariness" and uninterested in public discourse, wrote letters and diaries in a way opposite to that enjoined by any theories of women's language that have subsequently emerged to locate and, I believe, enforce sexual difference.

iii. The Father

It becomes clear that the theory of women's language is closely tied to a theory of the feminine personality; and because Freud is the originator of modern psychological theorizing on the feminine, an encounter with Freud might seem unavoidable. Yet we live in an age in which Freud is much questioned. As science, of course, his theories have yet to win respectability. As cure, his methods do no better than chance. As a body of philosophical writings, his works are shot through with inconsistencies and vaguenesses. And from various sources within the profession he founded, there are now serious doubts expressed about his integrity. What cannot be doubted, however, is the profound misogyny that underlies his descriptions of and prescriptions for women.

Thus, one would think that he could have been ignored by feminists interested in a theoretical base for their own forays into a theory of women's writing. On the contrary, however, literary feminist theorists have elevated him (and Lacan, his up-to-date surrogate) and in so doing have probably given his ideas new currency and prestige. To my perception (and at the risk of undercutting my own position I have to say it) this attachment to Freud—assuming that it is not simply opportunistic—manifests precisely that masochism that Freud and his followers identified with the female. We are most "daddy's girl" when we seek—as Jane Gallop not long ago expressed it—to seduce him.[13] Our attempt to seduce him, or our compliance with his attempt to seduce us, guarantees his authority. If Freud is right, there is no feminism.

Observing the Lacanian basis of contemporary French feminist theory, Christiane Makward roots "the problem of the feminine" in psychoanalytic theory because "the vast majority of those critics and writers—female or male—which [sic] have attempted to rationalize their perception of the different in the relation of women to language have done so on the basis of neo-Freudian postulates."[14] The key phrase here is "perception of the different." The most important questions (to me) for research and analysis—what differences there "really" are, how they are constituted, and what they "signify," not to mention the problematic role of language in the very framing of the questions—are all bypassed by this axiomatic assumption of known, immutable difference. To the extent that any idea of a recuperated future, no matter how modest, is an inalienable part of the concept of "feminism," we have here a program that, despite its claims, must be named anti-feminist.

The program is not unique to French feminists, with their particular historical relation to Lacan. In England, Juliet Mitchell has been a strong exponent of the need to retain Freud in a feminist vision of the female personality, and in this country the more recent work of Nancy Chodorow has had a striking impact on feminist literary criticism.[15] Chodorow argued that the questions "why do women want to be mothers?" and "why do they raise daughters who want to be mothers in turn?" could not be accounted for by any combination of biological marking and upbringing, but required an intrapsychic, specifically Freudian explanation. She proposed that girls failed to separate from their mothers because the mothers failed to separate from them with a resulting fluidity of boundary between self and others. In effect, Chodorow answered her questions by adducing the stereotyped notion of the female personality, which, to be sure, she rearticulated in somewhat more timely language; in so doing she gave that stereotype a new efficacy in the construction of a feminine reality. Despite the comments of feminist psychologists that at best Chodorow's was an untested hypothesis, this theory must have satisfied a need among literary feminist critics, for it has inspired numerous readings of women writers based on the assumption of their less organized, more connected and fluid personalities.

It is certainly no secret that the historical Freud was both misogynist and anti-feminist. It is demonstrable, too, that the misogynist and anti-feminist tendencies in Freud's writings became much more pronounced in his work after World War I, when he broke with many of his followers because of his new emphasis on the castration complex. The post-World War I malaise, exacerbated by the relatively rapid emancipation of women after 1920, manifested itself in his case by defection and dissent of his followers precisely on the question of the feminine; by the virtual disappearance of that kind of female patient who had made his reputation and on whom, therefore, he depended (the hysteric, who did indeed use "body language" as her means of speaking); and by the appearance of women psychoanalysts. One might say that the obedient daughter who could only speak with and through her body, and who was released into speech by Freud thus becoming his creation, gave way to or was supplanted by the rebellious daughter who dared to match him word for word. Her rebellion, of course, was no more than the representation of herself as an equal, rejecting his stewardship, his fatherhood. It is not really surprising that

Freud reacted with a marked intensification of his ideas about female inferiority, but he might have done differently.

For example, the Oedipus complex (itself, now, an ever more problematic concept) shifted attention from the boy's loving attachment to his mother to his fearful relation with his father. The mother was altered from the subject of a compelling heterosexual love to the object of a same-sex rivalry. And the castration complex, introduced to explain how the Oedipus complex came to an end, made it impossible for girls, who cannot be castrated, to become adults.[16] "In the absence of fear of castration the chief motive is lacking which leads boys to surmount the Oedipus complex," Freud wrote in "Femininity" (1933). "Girls remain in it for an indeterminate length of time; they demolish it late and, even so, incompletely. In these circumstances the formation of the super-ego must suffer; it cannot attain the strength and independence which give it its cultural significance, and feminists are not pleased when we point out to them the effects of this factor upon the average feminine character."[17] Freud's gibe at the feminists makes his purpose clear; he catches feminists in the double bind, denying that they are women, and asserting that as women, these feminists cannot be the rational beings they claim to be, capable of original thought. It was part of Freud's intellectual *machismo* to reserve original thought for the male; that is a reservation still immensely powerful in all academia.

Freud's late writing—"Some Psychical Consequences of the Anatomical Distinction between the Sexes" (1925), "Female Sexuality" (1931), and "Femininity" (an essay added to the *New Introductory Lectures* in 1933)—greatly exaggerated his never slight attention to the penis. Not having a penis is a *lack*, an objectively real *inferiority*, a castration *in fact*.[18] The little girl on first seeing a little boy's penis is instantly struck with her shame and inferiority while the boy regards the naked little girl with "horror at the mutilated creature or triumphant contempt for her."[19] Those without the penis can never be initiated into the culture's higher life, nor contribute to it. The aims of therapy are different according to the genital apparatus of the patient: those with a penis are helped to enter the world, those with a vagina are taught to "resign" themselves to marginality. Any woman's attempt to overcome feelings of inferiority vis-a-vis men is interpreted as the wish for a penis which, "unrealizable," is, or can be, the "beginning of a psychosis."[20] Of course this is all a fantasy; yet claiming that fantasy overrode the real world, Freud advanced this fantastic difference as the legitimizing basis of every sexist stereotype and proscription. This fantasy, or so it seems to me, is too patently useful, too crassly interested, and too culturally sophisticated, to qualify as an emanation from the Unconscious.

Lacan too—or perhaps, Lacan even more. At least Freud knew that his "laws" of human development were mostly broken; his livelihood depended on the broken law. Lacan's laws are unbreakable, and he is hence a far less "forgiving" father than Freud. With Lacan, we are always and forever outside. Lacan's deployment of the castration complex as the basis of the model for the symbolic order into which children—boys—are initiated, takes one particularly "sexist" element in Freud's rich system (which contained many ungendered insights) and makes it the whole story. Lacan claimed throughout his career that he had rescued Freud from a dated biologism by reformulating his theory as linguistics, but he resorted to biologism shamelessly when it suited him. Thus, in his 1972 seminar, produced in an ambience not unlike that faced by Freud in the 1920s— the growth of feminism, the arrival of female analysts as competition—he *pronounced* women into silence:

> There is no woman but excluded by the nature of things which is the nature of words, and it has to be said that if there is one thing about which women them- selves are complaining at the moment, it's well and truly that—it's just that they don't know what they are saying, which is all the difference between them and me.[21]

Them and me: the difference (since women are clearly doing just what Lacan's theory says they can't do) is not how women act but what they essentially are and cannot help but be. Lacan's defenders, including Juliet Mitchell and Jac- queline Rose, have claimed that he was attempting, here and elsewhere in his attacks on the French feminists, to counter their return to an overt biologism and a worship of the Eternal Feminine. But I find linguistic essentialism no improvement on the biological. Lacan's ideas of women belong neither to his realms of the real nor the symbolic, but to his imaginary. Both Freud and Lacan make haste to correct the fantasies of *others* in order that their own prevail. Not truth, but power, is the issue.

iv. The Mother

In attempting to save Freud for feminism (to save him more generally for today's world), many have turned to the concept of the pre-Oedipal mother and proposed her to balance the Oedipal father in the life-history of the child. But it seems to me that the pre-Oedipal mother plays, in such thinking, the role that patriarchs always allot to mothers: she shores up the father. Since the aim is to help out Freud rather than to help out women, such a result may have been inherent in the project.

The very term pre-Oedipal suggests the primacy of the Oedipal phase. Why not call the Oedipal phase the "post-Cerean"? Even more bizarre is the coinage "phallic mother," which suggests that the child responds to the pre-Oedipal mother only because she or he believes that the mother has a penis. The pre-

Oedipal mother is rudely rejected when the child discovers the mother's appalling "lack," such rejection indicating that the attachment to the mother was
based on fantasy, now to be rectified by the Oedipal phase. In a word, the
child was never "really" attached to the mother, only fantasized such an attachment; the"real" attachment was always to the father.

The concept also affirms the mother's disappearance as agent and subject
from the child's life early on—by age five if development is "normal." And,
while allowing influence, it limits it to a global, non-verbal or pre-verbal, endlessly supportive, passively nurturing presence. Here is one source for the idea
of the *adult* woman's language as unbounded, polysemous, and the like—a
residual memory of our mother in the days before we understood her language,
that is, in the days before we had a language of our own. Many feminists
celebrate the mother's body fluids as her "language."

Of course we all know, in our rational moments, that the mother's influence
lasts far beyond the age of five. But even if we were to grant its waning at that
age, we surely know that the mother's role in the child's earliest life is not so
simple as this pre-Oedipal model makes it out to be. (At least we who have
been mothers know.) To take the matter of most concern for literary theory,
we know that the mother is the language teacher, and begins her task before
the child is even a year old; normal children in all cultures are thoroughly
verbal though not yet fully syntactical by the age of three. And there is—*pace*
Lacan—no sudden break, no startling initiation into the order dominated or
constructed by language; language from the first is part of the child's relation
to the mother. What purpose does the theory of an exclusively nonverbal stage
serve? It minimizes the mother.

As the mother's influence on children of both sexes persists long beyond the
age of five, so does that influence on a maturing child become yet more complex,
albeit increasingly diluted, encompassing many activities that patriarchal rhetoric attributes to the father. Mothers make children into human and social
beings through a continuous process in which instruction and nurturance are
indistinguishable. No doubt, the social world into which our mothers initiated
us, and into which we initiate our sons and daughters, is dominated by men
and supported by a rationalizing symbol system; but it differs crucially from
the patriarchal social world of Freud and Lacan, in that mothers are demonstrably unlike the mothers of their theories.

Pre-Oedipal, then, is an interested fantasy of the maternal. Its purpose—to
contain and confine mothers and hence women within the field of the irrational—is evident; to espouse such a fantasy is to accede to a male appropriation
of the mother and her language. Why do feminists do it? Perhaps it is no more
than hegemonic fatigue. I offer two other possibilities: first, women feel the
same fear and jealousy of the mother that appears in part to underlie Freud's

writing (this is the thesis of Dorothy Dinnerstein's *The Mermaid and the Minotaur*);[22] second, a theory in which women have had nothing to do with the world is comforting and inspiring. To put this somewhat differently: the Freudian and the feminist agendas may coincide because feminists do not like their mothers, or because feminists prefer to endow women with a revolutionary power that we cannot have if we have been part of the system all along. To say this is not to blame the victim, but rather to question our ability to carry, after so many centuries of implication, any pure revitalizing force. Our powers are limited, and our agendas for change will have to take internal limitation into account.

These issues are sharply evident in recent feminist literary work on mothers and daughters. It provides testimony, often unwitting and in contradiction to its stated intentions, of the deep-seated hostility of daughters to mothers. (Mothers do not speak of daughters in this discourse.) Adrienne Rich's *Of Woman Born* excoriates the male establishment for forcing the *role* of motherhood on women while denying us the *experience* of it, but is strikingly cold when not silent on the writer's own mother. Nor does Rich's poetry speak to her mother, committed to women though it may be.[23] Even at the moment when the daughter-writer or daughter-feminist claims that she is seeking the mother in order to make strengthening contact she reveals that the mother she seeks is not *her* mother, but another mother, preferably an imaginary mother. Perhaps feminism has become confused with maturation.

In much criticism, it is the pre-Oedipal mother who is looked for, sought not to combat patriarchy, but to defend against the real mother. Here, for example, from *The Lost Tradition*, a collection of essays on the mother-daughter relation (all written from the standpoint of daughters): "confronting the Terrible Mother in order to move beyond the entanglements of the mother/daughter relationship . . . claiming her as metaphor for the sources of our own creative powers, women are creating new self-configurations in which the mother is no longer the necessary comfort but the seed of a new being, and in which we are no longer the protected child but the carriers of the new woman whose birth is our own."[24] We have made the mother our child, we are self-mothered, we move beyond the entanglements of our real mother by imprisoning her in metaphor. The Terrible Mother is called on to perform a matricide.

Karen Elias-Button also comments that the mothers portrayed in contemporary fiction by women "seem to have little existence apart from their children and dread their daughters' independence as if it means their own death."[25] If works with such images were written by men, no feminist would hesitate to label them projections: how like a male to imagine that his mother has no life except in him! "The most disturbing villain in recent women's fiction is not the selfish or oppressive male but instead the bad mother."[26] The author may

"dispose of" fear of the mother "by rendering the mother so repulsive or ridiculous that the reader must reject her as her fictional daughter does. Another
tactic is for the author to kill the mother in the course of the narrative."[27] The
matricidal impulse could not be plainer. Moving into the past, we find that
today's women writers join a long tradition. The mothers of fictional heroines
in the period ending with Jane Austen "are usually bad and living, or good and
dead."[28] "The women novelists of the period from Fanny Burney to Mrs. Gaskell
and George Eliot create very few positive images of motherhood."[29] Real
mothers—of Harriet Martineau, George Eliot, Emily Dickinson, Ellen Glas-
gow, Edith Wharton, Willa Cather—all are faulted by their daughters for failing
them, and these daughters are taken at their word by today's feminist daughter-
critic.

Think, now, for a moment, about Jane Eyre and Bertha Mason. Who, after
all, might Bertha Mason be—she to whom Rochester *is already married? Jane
Eyre* is replete with images of ferocious female power and Jane turns to Rochester, at first, as to a refuge. That refuge is sullied by the presence in the nest
of another woman, who is made repulsive and ridiculous so that the reader
must reject her; and is killed before the narrative is out, so that the daughter
can replace her. Even Gilbert and Gubar perform an unconscious matricide
when they define a literary tradition, "handed down not from one woman to
another but from the stern literary 'fathers' of patriarchy to all their 'inferiorized'
female descendents" (*Madwoman*, 50). Evidently by the time of the Brontës
and George Eliot there were literary mothers available; either these nineteenth-
century women rejected them as Jane rejected Bertha; or Gilbert and Gubar
forgot about them as they were caught up in the challenge of producing a
respectable (fathered rather than mothered) feminist literary theory.

A difference more profound for feminism than the male-female difference
emerges: the difference between woman and woman. If the speaking woman
sees other women as her mother, sees herself but not her mother as a woman,
then she can see her mother (other women) only as men or monsters. There
is no future for a commonality of women if we cannot traverse the generations.
One sees only here and there signs of something different. Julia Kristeva says
that we must challenge "the myth of the archaic mother"[30] in order for women
to enter society as participant beings—but her language is aggressive toward
the myth, not its patriarchal perpetrators; Dinnerstein writes that one must
come to see the "first parent" as "no more and no less than a fellow creature."[31]
Dinnerstein seems sentimental here, but her point is crucial. It goes beyond
her own Freudian emphasis to imply that the family model of daddy, mommy,
and me, is inimical to the human future. And, since the family triangle, and
its inevitable oddly-named "romance," is the veritable nurturing ground of
patriarchy, it "must" be abandoned before there can be a "true" feminist theory.

It has probably never existed in reality; one can wonder what a theory deliberately developed from childhood fantasies describes other than childish fantasies, and how such a theory serves feminist intentions. Indeed, whether children "see" the world as Freudians say they do is something we will never know so long as Freudian scholars are the only ones to ask the question.

I am, evidently, a pluralist. Essays in feminist journals are permeated with musts and shoulds,[32] with homily and exhortation and a fractiousness that at most puts "sisterhood" under erasure and at least means that the totalizing assumptions of theory are fictions. In the late sixties, feminism was called "women's liberation." It seemed to promise us that we could, at last, try to be and do what we wanted; it proposed that women could help each other to become what they wanted. "Women's liberation" didn't suggest we all had to be one thing. To find oneself again a conscript, within a decade, is sad.

NOTES

1. Elaine Showalter, "Feminist Criticism in the Wilderness," *Critical Inquiry*, 8 (1981), 181.

2. I borrow these terms from Wendy Martin, *An American Triptych: Ann Bradstreet, Emily Dickinson, Adrienne Rich* (Chapel Hill: University of North Carolina Press, 1983), p. 229. These terms do not apply to theories as such, but to styles that appear to override theories.

3. These words were originally written before the appalling account of life in the French Mouvement Libération des Femmes—a feminist ideal for many literary theorists—appeared in *Signs*. See Dorothy Kaufmann-McCall, "Politics of Difference: The Women's Movement in France from May 1968 to Mitterand," *Signs*, 9 (1983), 282–93.

4. See Lillian S. Robinson, "Treason our Text: Feminist Challenges to the Literary Canon," *Tulsa Studies in Women's Literature*, 2 (1983), 83–98.

5. Sandra M. Gilbert and Susan Gubar, *The Madwoman in the Attic: The Woman Writer and the Nineteenth-Century Imagination* (New Haven: Yale University Press, 1979). Subsequent references are cited parenthetically in the text.

6. Christiane Makward, "To Be or Not to Be . . . a Feminist Speaker," in *The Future of Difference*, eds. Alice Jardine and Hester Eisenstein (Boston: G. K. Hall, 1980), p. 96.

7. Mary Jacobus, "The Questions of Language: Men or Maxims and *The Mill on the Floss*," *Critical Inquiry*, 8 (1981), 222.

8. Domna C. Stanton, "Language and Revolution: The Franco-American Disconnection," in *The Future of Difference*, p. 86.

9. Makward, p. 100.

10. Hélène Cixous, "The Laugh of the Medusa," *Signs*, 1 (1976), 885. As Diane Griffin Crowder, an expert on Cixous, has recently observed in a review in *Tulsa Studies*, "Cixous is not a feminist in any sense that the American movement would recognize." *Tulsa Studies in Women's Literature*, 4 (1985), 149. This being patently the case, the zeal of American literary feminists to put her at the apex of feminist theory is all the more puzzling.

11. Sandra M. Gilbert and Susan Gubar, "Sexual Linguistics," *New Literary History*, 16 (1985), 515–43.

12. Elizabeth Hampsten, *Read This Only to Yourself: The Private Writings of Midwestern Women* (Bloomington: Indiana University Press, 1982).

13. Jane Gallop, *The Daughter's Seduction: Feminism and Psychoanalysis* (Ithaca, N.Y.: Cornell University Press, 1982). A young literary-academic feminist of my acquaintance tells me that most feminists of her generation are feminists precisely because they recognize the abjectness of their attitudes toward men. That recognition has been the starting point for many of us; but a theory that valorizes or prescribes abjectness seems to me to confuse the starting point with the end.

14. Makward, p. 102.

15. Nancy Chodorow, *The Reproduction of Mothering* (Berkeley and Los Angeles: University of California Press, 1976). Another influential book of the same sort is Carol Gilligan, *In a Different Voice* (Cambridge, Mass.: Harvard University Press, 1982). Both of these works have had more impact on feminist literary studies than in their own social science fields, largely because the evidence on which their arguments are based are, by social science standards, deplorably weak.

16. The real Freudian scandal, however—one to shame a feminist advocate of a meeting of feminism and psychoanalysis—is the substitution of the Oedipus complex for the seduction theory on the grounds that it would be impossible for all those women (and men) to have been telling the truth when they testified to childhood sexual abuse. What we are learning of child abuse these days exposes this uncharacteristic eruption of "common sense" into Freud's discourse as a dreadful hypocrisy. And indeed, the logic of this replacement was always poor—much like saying that it would be impossible for all those cases of tuberculosis to have been caused by the same bacteria.

17. Sigmund Freud, "Femininity," in *Psychoanalysis and Feminism*, ed. Juliet Mitchell (New York: Pantheon, 1974), p. 88.

18. Sigmund Freud, "Analysis Terminable and Interminable," in *The Collected Writings of Sigmund Freud*, 5 (London: Hogarth Press, 1953–1974), p. 356.

19. Sigmund Freud, "Some Psychical Consequences of the Anatomical Distinction Between the Sexes," in *Psychoanalysis and Feminism*, p. 191. Note that for Freud there is only "the" distinction. I hope it is clear that my argument does not deny differences; I stress the plural. I believe that differences are multiple, variable, and largely unresearched and not understood; therefore any theory based on only one is pernicious.

20. Freud, "Analysis Terminable and Interminable," p. 357.

21. Quoted in Juliet Mitchell and Jacqueline Rose, eds., *Feminine Psychology: Jacques Lacan and the école freudienne* (New York: Norton, 1982), p. 144.

22. Dorothy Dinnerstein, *The Mermaid and the Minotaur: Sexual Arrangements and Human Malaise* (New York: Harper, 1976).

23. Adrienne Rich, *Of Woman Born* (New York: Norton, 1976).

24. Karen Elias-Button, "The Muse as Medusa," in *The Lost Tradition: Mothers and Daughters in Literature*, eds. Cathy N. Davidson and E. M. Broner (New York: Ungar, 1980), p. 205.

25. Elias-Button, p. 192.

26. Judith Kegan Gardiner, "On Female Identity and Writing By Women," *Critical Inquiry*, 8 (1981), 356.

27. Ibid.

28. Janet Todd, *Women's Friendship in Literature* (New York: Columbia University Press, 1980), p. 2.

29. Susan Peck MacDonald, "Jane Austen and the Tradition of the Absent Mother," in *The Lost Tradition*, p. 58.

30. Julia Kristeva, "Women's Time," *Signs*, 7 (1981), 29.

31. Dinnerstein, p. 164.

32. See Jane Marcus in her attack on pluralism, "Storming the Toolshed," *Signs*, 7 (1982), 622–40, especially p. 626: "she must . . . she must . . . she must." If that *she* is *me*, somebody (once again) is telling me what I "*must*" do to be a true woman, and that somebody is asserting (not incidentally) her own monopoly on truth as she does so. I've been here before.

ESCAPING THE SENTENCE
Diagnosis and Discourse in "The Yellow Wallpaper"

Paula A. Treichler

Almost immediately in Charlotte Perkins Gilman's story "The Yellow Wall-paper," the female narrator tells us she is "sick." Her husband, "a physician of high standing," has diagnosed her as having a "temporary nervous depression—a slight hysterical tendency."[1] Yet her journal—in whose words the story unfolds—records her own resistance to this diagnosis and, tentatively, her suspicion that the medical treatment it dictates—treatment that confines her to a room in an isolated country estate—will not cure her. She suggests that the diagnosis itself, by undermining her own conviction that her "condition" is serious and real, may indeed be one reason why she does not get well.

A medical diagnosis is a verbal formula representing a constellation of physical symptoms and observable behaviors. Once formulated, it dictates a series of therapeutic actions. In "The Yellow Wallpaper," the diagnosis of hysteria or depression, conventional "women's diseases" of the nineteenth century, sets in motion a therapeutic regimen which involves language in several ways. The narrator is forbidden to engage in normal social conversation; her physical isolation is in part designed to remove her from the possibility of over-stimulating intellectual discussion. She is further encouraged to exercise "self-control" and avoid expressing negative thoughts and fears about her illness; she is also urged to keep her fancies and superstitions in check. Above all, she is forbidden to "work"—to write. Learning to monitor her own speech, she develops an artificial feminine self who reinforces the terms of her husband's expert diagnosis: this self attempts to speak reasonably and in "a very quiet voice," refrains from crying in his presence, and hides the fact that she is keeping a journal. This male-identified self disguises the true underground narrative: a confrontation with language.

Because she does not feel free to speak truthfully "to a living soul," she confides her thoughts to a journal—"dead paper"—instead. The only safe lan-

guage is dead language. But even the journal is not altogether safe. The opening
passages are fragmented as the narrator retreats from topic after topic (the first
journal entry consists of 39 separate paragraphs). The three points at which her
language becomes more discursive carry more weight by contrast. These passages seem at first to involve seemingly unobjectionable, safe topics: the house,
her room, and the room's yellow wallpaper. Indeed, the very first mention of
the wallpaper expresses conventional hyperbole: "I never saw worse paper in
my life." But the language at once grows unexpected and intense:

> One of those sprawling flamboyant patterns committing every artistic sin.
> It is dull enough to confuse the eye in following, pronounced enough to constantly
> irritate and provoke study, and when you follow the lame uncertain curves for
> a little distance they suddenly commit suicide—plunge off at outrageous angles,
> destroy themselves in unheard of contradictions.(13)

Disguised as an acceptable feminine topic (interest in decor), the yellow wallpaper comes to occupy the narrator's entire reality. Finally, she rips it from
the walls to reveal its real meaning. Unveiled, the yellow wallpaper is a metaphor for women's discourse. From a conventional perspective, it first seems
strange, flamboyant, confusing, outrageous: the very act of women's writing
produces discourse which embodies "unheard of contradictions." Once freed,
it expresses what is elsewhere kept hidden and embodies patterns that the
patriarchal order ignores, suppresses, fears as grotesque, or fails to perceive at
all. Like all good metaphors, the yellow wallpaper is variously interpreted by
readers to represent (among other things) the "pattern" which underlies sexual
inequality, the external manifestation of neurasthenia, the narrator's unconscious, the narrator's situation within patriarchy.[2] But an emphasis on discourse—writing, the act of speaking, language—draws us to the central issue
in this particular story: the narrator's alienation from work, writing, and intellectual life. Thus the story is inevitably concerned with the complicated and
charged relationship between women and language: analysis then illuminates
particular points of conflict between patriarchal language and women's discourse. This conflict in turn raises a number of questions relevant for both
literary and feminist scholarship: In what senses can language be said to be
oppressive to women? How do feminist linguistic innovations seek to escape
this oppression? What is the relationship of innovation to material conditions?
And what does it mean, theoretically, to escape the sentence that the structure
of patriarchal language imposes?

i. The Yellow Wallpaper

The narrator of "The Yellow Wallpaper" has come with her husband to an

isolated country estate for the summer. The house, a "colonial mansion," has
been untenanted for years through some problem with inheritance. It is "the
most beautiful place!" The grounds contain "hedges and walls and gates that
lock, and lots of separate little houses for the gardeners and people" (11).
Despite this palatial potential to accommodate many people, the estate is virtually deserted with nothing growing in its greenhouses. The narrator perceives
"something queer about it" and believes it may be haunted.

   She is discouraged in this and other fancies by her sensible physician-husband
who credits only what is observable, scientific, or demonstrable through facts
and figures. He has scientifically diagnosed his wife's condition as merely "a
temporary nervous depression"; her brother, also a noted physician, concurs
in this opinion. Hence husband and wife have come as physician and patient
to this solitary summer mansion in quest of cure. The narrator reports her
medical regimen to her journal, together with her own view of the problem:

> So I take phosphates or phosphites—whichever it is, and tonics, and journeys,
> and air, and exercise, and am absolutely forbidden to "work" until I am well
> again.
> Personally, I disagree with their ideas.
> Personally, I believe that congenial work, with excitement and change, would
> do me good.
> But what is one to do? (10)

   Her room at the top of the house seems once to have been a nursery or a
playroom with bars on the windows and "rings and things on the walls." The
room contains not much more than a mammoth metal bed. The ugly yellow
wallpaper has been stripped off in patches—perhaps by the children who for-
merly inhabited the room. In this "atrocious nursery" the narrator increasingly
spends her time. Her husband is often away on medical cases, her baby makes
her nervous, and no other company is permitted her. Disturbed by the wallpaper, she asks for another room or for different paper; her husband urges her
not to give way to her "fancies." Further, he claims that any change would lead
to more change: "after the wall-paper was changed it would be the heavy
bedstead, and then the barred windows, and then that gate at the head of the
stairs, and so on" (14). So no changes are made, and the narrator is left alone
with her "imaginative power and habit of story-making" (15). In this stimulus-
deprived environment, the "pattern" of the wallpaper becomes increasingly
compelling: the narrator gradually becomes intimate with its "principle of design" and unconventional connections. The figure of a woman begins to take
shape behind the superficial pattern of the paper. The more the wallpaper
comes alive, the less inclined is the narrator to write in her journal—"dead
paper." Now with three weeks left of the summer and her relationship with

the wallpaper more and more intense, she asks once more to be allowed to leave. Her husband refuses: "I cannot possibly leave town just now. Of course if you were in any danger, I could and would, but you really are better, dear, whether you can see it or not. I am a doctor, dear, and I know" (23). She expresses the fear that she is not getting well. "Bless her little heart!" he responds, "She shall be as sick as she pleases" (24). When she hesitantly voices the belief that she may be losing her mind, he reproaches her so vehemently that she says no more. Instead, in the final weeks of the summer, she gives herself up to the wallpaper. "Life is very much more exciting now than it used to be," she tells her journal. "You see I have something more to expect, to look forward to, to watch. I really do eat better, and am more quiet than I was" (27). She reports that her husband judges her "to be flourishing in spite of my wall-paper."

She begins to strip off the wallpaper at every opportunity in order to free the woman she perceives is trapped inside. She becomes increasingly aware of this woman and other female figures creeping behind the surface pattern of the wallpaper: there is a hint that the room's previous female occupant has left behind the marks of her struggle for freedom. Paranoid by now, the narrator attempts to disguise her obsession with the wallpaper. On the last day, she locks herself in the room and succeeds in stripping off most of the remaining paper. When her husband comes home and finally unlocks the door, he is horrified to find her creeping along the walls of the room. "I've got out at last," she tells him triumphantly, "And I've pulled off most of the paper, so you can't put me back" (36). Her husband faints, and she is obliged to step over him each time she circles the room.

"The Yellow Wallpaper" was read by nineteenth-century readers as a harrowing case study of neurasthenia. Even recent readings have treated the narrator's madness as a function of her individual psychological situation. A feminist reading emphasizes the social and economic conditions which drive the narrator—and potentially all women—to madness. In these readings, the yellow wallpaper represents (1) the narrator's own mind, (2) the narrator's unconscious, (3) the "pattern" of social and economic dependence which reduces women to domestic slavery. The woman in the wallpaper represents (1) the narrator herself, gone mad, (2) the narrator's unconscious, (3) all women. While these interpretations are plausible and fruitful, I interpret the wallpaper to be women's writing or women's discourse, and the woman in the wallpaper to be the representation of women that becomes possible only after women obtain the right to speak. In this reading, the yellow wallpaper stands for a new vision of women—one which is constructed differently from the representation of women in patriarchal language. The story is thus in part about the clash between two modes of discourse: one powerful, "ancestral," and dominant; the other new, "impertinent," and visionary. The story's outcome makes a statement about the relationship of a visionary feminist project to material reality.

ii. Diagnosis and Discourse

It is significant that the narrator of "The Yellow Wallpaper" is keeping a journal, confiding to "dead paper" the unorthodox thoughts and perceptions she is reluctant to tell to a "living soul." Challenging and subverting the expert prescription that forbids her to write, the journal evokes a sense of urgency and danger. "There comes John," she tells us at the end of her first entry, "and I must put this away,—he hates to have me write a word" (13). We, her readers, are thus from the beginning her confidantes, implicated in forbidden discourse.

Contributing to our suspense and sense of urgency is the ambiguity of the narrator's "condition," whose etiology is left unstated in the story. For her physician-husband, it is a medical condition of unknown origin to be medically managed. Certain imagery (the "ghostliness" of the estate, the "trouble" with the heirs) suggests hereditary disease. Other evidence points toward psychological causes (e.g., postpartum depression, failure to adjust to marriage and motherhood). A feminist analysis moves beyond such localized causes to implicate the economic and social conditions which, under patriarchy, make women domestic slaves. In any case, the fact that the origin of the narrator's condition is never made explicit intensifies the role of diagnosis in putting a name to her "condition."

Symptoms are crucial for the diagnostic process. The narrator reports, among other things, exhaustion, crying, nervousness, synesthesia, anger, paranoia, and hallucination. "Temporary nervous depression" (coupled with a "slight hysterical tendency") is the medical term that serves to diagnose or define these symptoms. Once pronounced, and reinforced by the second opinion of the narrator's brother, this diagnosis not only names reality but also has considerable power over what that reality is now to be: it dictates the narrator's removal to the "ancestral halls" where the story is set and generates a medical therapeutic regimen that includes physical isolation, "phosphates and phosphites," air, and rest. Above all, it forbids her to "work." The quotation marks, registering her husband's perspective, discredit the equation of writing with true work. The diagnostic language of the physician is coupled with the paternalistic language of the husband to create a formidable array of controls over her behavior.

I use "diagnosis," then, as a metaphor for the voice of medicine or science that speaks to define women's condition. Diagnosis is powerful and public; representing institutional authority, it dictates that money, resources, and space are to be expended as consequences in the "real world." It is a male voice that privileges the rational, the practical, and the observable. It is the voice of male logic and male judgment which dismisses superstition and refuses to see the house as haunted or the narrator's condition as serious. It imposes controls on the female narrator and dictates how she is to perceive and talk about the world. It is enforced by the "ancestral halls" themselves: the rules are followed even when the physician-husband is absent. In fact, the opening imagery—"ancestral halls," "a colonial mansion," "a haunted house"—legitimizes the diagnostic process by placing it firmly within an institutional frame: medicine, marriage, patriarchy. All function in the story to define and prescribe.

In contrast, the narrator in her nursery room speaks privately to her journal. At first she expresses her views hesitantly, "personally." Her language includes a number of stereotypical features of "women's language": not only are its topics limited, it is marked formally by exclamation marks, italics, intensifiers, and repetition of the impotent refrain, "What is one to do?"[3] The journal entries at this early stage are very tentative and clearly shaped under the stern eye of male judgment. Oblique references only hint at an alternative reality. The narrator writes, for example, that the wallpaper has been "torn off" and "stripped away," yet she does not say by whom. Her qualms about her medical diagnosis and treatment remain unspoken except in her journal, which functions only as a private respite, a temporary relief. "Dead paper," it is not truly subversive.

Nevertheless, the narrator's language almost from the first does serve to call into question both the diagnosis of her condition and the rules established to treat it. As readers, therefore, we are not permitted wholehearted confidence in the medical assessment of the problem. It is not that we doubt the existence of her "condition," for it obviously causes genuine suffering; but we come to doubt that the diagnosis names the real problem—the narrator seems to place her own inverted commas around the words "temporary nervous depression" and "slight hysterical tendency"—and perceive that whatever its nature it is exacerbated by the rules established for its cure.

For this reason, we are alert to the possibility of an alternative vision. The yellow wallpaper provides it. Representing a different reality, it is "living paper," aggressively alive: "You think you have mastered it, but just as you get well underway in following, it turns a back-somersault and there you are. It slaps you in the face, knocks you down, and tramples upon you. It is like a bad dream" (25). The narrator's husband refuses to replace the wallpaper, "whitewash" the room, or let her change rooms altogether on the grounds that other changes will then be demanded. The wallpaper is to remain: acknowledgment of its reality is the first step toward freedom. Confronting it at first through male eyes, the narrator is repelled and speculates that the children who inhabited the room before her attacked it for its ugliness. There is thus considerable resistance to the wallpaper and an implied rejection of what it represents, even by young children.

But the wallpaper exerts its power and, at the same time, the narrator's journal entries falter; "I don't know why I should write this" (21), she says, about halfway through the story. She makes a final effort to be allowed to leave the room; when this fails, she becomes increasingly absorbed by the wallpaper and by the figure of a woman that exists behind its confusing surface pattern. This figure grows clearer to her, to the point where she can join her behind the paper and literally act within it. At this point, her language becomes bolder: she completes the predicates that were earlier left passively hanging. Describing joint action with the woman in the wallpaper, she tells us that the room has come to be damaged at the hands of women: "I pulled and she shook, I shook and she pulled, and before morning we had peeled off yards of that paper" (32); "I am getting angry enough to do something desperate" (34). From an increasingly distinctive perspective, she sees an alternative reality beneath the repellent surface pattern in which the figures of women are emerging. Her original perception is confirmed: the patriarchal house is indeed "haunted" by figures of women. The room is revealed as a prison inhabited by its former inmates, whose struggles have nearly destroyed it. Absorbed almost physically by "living paper"—writing—she strives to liberate the women trapped within the ancestral halls, women with whom she increasingly identifies. Once begun, liberation and identification are irreversible: "I've got out at last . . . " cries the narrator, "And I've pulled off most of the paper, so you can't put me back!" (36).

This ending of "The Yellow Wallpaper" is ambiguous and complex. Because the narrator's final proclamation is both triumphant and horrifying, madness in the story is both positive and negative. On the one hand, it testifies to an alternative reality and challenges patriarchy head on. The fact that her unflappable husband faints when he finds her establishes the dramatic power of her new freedom. Defying the judgment that she suffers from a "temporary nervous depression," she has followed her own logic, her own perceptions, her own projects to this final scene in which madness is seen as a kind of transcendent sanity. This engagement with the yellow wallpaper constitutes a form of the "work" which has been forbidden—women's writing. As she steps over the patriarchal body, she leaves the authoritative voice of diagnosis in shambles at her feet. Forsaking "women's language" forever, her new mode of speaking—an unlawful language—escapes "the sentence" imposed by patriarchy.

On the other hand, there are consequences to be paid for this escape. As the ending of the narrative, her madness will no doubt commit her to more intense medical treatment, perhaps to the dreaded Weir Mitchell of whom her husband has spoken. The surrender of patriarchy is only temporary: her husband has merely fainted, after all, not died, and will no doubt move swiftly and severely to deal with her. Her individual escape is temporary and compromised.

But there is yet another sense in which "The Yellow Wallpaper" enacts a clash between diagnosis and women's discourse. Asked once whether the story was based on fact, Gilman replied "I had been as far as one could go and get back."[4] Gillman based the story on her own experience of depression and treatment. For her first visit to the noted neurologist S. Weir Mitchell, she prepared a detailed case history of her own illness, constructed in part from her journal entries. Mitchell was not impressed: he "only thought it proved conceit" (*The Living*, 95). He wanted obedience from patients, not information. "Wise women," he wrote elsewhere, "choose their doctors and trust them. The wisest ask the fewest questions."[5] Gilman reproduced in her journal Mitchell's prescription for her:

> Live as domestic a life as possible. Have your child with you all the time. (Be it remarked that if I did but dress the baby it left me shaking and crying—certainly far from a healthy companionship for her, to say nothing of the effect on me.) Lie down an hour after every meal. Have but two hours intellectual life a day. And never touch pen, brush or pencil as long as you live. (*The Living*, 96)

Gilman spent several months trying to follow Mitchell's prescription, a period of intense suffering for her:

> I could not read nor write nor paint nor sew nor talk nor listen to talking, nor anything. I lay on that lounge and wept all day. The tears ran down into my ears on either side. I went to bed crying, woke in the night crying, sat on the edge of the bed in the morning and cried—from sheer continuous pain. (*The Living*, 121)

At last in a "moment of clear vision," Gilman realized that for her the traditional domestic role was at least in part the cause of her distress. She left her husband and with her baby went to California to be a writer and a feminist activist. Three years later she wrote "The Yellow Wallpaper." After the story was published, she sent a copy to Mitchell. If it in any way influenced his treatment of women in the future, she wrote, "I have not lived in vain" (*The Living*, 121).

There are several points to note here with respect to women's discourse. Gilman's use of her own journal to create a fictional journal which in turn becomes a published short story problematizes and calls our attention to the journal form. The terms "depression" and "hysteria" signal a non-textual as well as a textual conundrum: contemporary readers could (and some did) read the story as a realistic account of madness; for feminist readers (then and now) who bring to the text some comprehension of medical attitudes toward women in the nineteenth century, such a non-ironic reading is not possible. Lest we miss Gilman's point, her use of a real proper name in her story, Weir Mitchell's, draws explicit attention to the world outside the text.[6]

Thus "The Yellow Wallpaper" is not merely a fictional challenge to the patriarchal diagnosis of women's condition. it is also a public critique of a real medical treatment. Publication of the story added power and status to Gilman's words and transformed the journal form from a private to a public setting. Her published challenge to diagnosis has now been read by thousands of readers. By living to tell the tale, the woman who writes escapes the sentence that condemns her to silence.

iii. Escaping the Sentence

To call "The Yellow Wallpaper" a struggle between diagnosis and discourse is to characterize the story in terms of language. More precisely, it is to contrast the signification procedures of patriarchal medicine with discursive disruptions that call those procedures into question. A major problem in "The Yellow Wallpaper" involves the relationship of the linguistic sign to the signified, of language to "reality." Diagnosis, highlighted from the beginning by the implicit inverted commas around diagnostic phrases ("a slight hysterical tendency"), stands in the middle of an equation which translates a phenomenological perception of the human body into a finite set of signs called "symptoms"—fever, exhaustion, nervousness, pallor, and so on—which are in turn assembled to produce a "diagnosis"; this sign generates treatment, a set of prescriptions that impinge once more upon the "real" human body. Part of the power of diagnosis as a scientific process depends upon a notion of language as transparent, as *not* the issue. Rather the issue is the precision, efficiency, and plausibility with which a correct diagnostic sign is generated by a particular state of affairs that is assumed to exist in reality. In turn, the diagnostic sign is not complete until its clinical implications have been elaborated as a set of concrete therapeutic practices designed not merely to refer to but actually to change the original physical reality. Chary with its diagnostic categories (as specialized lexicons go), medicine's rich and intricate descriptive vocabulary testifies to the history of its mission: to translate the realities of the human body into human language and back again. As such, it is a perfect example of language which "reflects" reality and simultaneously "produces" it.[7]

Why is this interesting? And why is this process important in "The Yellow Wallpaper"? Medical diagnosis stands as a prime example of an authorized linguistic process (distilled, respected, high-paying) whose representational claims are strongly supported by social, cultural, and economic practices. Even more than most forms of male discourse, the diagnostic process is multiply-sanctioned.[8] "The Yellow Wallpaper" challenges both the particular "sentence" passed on the narrator and the elaborate sentencing process whose presumed representational power can sentence women to isolation, deprivation, and alienation from their own sentencing possibilities. The right to author or originate sentences is at the heart of the story and what the yellow wallpaper represents: a figure for women's discourse, it seeks to escape the sentence passed by medicine and patriarchy. Before looking more closely at what the story suggests about the nature of women's discourse, we need to place somewhat more precisely this notion of "the sentence."

Diagnosis is a "sentence" in that it is simultaneously a linguistic entity, a declaration or judgment, and a plan for action in the real world whose clinical consequences may spell dullness, drama, or doom for the diagnosed. Diagnosis may be, then, not merely a sentence but a death sentence. This doubling of the word "sentence" is not mere playfulness. "I sat down and began to speak," wrote Anna Kavan in *Asylum Piece*, describing the beginning of a woman's mental breakdown, "driving my sluggish tongue to frame words that seemed useless even before they were uttered." This physically exhausting process of producing sentences is generalized: "Sometimes I think that some secret court must have tried and condemned me, unheard, to this heavy sentence."[9] The word "sentence" is both sign and signified, word and act, declaration and discursive consequence. Its duality emphasizes the difficulty of an analysis which privileges purely semiotic relationships on the one hand or the representational nature of language on the other. In "The Yellow Wallpaper," the diagnosis of hysteria may be a sham: it may be socially constituted or merely individually expedient quite apart from even a conventional representational relationship. But it dictates a rearrangement of material reality nevertheless. The sentence may be unjust, inaccurate, or irrelevant, but the sentence is served anyway.[10]

The sentence is of particular importance in modern linguistics, where it has dominated inquiry for twenty-five years and for more than seventy years has been the upper cut-off point for the study of language: consideration of word sequences and meaning beyond the sentence has been typically dismissed as too untidy and speculative for linguistic science. The word "sentence" also emphasizes the technical concentration, initiated by structuralism but powerfully developed by transformational grammar, on syntax (formal grammatical structure at the sentence level). The formulaic sentence $S \rightarrow NP + VP$ which initiates the familiar tree diagram of linguistic analysis could well be said to exemplify the tyranny of syntax over the study of semantics (meaning) and pragmatics (usage). As a result, as Sally McConnell-Ginet has argued, linguistics has often failed to address those aspects of language with which women have been most concerned: on the one hand, the semantic or non-linguistic conditions underlying given grammatical structures, and on the other, the contextual circumstances in which linguistic structures are actually used.[11] One can generalize and say that signs alone are of less interest to women than are the processes of signification which link signs to semantic and pragmatic aspects of speaking. To "escape the sentence" is to move beyond the boundaries of formal syntax.

But is it to move beyond language? In writing about language over the last fifteen years, most feminist scholars in the United States have argued that language creates as well as reflects reality and hence that feminist linguistic innovation helps foster more enlightened social conditions for women. A more conservative position holds that language merely reflects social reality and that linguistic reform is hollow unless accompanied by changes in attitudes and socio-economic conditions that also favor women's equality. Though different, particularly in their support for innovation, both positions more or less embody a view that there *is* a non-linguistic reality to which language is related in systematic ways.[12] Recent European writing challenges the transparency of such a division, arguing that at some level reality is inescapably linguistic. The account of female development within this framework emphasizes the point at which the female child comes into language (and becomes a being now called female); because she is female, she is from the first alienated from the processes of symbolic representation. Within this symbolic order, a phallocentric order, she is frozen, confined, curtailed, limited, and represented as "lack," as "other." To make a long story short, there is as yet no escaping the sentence of male-determining discourse.[13]

According to this account, "the sentence," for women, is inescapably bound up with the symbolic order. Within language, says Luce Irigaray for example, women's fate is a "death sentence."[14] Irigaray's linguistic innovations attempt to disrupt this "law of the father" and exemplify the possibilities for a female language which "has nothing to do with the syntax which we have used for centuries, namely, that constructed according to the following organization: subject, predicate, or, subject, verb, object."[15] Whatever the realities of that particular claim, at the moment there are persuasive theoretical, professional, and political reasons for feminists to pay attention to what I will now more officially call discourse, which encompasses linguistic and formalistic considerations, yet goes beyond strict formalism to include both semantics and pragmatics. It is thus concerned not merely with speech, but with the conditions of speaking. With this notion of "sentencing," I have tried to suggest a process of language production in which an individual word, speech, or text is linked to the conditions under which it was (and could have been) produced as well as to those under which it is (and could be) read and interpreted. Thus the examination of diagnosis and discourse in a text is at once a study of a set of

representational practices, of mechanisms for control and opportunities for resistance, and of communicational possibilities in fiction and elsewhere.[16]

In "The Yellow Wallpaper" we see consequences of the "death sentence."
Woman is represented as childlike and dysfunctional. Her complaints are wholly
circular, merely confirming the already-spoken patriarchal diagnosis. She is
constituted and defined within the patriarchal order of language and destined,
like Athena in Irigaray's analysis, to repeat her father's discourse "without much
understanding."[17] "Personally," she says, and "I sometimes fancy": this is acceptable language in the ancestral halls. Her attempts to engage in different,
serious language—self-authored—are given up; to write in the absence of patriarchal sanction requires "having to be so sly about it, or else meet with heavy
opposition" (10) and is too exhausting. Therefore, the narrator speaks the law
of the father in the form of a "women's language" which is prescribed by patriarchy and exacts its sentence upon her: not to author sentences of her own.

The yellow wallpaper challenges this sentence. In contrast to the orderly,
evacuated patriarchal estate, the female lineage that the wallpaper represents
is thick with life, expression, and suffering. Masquerading as a symptom of
"madness," language animates what had been merely an irritating and distract-
ing pattern:

> This paper looks to me as if it *knew* what a vicious influence it had!
> There is a recurrent spot where the pattern lolls like a broken neck and two
> bulbous eyes stare at you upside down.
> I get positively angry with the impertinence of it and the everlastingness. Up
> and down and sideways they crawl, and those absurd, unblinking eyes are every-
> where. (16)

The silly and grotesque surface pattern reflects women's conventional representation; one juxtaposition identifies "that silly and conspicuous front design"
with "sister on the stairs!" (18). In the middle section of the story, where the
narrator attempts to convey her belief that she is seriously ill, the husband-
physician is quoted verbatim (23–25), enabling us to see the operation of male
judgment at first hand. He notes an improvement in her symptoms: "You are
gaining flesh and color, your appetite is better, I feel really much easier about
you." The narrator disputes these statements: "I don't weigh a bit more, nor
as much; and my appetite may be better in the evening when you are here,
but it is worse in the morning when you are away!" His response not only pre-
empts further talk of facts, it reinforces the certainty of his original diagnosis
and confirms his view of her illness as non-serious: " 'Bless her little heart!'
said he with a big hug, 'she shall be as sick as she pleases!' " (24).

His failure to let her leave the estate initiates a new relationship to the
wallpaper. She begins to see women in the pattern. Until now, we as readers
have acquiesced in the fiction that the protagonist is keeping a journal, a fiction

initially supported by journal-like textual references. This now becomes difficult
to sustain: how can the narrator keep a journal when, as she tells us, she is
sleeping, creeping, or watching the wallpaper the whole time? In her growing
paranoia, would she confide in a journal she could not lock up? How did the
journal get into our hands? Because we are nevertheless reading this "journal,"
we are forced to experience a contradiction: the narrative is unfolding in an
impossible form. This embeds our experience of the story in self-conscious
attention to its construction. A new tone enters as she reports that she defies
orders to take naps by not actually sleeping: "And that cultivates deceit, for I
don't tell them I'm awake—O no!" (26). This crowing tone announces a decisive
break from the patriarchal order. She mocks her husband's diagnosis by di-
agnosing for herself why he "seems very queer sometimes": "It strikes me
occasionally, just as a scientific hypothesis,—that perhaps it is the paper!"
(26–27).

The wallpaper never becomes attractive. It remains indeterminate, complex,
unresolved, disturbing; it continues to embody, like the form of the story we
are reading, "unheard of contradictions." By now the narrator is fully engrossed
by it and determined to find out its meaning. During the day—by "normal"
standards—it remains "tiresome and perplexing" (28). But at night she sees a
woman, or many women, shaking the pattern and trying to climb through it.
Women "get through," she perceives, "and then the pattern strangles them
off and turns them upside down, and makes their eyes white!" (30). The death
sentence imposed by patriarchy is violent and relentless. No one escapes.

The story is now at its final turning point: "I have found out another funny
thing," reports the narrator, "but I shan't tell it this time! It does not do to
trust people too much" (31). This is a break with patriarchy—and a break with
us. What she has discovered, which she does not state, is that she and the
woman behind the paper are the same. This is communicated syntactically by
contrasting sentences: "This bedstead is fairly gnawed!" she tells us, and then:
"I bit off a little piece (of the bedstead) at one corner" (34). "If that woman
does get out, and tries to get away, I can tie her!" and "But I am securely
fastened now by my well-hidden rope" (34–35). The final passages are filled
with crowing, "impertinent" language: "Hurrah!" "The sly thing!" "No person
touches this paper but me,—not *alive!*" (32–33). Locked in the room, she addresses her husband in a dramatically different way: "It is no use, young man,
you can't open it!"

She does not make this declaration aloud. In fact, she appears to have difficulty even making herself understood and must repeat several times the instructions to her husband for finding the key to the room. At first we think she
may be too mad to speak proper English. But then we realize that he simply
is unable to accept a statement of fact from her, his little goose, until she has

"said it so often that he had to go and see" (36). Her final triumph is her public proclamation, "I've got out at last . . . you can't put me back!" (36).

There is a dramatic shift here both in *what* is said and in *who* is speaking. Not only has a new "impertinent" self emerged, but this final voice is collective, representing the narrator, the woman behind the wallpaper, and women elsewhere and everywhere. The final vision itself is one of physical enslavement, not liberation: the woman, bound by a rope, circles the room like an animal in a yoke. Yet that this vision has come to exist and to be expressed changes the terms of the representational process. That the husband-physician must at last listen to a woman speaking—no matter what she says—significantly changes conditions for speaking. Though patriarchy may be only temporarily unconscious, its ancestral halls will never be precisely the same again.

We can return now to the questions raised at the outset. Language in "The Yellow Wallpaper" is oppressive to women in the particular form of a medical diagnosis, a set of linguistic signs whose representational claims are authorized by society and whose power to control women's fate, whether or not those claims are valid, is real. Representation has real, material consequences. In contrast, women's power to originate signs is monitored; and, once produced, no legitimating social apparatus is available to give those signs substance in the real world.

Linguistic innovation, then, has a dual fate. The narrator in "The Yellow Wallpaper" initially speaks a language authorized by patriarchy, with genuine language ("work") forbidden her. But as the wallpaper comes alive she devises a different, "impertinent" language which defies patriarchal control and confounds the predictions of male judgment (diagnosis). The fact that she becomes a creative and involved language user, producing sentences which break established rules, *in and of itself* changes the terms in which women are represented in language and extends the conditions under which women will speak.

Yet language is intimately connected to material reality, despite the fact that no direct correspondence exists. The word is theory to the deed: but the deed's existence will depend upon a complicated set of material conditions. The narrator of "The Yellow Wallpaper" is not free at the end of the story because she has temporarily escaped her sentence: though she has "got out at last," her triumph is to have sharpened and articulated the nature of women's condition; she remains physically bound by a rope and locked in a room. The conditions she has diagnosed must change before she and other women will be free. Thus women's control of language is left metaphorical and evocative: the story only hints at possibilities for change. Woman is both passive and active, subject and object, sane and mad. Contradictions remain, for they are inherent in women's current "condition."

Thus to "escape the sentence" involves both linguistic innovation and change in material conditions: both change in what is said and change in the conditions of speaking. The escape of individual women may constitute a kind of linguistic self-help which has intrinsic value as a contribution to language but which functions socially and politically to isolate deviance rather than to introduce change. Representation is not without consequences. The study of women and language must involve the study of discourse, which encompasses both form and function as well as the representational uncertainty their relationship entails. As a metaphor, the yellow wallpaper is never fully resolved: it can be described, but its meaning cannot be fixed. It remains trivial and dramatic, vivid and dowdy, compelling and repulsive: these multiple meanings run throughout the story in contrast to the one certain meaning of patriarchal diagnosis. If diagnosis is the middle of an equation that freezes material flux in a certain sign, the wallpaper is a disruptive center that chaotically fragments any attempt to fix on it a single meaning. It offers a lesson in language, whose sentence is perhaps not always destined to escape us.

NOTES

1. Charlotte Perkins Gilman, *The Yellow Wallpaper* (Old Westbury, N.Y.: The Feminist Press, 1973), p. 13. Subsequent references are cited parenthetically in the text.

2. Umberto Eco describes a "good metaphor" as one which, like a good joke, offers a shortcut through the labyrinth of limitless semiosis. "Metaphor, Dictionary, and Encyclopedia," *New Literary History*, 15 (Winter 1984), 255–71. Though there is relatively little criticism on "The Yellow Wallpaper" to date, the wallpaper seems to be a fruitful metaphor for discussions of madness, women's relationship to medicine, sexual inequality, marriage, economic dependence, and sexuality. An introduction to these issues is provided by Elaine R. Hedges in her "Afterword," *The Yellow Wallpaper*, pp. 37–63. Hedges also cites a number of nineteenth-century responses to the story. A useful though condescending discussion of the story in the light of Gilman's own life is Mary A. Hill, "Charlotte Perkins Gilman: A Feminist's Struggle with Womanhood," *Massachusetts Review*, 21 (Fall 1980), 503–26. A Bachelardian critical reading is Mary Beth Pringle, " 'La Poétique de l'Espace' in Charlotte Perkins Gilman's 'The Yellow Wallpaper,' " *The French-American Review*, 3 (Winter 1978/Spring 1979), 15–22. See also Loralee MacPike, "Environment as Psychopathological Symbolism in the 'The Yellow Wallpaper,' " *American Literary Realism 1870–1910*, 8 (Summer 1975), 286–88, and Beate Schopp-Schilling, " 'The Yellow Wallpaper': A Rediscovered 'Realistic' Story," *American Literary Realism 1870–1910*, 8 (Summer 1975), 284–86.

3. "Women's language" is discussed in Robin Lakoff, *Language and Woman's Place* (New York: Harper and Row, 1975); Casey Miller and Kate Swift, *Words and Women* (New York: Anchor/ Doubleday, 1976); Barrie Thorne, Cheris Kramarae, and Nancy Henley, eds., "Introduction," *Language, Gender and Society* (Rowley, Mass.: Newbury House, 1983); Cheris Kramarae, *Women and Men Speaking* (Rowley, Mass.: Newbury

House, 1981); Sally McConnell-Ginet, Ruth Borker, and Nelly Furman, eds., *Women and Language in Literature and Society* (New York: Praeger, 1980); Mary Ritchie Key, *Male/Female Language* (Metuchen, New Jersey: Scarecrow Press, 1975); and Paula A. Treichler, "Verbal Subversions in Dorothy Parker: 'Trapped like a Trap in a Trap,'" *Language and Style*, 13 (Fall 1980), 46–61.

4. Charlotte Perkins Gilman, *The Living of Charlotte Perkins Gilman: An Autobiography* (New York: Appleton-Century, 1935), p. 121. Subsequent references are cited parenthetically in the text.

5. S. Weir Mitchell, *Doctor and Patient* (Philadelphia: Lippincott, 1888), p. 48.

6. A feminist understanding of medical treatment of women in the nineteenth century is, however, by no means uncomplicated. An analysis frequently quoted is that by Barbara Ehrenreich and Deirdre English, *For Her Own Good: 150 Years of the Experts' Advice to Women* (Garden City, N.Y.: Anchor/Doubleday, 1979). Their analysis is critiqued by Regina Morantz, "The Lady and Her Physician," in *Clio's Consciousness Raised: New Perspectives on the History of Women*, eds. Mary S. Hartman and Lois Banner (New York: Harper Colophon, 1974), pp. 38–53; as well as by Ludi Jordanova, "Conceptualizing Power Over Women," *Radical Science Journal*, 12 (1982), 124–28. Attention to the progressive aspects of Weir Mitchell's treatment of women is given by Morantz and by Suzanne Poirier, "The Weir Mitchell Rest Cure: Four Women Who 'Took Charge,'" paper presented at the conference Women's Health: Taking Care and Taking Charge, Morgantown, West Virginia, 1982 [Author's affiliation: Humanistic Studies Program, Health Sciences Center, University of Illinois at Chicago.] See also Barbara Sicherman, "The Uses of Diagnosis: Doctors, Patients, and Neurasthenia," *Journal of the History of Medicine and Allied Sciences*, 32 (January 1977), 33–54; Carroll Smith-Rosenberg and Charles Rosenberg, "The Female Animal: Medical and Biological Views of Woman and Her Role in Nineteenth-Century America," rpt. in *Concepts of Health and Disease; Interdisciplinary Perspectives*, eds. Arthur Caplan, H. Tristram Engelhardt, Jr. and James J. McCartney (Reading, Mass.: Addison-Wesley, 1981), pp. 281–303; and Ann Douglas Wood, "'The Fashionable Diseases': Women's Complaints and Their Treatment in Nineteenth-Century America," in *Clio's Conciousness Raised: New Perspectives on the History of Women*, pp. 1–22.

7. The notion that diagnosis is socially constituted through doctor-patient interaction is discussed by Marianne A. Paget, "On the Work of Talk: Studies in Misunderstanding," in *The Social Organization of Doctor-Patient Communication*, eds. Sue Fisher and Alexandra Dundas Todd (Washington, D.C.: Center for Applied Linguistics, 1983), pp. 55–74. See also Barbara Sicherman, "The Uses of Diagnosis."

8. Discussions of the multiple sanctions for medicine and science include Shelley Day, "Is Obstetric Technology Depressing?" *Radical Science Journal*, 12 (1982), 17–45; Donna J. Haraway, "In the Beginning was the Word: The Genesis of Biological Theory," *Signs*, 6 (Spring 1981), 469–81; Bruno Latour and Steve Woolgar, *Laboratory Life: Social Contruction of Scientific Facts* (Beverly Hills: Sage, 1979); Evan Stark, "What is Medicine?" *Radical Science Journal*, 12 (1982), 46–89; and P. Wright and A. Treacher, eds., *The Problem of Medical Knowledge* (Edinburgh: Edinburgh University Press, 1982).

9. Anna Kavan, *Asylum Piece* (1940; rpt. New York: Michael Kesend, 1981), pp. 63, 65.

10. Reviewing medical evidence in "The Yellow Wallpaper," Suzanne Poirier suggests that a diagnosis of "neurasthenia" would have been more precise but that in any case, given the narrator's symptoms, the treatment was inappropriate and probably harmful. "'The Yellow Wallpaper' as Medical Case History," paper presented to the Faculty Seminar in Medicine and Society, University of Illinois College of Medicine at Urbana-Champaign, April 13, 1983. On the more general point, two recent contrasting analyses are offered by Umberto Eco, "Metaphor, Dictionary, Encyclopedia," who poses a world

of language resonant with purely semiotic, intertextual relationships, and John Haiman, "Dictionaries and Encyclopedias," *Lingua*, 50 (1980), 329–57, who argues for the total interrelatedness of linguistic and cultural knowledge.

11. Sally McConnell-Ginet, "Linguistics and the Feminist Challenge," in *Women and Language in Literature and Society*, pp. 3–25. The linguistic formula S→NP + VP means that Sentence is rewritten from this formula. Sentences are "generated" as tree diagrams that move downward from the abstract entity S to individual components of actual sentences. it could be said that linguistics misses the forest for the trees. But the fact that the study of women and language *has* concentrated on meaning and usage does not mean that syntax might not be relevant for feminist analysis. Potentially fruitful areas might include analysis of passive versus active voice (for example, see my "The Construction of Ambiguity in *The Awakening*: A Linguistic Analysis," in *Women and Language in Literature and Society*, pp. 239–57), of nominalization (a linguistic process particularly characteristic of male bureaucracies and technologies), of cases (showing underlying agency and other relationships), of negation and interrogation (two grammatical processes implicated by "women's language," Note 3), and of the relationship between deep and surface structure. Julia Penelope Stanley has addressed a number of these areas; see, for example, "Passive Motivation," *Foundations of Language*, 13 (1975), 25–39. Pronominalization, of course, has been a focus for feminist analysis for some time.

12. See, for example, Maija Blaubergs, "An Analysis of Classic Arguments Against Changing Sexist Language," in *The Voices and Words of Women and Men*, ed. Cheris Kramarae (Oxford: Pergamon Press, 1980), pp. 135–47; Francine Frank, "Women's Language in America: Myth and Reality," in *Women's Language and Style*, eds. Douglas Butturff and Edmund L. Epstein (Akron, Ohio: L&S Books, 1978), pp. 47–61; Mary Daly, *Gyn/Ecology* (Boston: Beacon, 1978); and Wendy Martyna, "The Psychology of the Generic Masculine," in *Women and Language in Literature and Society*, pp. 69–78. A general source is Barrie Thorne, Cheris Kramarae, and Nancy Henley, eds., *Language, Gender and Society* (Rowley, Mass.: Newbury House, 1983).

13. See, for example, Juliet Mitchell and Jacqueline Rose, eds., *Feminine Sexuality: Jacques Lacan and the école freudienne* (New York: W.W. Norton, 1982), pp. 1–57.

14. Luce Irigaray, "Veiled Lips," trans. Sara Speidel, *Mississippi Review*, 33 (Winter/Spring 1983), 99. See also Luce Irigaray, "Women's Exile: Interview with Luce Irigaray," trans. Couze Venn, *Ideololgy and Consciousness*, 1 (1977), 62–76; and Cary Nelson, "Envoys of Otherness: Difference and Continuity in Feminist Criticism," in *For Alma Mater: Theory and Practice in Feminist Scholarship*, eds. Paula A. Treichler, Cheris Kramarae, and Beth Stafford (Urbana: University of Illinois Press, 1985), pp. 91–118.

15. Luce Irigaray, "Women's Exile," 64.

16. See the discussion of discourse in Meaghan Morris, "A-Mazing Grace: Notes on Mary Daly's Poetics," *Intervention*, 16 (1982), 70–92.

17. Luce Irigaray, "Veiled Lips," 99–101. According to Irigaray's account, Apollo, "the always-already-speaking," drives away the chorus of women (the Furies) who want revenge for Clytemnestra's murder. His words convey his repulsion for the chaotic, non-hierarchical female voice: "Heave in torment, black froth erupting from your lungs"; "Never touch my halls, you have no right"; "Out you flock without a herdsman—out!" Calling for the forgetting of bloodshed, Athena, embodying the father's voice and the father's law, pronounces the patriarchal sentence on the matriarchal chorus: the women will withdraw to a subterranean cavern where they will be permitted to establish a cult, perform religious rites and sacrifices, and remain "loyal and propitious to the land." They are removed from positions of influence, their words destined to have only subterranean meaning.

STILL PRACTICE, A/WRESTED ALPHABET
Toward a Feminist Aesthetic

Jane Marcus

In *Between the Acts* Virginia Woolf uses Ovid's telling of the Procne and Philomel myth as an appropriate metaphor for the silencing of the female, for rape and male violence against women. I see Woolf as Procne to Philomel's text, the socialist feminist critic as reader of the *peplos*, the woven story of her silenced sister's rape.[1] The reading of the weaving is a model for a contemporary socialist feminist criticism. It gives us an aesthetics of political commitment to offer in place of current theories based in psychology or in formalism.

The voice of the nightingale, the voice of the shuttle weaving its story of oppression, is the voice which cries for freedom. An appropriate voice for women of color and lesbians, it speaks from the place of imprisonment as political resistance. The voice of the swallow, however, Procne's voice, is the voice of the reader, the translator, the middle-class feminist speaking for her sisters; in a sense, the voice which demands justice. The socialist feminist critic's voice is a voice of revenge, collaboration, defiance, and solidarity with her oppressed sister's struggle. She chooses to attend to her sister's story or even to explicate its absence, as Virginia Woolf told the story of Shakespeare's sister.

A Room of One's Own is the first modern text of feminist criticism, the model in both theory and practice, of a specifically socialist feminist criticism. The collective narrative voice of *A Room of One's Own* is a strategic rhetoric for feminist intellectuals. It solves the problem, moral and intellectual, of being one's sister's keeper, one's voiceless sister's voice.[2] Woolf has transformed the formidable lecture form into an intimate conversation among female equals.[3] Men are excluded. Shakespeare is important to *A Room of One's Own* because he is used as a barrier to the text for the male reader. In order to gain entry to the closed circle of female readers and writer, the male reader must pass a test, give the correct password; he must agree that Shakespeare's gender has nothing to do with his greatness. Shakespeare himself retold the story of Procne and Philomel in *Titus Andronicus* and in it there is an even clearer statement of the role of the critic.[4]

In *Titus Andronicus*, Shakespeare explores the rape victim as a "speaking text" and the problem of how to read her to its bloodiest degree. Lavinia is a "map of woe" to be read by her father and nephew. She is gang-raped by the sons of her father's captive in war. Not only is her tongue cut out but her arms are cut off to prevent her writing her tale. Her *peplos* is a bloody napkin (a reminder of the bridal sheet stained only the night before), and she makes bodily gestures and signs to her father: "But I, of these, will wrest an alphabet,/ And by still practice learn to know thy meaning" (III.ii.44–45). With her stumps, Lavinia points to the Procne and Philomel story in her nephew's Ovid and writes the names of her rapists in the sand with a stick held between her teeth. The story is not a pretty one, but it does give us a vivid image for the feminist critic and her relation to oppressed women. *A Room of One's Own* is "still practice," a reading of the signs, the dumb show of all the women between Sappho and Jane Austen who wrote in sand with a stick between their teeth. It tries to "wrest an alphabet" from the "speaking text" of women's bodies. This concept of "still practice," the patient struggle to "read" the body of the text of the oppressed and silenced, is a model for feminist criticism. It demands the suppression of the critic's ego in a genuine attempt at explicating the signs of the subject, her body, her text. It is a frustrating and selfless activity that must include, as in the case of Titus, a recognition of one's own complicity in the silencing of the subject. The focus of the critic must fix on forms foreign to the common practice of communication and art as Titus reads Lavinia's sand-writing and Procne interprets Philomel's message in the tapestry. The white woman critic must be careful not to impose her own alphabet on the art of women of color; the heterosexual critic must not impose her own alphabet on the lesbian writer. She must learn to read their languages. The alphabet she wrests from these signs may spell out Woolf's "little language unknown to men." Lavinia's lament, written in the sand, and the picture in Procne's *peplos*, not only ask for interpretation, they demand action. Thus the socialist feminist critic's desire to change the world as well as the hearts and minds of readers is included in its challenge. Reading that "map of woe" in such a way reverses the current practice of much literary criticism, where the initial act of the critic is an aggressive forced entry into the text of the writer with a reading of one's own and a subsequent silence regarding the impulse to political action as a result of one's reading. "Still practice" is not always "still," not entirely pacifist, for certainly Procne and Titus are moved to violent revenge on reading these texts of sister and daughter. A revolutionary criticism would perhaps insist that it is the critic's role to follow Procne and Titus in redressing the wrongs committed against the violated victim. We are at the very least forced to recognize that the suppression of women's writing is historically and psychologically directly related to male sexual violence against women, that men have cut out the tongues of the speaking woman and cut off the hands of the writing woman for fear of what she will say about them and about the world. If we arrest the alphabet we wrest from the tapestry and translate the voice of the stick in the sand, the poem is a four letter word, R A P E. The unwritten poems of Philomel and Lavinia, the stories of their lives before they were brutalized as women and as poets, are tragically lost. Woman is thus imaginatively fixed on a point which conflates her art with man's perception of her sexuality. Because man wishes to repress her power to accuse him and to remake the world, he has also repressed all her powers of celebration and limited her expression to the depiction of the scene of raping and the naming of her oppressors. Male patriarchal writing in its aggressiveness often rings with guilt for its history of robbing women of language and art. These stories reinforce a vision of one primal scene in the history of women in which both her sexual power and her creative power are attacked and destroyed. Her desire and her art are intimately related in their suppression. She writes on sand or weaves cloth for the reader who can see something other than the printed page as a text.

In "Aristotle's Sister," Lawrence Lipking laments the lack of a woman's poetics, imagining Aristotle's sister, Arimneste, and inventing a poetic for her, as well as reintroducing us to Madame de Staël's radical proposals for a community of readers reading society as well as literature.[5] Lipking is sympathetic to such a project, but his "poetics of abandonment" merely fits his theory of women into the existing male hierarchical structure, where it is clearly less important than men's. It does have the advantage, however, of extending the range of the male critic's possibilities for study into the fiction of feeling and the reading practice of women. Like the ubiquitous recreations of the androgyne in art (always as a feminized male) in the 1890s in response to the last wave of European feminism, this proposal extends the range of male critical action into the female. The opposite figure, the mannish woman, was given no such liberating exposure, in life or art. Yet the feminist critic who concentrates on male texts, as Nina Auerbach does, is often seen as a trespasser on male territory.

Elaine Showalter, in her discussion of Jonathan Culler's and Terry Eagleton's attempts at feminist criticism, asks, "But can a *man* read as a woman?"[6] and points out their essentialist bind in trying to imitate a woman's reading practice, as if this were an eternal Platonic state undetermined by class, time, history, gender, ethnicity, or place, as well as by the male critics' confusion about what has become clear to feminist critics—that any number of "women's" readings may not be feminist readings. Showalter asks the male would-be feminist to confront what reading as a man entails, to surrender his "paternal privileges." Otherwise, she claims, "we get a phallic 'feminist' criticism that competes with women instead of breaking out of patriarchal bounds" (143). The unexamined paternal privilege of Lipking's poetics of abandonment leads him into this trap. We valorize the victim at our own peril. The suffering posture of the abandoned woman is appealing to the phallic feminist because the absent male is at the center of the woman writer's text. But, as Judith Newton argues, feminist criticism has abandoned the posture of seeing history as a story of "individual and inevitable suffering."[7] Literary texts are, for this kind of committed criticism, "gestures toward history and gestures with political effect," and feminist criticism is "an act of political intervention, a mode of shaping the cultural use to which women's writing and men's will be put." Lipking's tragic essentialism focuses on eternal victimization, ignoring the fact that the power relations which construct gender do change over time. Victimization in his view seems to be woman's natural condition.

Elevating sexual victimization as a woman's poetics is a political act of phallic feminism that robs women of a sense of agency in history. Women have certainly gnashed their teeth and torn their hair and written good poems about it, but one could offer instead a feminist aesthetics of power with, say, Judith beheading Holofernes and Artemisia Gentileschi's depiction of the scene as its paradigm. Or, an aesthetics of maternal protection, an aesthetics of sisterhood, an aesthetics of virgin vengeance from the Amazons to Joan of Arc to Christabel Pankhurst, an aesthetics of woman's critique of male domination. Any one of these structures of literary history would have the virtue of melting the current thinking about the virtuous subjugated woman and the eternally dominating male. Nina Auerbach's *Woman and the Demon* is a brilliantly over-determined and insistently feminist reading of men's female literary monsters as powerful; Auerbach's study is far more valuable as a political tool for changing gender relations, however much it may resist the intended meanings of Victorian men, than the *ethos* of suffering and romantic love which haunts Lipking's nostalgic vision.[8] Auerbach's rereadings and misreadings urge her own readers to similar subversive acts.

Challenging and revising the canon is often an effective weapon in a campaign of criticism as political intervention. The most challenging critique of the canon comes from feminism, hence one's shock at the omission of such a critique from the *Critical Inquiry* canon issue. (Lillian Robinson's essay, invited but not published by that journal, appears in *Tulsa Studies in Women's Literature*).[9] The use of four new texts in my Women's Studies course this year leads me to believe, perhaps too optimistically, that our students' intellectual lives will be less shadowed by Milton's and other patriarchal bogeys than our own. Barbara Taylor's *Eve and the New Jerusalem* makes clear that there always was a feminism at the heart of British socialism, but male historians left it out. Marta Wiegle's *Spiders and Spinsters* exposes the ethnocentricity of our cultural studies. How deflated is Greek myth when seen in the context of world mythology, how interesting the place of women and goddesses in non-western cultures or the lore of American Indians. And the Bankier and Lashgari *Women Poets of the World* gives any would-be poet a rich and exciting heritage in which to place herself.[10] Any young woman dipping into this extraordinary volume has a poetic past of glorious words belonging to her sex, perhaps a *cliterologos* to think and write back through her many singing mothers. At her age I had only Sappho, Emily Dickinson, and Amy Lowell, and felt I had to choose an ethnic heritage for a writing identity rather than a gendered one. An important event in the history of women's literature is the publication of *Inanna*.[11] It may take several generations before Inanna as the *cliterologos* becomes flesh in the hearts and minds of readers or on the pages of a Norton Anthology of Literature, but her advent is a prologue to an emancipation proclamation for a whole sex. Scholars are not satisfied with the popular paperback text, but it has caused such a stir that a more authentic scholarly version of these fragments is sure to emerge from the controversy. It is Inanna's anteriority—2,000 years before the Hebrew biblical narrative—that is part of her aura. Given the chronological nature of patriarchal thinking, an authentic *Inanna*, when read before Homer or the Hebrew and Christian biblical narratives, will cause Eve's firstness to fade, and young women will read aloud to one another Inanna's stirring celebration of the power of her vulva under the apple tree: "Rejoicing at her wondrous vulva, the young woman Inanna applauded herself." The celebration of female sexuality is one of the wonders of this text. No guilt, no blame, no bearing of children in sorrow. In fact, this first written female epic has little to say about either motherhood or chastity; it stresses instead a powerful ethos of sisterhood and a sexuality both oral and genital. It presents a heroine who is politically powerful and sexually free. When Inanna demands that her brother fashion for her both a throne and a bed from the wood of the tree of life, which she has saved from the flood, female sexuality speaks as a blessing, not a curse, a sign of power, not of sin. Our students may then see the Greeks and Judeo-Christian biblical scribes as patriarchal revisers of a reality and a literature in which women were powerful. They will start to explore this first hanged goddess who descends into hell and rises again after three days as a prototype and will begin to ask *why* succeeding cultures inscribed, over and over again, female sexuality as evil.[12]

To return to Lipking's Arimneste, it appears probable that she could not read. However sympathetic male critics are to women, they never seem able to acknowledge that throughout history patriarchy has denied women (and many men) access to tools which make it possible to create written works of art or the written criticism of culture. Women have nevertheless produced and re-produced culture. Until male critics acknowledge their own patriarchal privi-

lege, built upon centuries of violent suppression of women's art, they will see
Arimneste as a shadow of Aristotle. Her fate was doubtless the fate of Freud's
female patients or Marx's daughters or Tolstoy's wife—Woolf's Shakespeare's
sister is less a fiction than we suppose.

Let us imagine a different scene. Let us suppose that Aristotle and his ilk
were unhappy in the communal culture of family and kinship, unhappy with
their roles as sons and husbands and fathers: that to escape a culture in which
art, work, religion, ritual, and community life were intertwined, they separated
themselves out by gender and class from women, slaves, and children, and
defined an art and a way of thinking which denied the connection between art
and work, and made themselves its priests. Women continued to make pots,
weave cloth, cook and serve food, prepare religious festivals, and sing the songs
of their oral tradition among each other in their own space. Lipking's most
shocking statement is the one he puts into Arimneste's mouth, that she achieves
"a momentary sense of not being alone, . . . through sharing the emotions of
loneliness and abandonment" (77). If I read this correctly, he means that the
woman artist achieves the radical sense of intimacy between speaker and listener
and the effect of the interconnected nature of human relations because and
only because her lover has left her. Certainly women have written great poems
on this theme, but to define a specifically female poetics in these terms seems
to deny the very existence of a female culture.

We could imagine another aesthetic, call it Penelope's, which grew out of a
female culture. Lipking says that Arimneste's "cannot compete, of course, with
her brother's tradition." Penelope's aesthetic does not wish to compete, is anti-
hierarchical, anti-theoretical, not aggressively exclusionary. *A real woman's
poetics is a poetics of commitment, not a poetics of abandonment.* Above all,
it does not separate art from work and daily life. Penelope weaves her tapestry
by day and takes it apart by night. Could Aristotle destroy his lectures and
start over again each day? This model of art, with repetition and dailiness at
the heart of it, with the teaching of other women the patient craft of one's
cultural heritage as the object of it, is a female poetic which women live and
accept. Penelope's art is work, as women cook food that is eaten, weave cloth
that is worn, clean houses that are dirtied. Transformation, rather than permanence, is at the heart of this aesthetic, as it is at the heart of most women's
lives.

History is preserved not in the art object, but in the tradition of *making* the
art object. Alice Walker's "Everyday Use" is the perfect modern example of
Penelope's poetic in practice. Penelope's poetic is based on the celebration of
the intimate connection between art and the labor which produced it. The
boeuf en daube or the embroidered robe is not produced to survive eternally.
It is eaten, it is worn; culture consists in passing on the technique of its making.

Stories are made to be told and songs to be sung. In the singing and the telling they are changed. Both Penelope's aesthetics and Procne's role as reader of her sister's text are rooted in the material base of female experience. A formalist criticism privileging the printed text cannot deal with its basic premises. The physical production of the work of art, studies of textual revision, censorship (by the poet and her editors, publishers, etc.), the historical conditions of the writing, biography, all the old-fashioned methodologies of literary history as well as the new ones which deal with maternal subtexts in women's fiction or mother-daughter relations, can contribute to a new criticism which presumes that a female culture has been produced and reproduced throughout history. As Dale Spender writes of women's ideas:

> We *can* produce knowledge, we have been doing so for centuries, but the fact that it is not part of our tradition, that it is not visible in our culture, is because we have little or no influence over where it goes. We are not the judges of what is significant or helpful, we are not influential members in those institutions which legitimate and distribute knowledge. We are women producing knowledge which is often different from that produced by men, in a society controlled by men. If they like what we produce they will appropriate it, if they can use what we produce (even against us) they will take it, if they do not want to know, they will lose it. But rarely, if ever, will they treat it as they treat their own.[13]

The same is true for women's works of art. Sandra M. Gilbert and Susan Gubar have written eloquently on the anxiety a woman writer feels in a patriarchal society when the pen is equated with the penis. Ovid's "Procne and Philomel" and Shakespeare's *Titus Andronicus* give us a *mythos* which explains the female artist's fear. Here is a poem by a sixteenth-century Frenchwoman who overcomes her anxiety, as I would argue most modern women writers have, by keeping a hand in both worlds. Penelope's spindle protects the writer as she attempts the pen:

To My Spindle

My spindle and my care, I promise you and swear
To love you forever, and never to exchange
Sweet domestic honor for a thing wild and strange,
Which, inconstant, wanders, and tends its foolish snare.

With you at my side, dear, I feel much more secure
Than with paper and ink arrayed all around me,
For, if I needed defending, there you would be,
To rebuff any danger, to help me endure.

But, spindle, my dearest, I do not believe
That, much as I love you, I will come to grief
If I do not quite let that good practice dwindle

Of writing sometimes, if I give you fair share,

If I write of your goodness, my friend and my care,
And hold in my hand both my pen and my spindle.[14]

Reading as Desire

Virginia Woolf believed that a woman's reading group was revolutionary; and in her edition of *Virginia Woolf's Reading Notebooks*, Brenda Silver describes a lifetime of intellectual and political obsession with reading and notetaking which belies the biographer's portrait of a lady.[15] Woolf's attitude (reading as desire) is perhaps best expressed in this letter to Ethel Smyth:

> Sometimes I think heaven must be one continuous unexhausted reading. It is a disembodied trance-like intense rapture that used to seize me as a girl, and comes back now and again down here, with a violence that lays me low . . . the state of reading consists in the complete elimination of the *ego*; and its the ego that erects itself like another part of the body I dont dare to name (Letter 2915).

It seems pointless to argue whether women are better readers than men because of their receptiveness and openness to the text. What is important is that Woolf saw gender as determining the roles of writer, speaker, and reader and privileged the female versions of these acts as more democratic than the male. Given contemporary male critics' descriptions of ravishing the text and deconstructionists' search for points of entry into the text, Woolf's critical "still practice" as the enraptured reader, ego-less and open to the text rather than aggressively attacking it, is consistent with the goals of feminist philosophy. The reader's desire to be enraptured by the writer, which Woolf celebrates, is very different from contemporary criticism's assertion of intellectual superiority over writers and books. It is difficult to imagine an American formalist deconstructive critic being laid low by a book. Woolf's imagined embrace of the common reader and the common writer comes from a desire for shared pleasure.

It is by the use of obscurantist language and labelling that formalist critics batter the text and bury it. They assert their egos and insult their own readers by making them feel ignorant. Much as they criticize anti-intellectual bourgeois society, they add to the contempt for art and thought by alienating readers even further. Their jargon, the hieroglyphics of a self-appointed priesthood, makes reading seem far more difficult than it is. In an age of declining literacy, it seems suicidal for the supposed champions of arts and letters to attack and incapacitate readers.

The language of current theoretical writing is a thicket of brambles; the reader must aggressively fight her way into it, emerging shaken and scratched. Those survivors in the central clearing congratulate themselves on being there. Everyone on the other side of the bushes is a coward or an intellectual weakling. Bleeding and exhausted from their struggle, they invent a new hierarchy, with theorists at the top, vying to be scientists and philosophers. Literary criticism and theory are somehow tougher and more rigorous than other forms of literary study. It is an ironic turn of events when one declares that a socialist feminist criticism should defend its old enemies, the very bibliographers, editors, textual scholars, biographers, and literary historians who wrote women writers out of history to begin with. But without the survival of these skills and the appropriation of them, women will again lose the history of their own culture. Theory is necessary and useful but is not superior to other literary practice or immune to historical forces. In fact, despite its birth in the left-wing beds of Europe, it has grown in practice to be an arrogant apolitical American adolescent with too much muscle and a big mouth. As the theorists constrict the world of readers and writers to ever tinier elites, the socialist feminist critic must reach out to expand and elasticize that world to include the illiterate, the watchers of television, the readers of romances, the participants in oral cultures—in short, our students.

When male theorists practice a feminist criticism, as Elaine Showalter brilliantly argues in "Critical Cross-Dressing," they are giving their abstract theory a body. One is as reluctant to lend them the materiality of our reading practice as ballast as one is to see good feminist critics throw that materiality overboard to soar in the high ether of theory with the men. If we are good enough to steal from, we are good enough to get published, get tenure, get grants. The male critics who find our work so interesting have put remarkably little effort into seeing that we survive professionally to write it. When a famous Yale professor who *is* the establishment refuses to recognize his power, in fact defines himself as an outsider, feminist critics have little hope of institutional comfort.[16] I agree with Gayatri Spivak that our marginality is important—but there is very little room in the margins when that space has been claimed by Marxists and theorists of all stripes. With all this jostling in the margins, who is in the center? Shari Benstock, discussing the appendages to Joanna Russ's *How to Suppress Women's Writing*, suggests that academic feminist critics are not marginal in the least, compared to black outsiders or writers excluded from the academy.[17] Yet hierarchy develops within feminist criticism itself. Are certain forms of feminist criticism more acceptable to the patriarchy? Obviously, yes. Are certain forms of feminist criticism more marginal than others? Obviously, yes. Note that Elizabeth Abel's feminist issue of *Critical Inquiry*, "Writing and Sexual Difference," contains essays by several left-wing women.[18] Yet none of them explicates a theory of socialist feminist or Marxist feminist criticism. Women of color and lesbians are working on their own theories of feminist criticism. A socialist feminist criticism that wishes to include them must overcome separatist notions of "more marginal than thou," and offer an umbrella of sisterhood under which to shield many writers who feel that their privileged, straight, white sisters are not sisters at all. Yet it must also have the courage to explicate its own tenets and assert its presence in public.

Shari Benstock challenges us: "Feminist criticism must be willing to pose the question of the *differences within* women's writing. . . . Feminist criticism must be a radical critique not only of women's writing but of women's *critical* writing." She calls for us to "inscribe the authority of our own experience" (147) and to question the assumptions of that authority. I am not sure that Shari Benstock realizes how dangerous this project can be. My own career began with such critiques of feminist criticism and I have concluded that years of joblessness were a direct result of that practice.[19] Old girl networks exist; hierarchy is imposed and some feminist journals have "better" reputations than others. Star feminist critics perform their acts on platforms all over the country. The only difference is that we like what they have to say, and fall asleep less easily than at a male critic's lecture. One feminist critic says that she would not have the "hubris" to criticize Gilbert and Gubar. It is not hubris but a pledge to our collective future as practicing critics to point out differences in theory and practice. I am sure that Sandra Gilbert and Susan Gubar would be the first to insist that such sisterly criticisms of their work be offered, for they continue to write, to grow, and to change. If feminist criticism has taught us anything, it has taught us to question authority, each other's as well as our oppressors'. There are some cases in which theorists ignore scholarship at their peril.

Benstock assumes a willingness on the part of feminist critics to change their practice, which may be as utopian as my wish for a historically sound, materially based, theoretically brilliant socialist feminist criticism. I assure her that several of my feminist colleagues, who agree with my analysis, have nevertheless urged me to delete some of the following remarks. Standing on tiptoe, under an umbrella, in the margin of the margin, can we really engage in dialogue with each other?

In "Unmaking and Making in *To the Lighthouse*," Gayatri Spivak places a Derridean box over the text and crushes and squeezes everything to fit.[20] Like Cinderella's stepsister cutting off a piece of her foot to fit the glass slipper, this technique distorts the text. Derrida's notion of sexual difference includes only male and female and cannot encompass Woolf's celebration of celibacy in Lily Briscoe. So the text is distorted to allow Spivak to see Lily's painting as analogous to gestation, where she uses Mr. Ramsey as an agent to complete the painting. That the text actually exults in Lily's *refusal* of Mr. Ramsey is ignored. The sexual and grammatical Derridean allegory of the copula in which the painting is the predicate of Mrs. Ramsay, imposes a male structure on female text which simply does not fit. The biographical reading of the "Time Passes" section as Woolf's "madness" depends entirely on Quentin Bell and is not only not an accurate picture of Woolf's mental states, but far from feminist criticism. The footnotes do not cite a single feminist reading of Woolf. Yet there is no more perfect example of "still practice" than Spivak's essay on, and translation of, an Indian revolutionary writer's story in the feminist issue of *Critical Inquiry*.[21]

Peggy Kamuf's suggestive essay, "Penelope at Work: Interruptions in *A Room of One's Own*," also fails to keep faith with its subject.[22] The politics of the footnote is the subject of another essay, but it is clear from Kamuf's reading of Woolf through Foucault, Descartes, and *The Odyssey*, like Spivak's reading through Derrida and Freud, that the critics reject the role of common reader to Woolf's common writer, and that they also reject the notion of a community or collective of feminist criticism.[23] It is not "still practice," and it does not try to wrest a woman's alphabet from the woman writer but spells her message in male letters. More importantly, these critics reject explicitly Woolf's role as foremother of feminist criticism in *A Room of One's Own*. There she outlines "thinking back through our mothers" as writing practice for feminist critics as well as novelists, and shows us how to do feminist criticism. By refusing to accept their role as inheritors of this tradition established by Woolf, seeing her only as a writer whose texts are decoded with male tools, whose premises they dare not enter without the support of male systems, they assert themselves as superior and isolated from their subject as well as from those other critics who have seen themselves as descendants of Woolf, the feminist critic. In *A Room* Woolf stakes out the territory for the practice of feminist criticism, includes the history of women writing before her, and prophesies the future. But these critics deny the authority of the female text. By taking father-guides to map the labyrinth of the female text, they deny the motherhood of the author of the text. These readings reinforce patriarchal authority. By reading Woolf through Foucault, Kamuf names Foucault's critique of the history of sexuality as more powerful than Woolf's. Reading Woolf through Derrida, Spivak serves patriarchy by insisting on a heterosexuality which the novel attacks by privileging chastity in the woman artist. The critic takes a position which is daughter to the father, not daughter to the mother. Is Woolf so frightening to the female critic, are her proposals so radical, that she must provide herself with a male medium through whom to approach the text? What they seem unable to accept is their own daughterhood as critics to Woolf's role as the mother of socialist feminist criticism. One of the major points of *A Room of One's Own* is the clear injunction to the audience of female students to avoid male mentors, the assertion with the story of Oscar Browning that the British academic world is a male homosexual hegemony which needs to deny women to stay in power. Woolf says when turned back from the university library, "Never will I wake

those echoes again." Why does the female critic wake those echoes? There is
a real problem, which I do not wish to minimize, for leftist feminist critics
regarding whether our Marxism or socialism is mediated through men. Certainly Jameson, Said, and Eagleton do not make things any easier for us.

I suggest that the course Woolf proposes, if taken seriously as intellectual
and political action, is often too difficult for women trained by men to do. In
effect, the critic says to the writer, "I cannot face your female authority without
a male guide; I cannot face the historical fact of the interrupted woman writer
without interrupting the woman telling me the story of woman's oppression."
There is a way of being a feminist critic without insisting on the role of daughter
of Derrida or *femme de* Foucault, a way of accepting and exploiting the marginality of women and of feminist literary criticism. It is a way described in
Three Guineas as the alternative institution built by women and working class
men. The critic must join the Outsiders' Society. I am not denying the brilliance
of Spivak and Kamuf as critics. It is because I have learned from them that I
want to ask them to reject male formalist models for criticism. I do not even
claim that a pragmatic historical feminist criticism is the only way to read a
text. But, as Elaine Showalter has pointed out in her English Institute paper
(which also appears in this volume), formalist and psychoanalytic models of
feminist criticism, using Lacan, Derrida, and Foucault, are currently fashionable. A materialist "still practice" may yet emerge.

I would also like to see a more sisterly relationship develop between feminist
theorists and feminist scholars. At present the scholars generously acknowledge
the theorists, but theorists, like their brothers, follow the fashionable practice
of minimalism in footnoting, often slighting years of scholarship, textual editing,
and interpretation without which their own work could not begin. This is a
denial of the place of one's own work in literary history, asserting as virgin
births interpretations which have ancestry. As Virginia Woolf claimed of art,
"masterpieces are not single and solitary births," so one may claim that criticism
itself has a familial and cultural history. Perhaps theorists, like the characters
in Oscar Wilde's plays, want to be orphaned. It increases the cachet of avant-
gardism. A look at feminist interpretations of Virginia Woolf's madness would
have altered Spivak's reading of the "Time Passes" section of *To the Lighthouse*.
It does not seem necessary for Peggy Kamuf to dismiss cavalierly the importance
of the historical authenticity of Heloise's letters to Abelard in her brilliant
Fictions of Feminine Desire.[24] That their authenticity is questioned is surely
part of the historical suppression of the idea or evidence of female desire.
Whether Heloise wrote the letters or the Portuguese Nun was a man is of
interest to the argument about female desire. Why this defensive bristling at
the historical nature of our enterprise as well as its collectivity? Who profits
when departments of literature reward theorists more than scholars? As Virginia

Woolf wrote, one must beware of the headmaster with a measuring rod up his sleeve. Who set us in competition with one another, and for such small stakes? The prize is only, as Woolf dryly remarks, an ornamental pot. In the current atmosphere of anti-intellectualism, we are all lumped together anyway.

What would a truly socialist feminist criticism look like? We do have some examples in Virginia Woolf and Sylvia Townsend Warner. What Sylvia Townsend Warner calls the "Backstairs or pantry-door" marginality of the feminist critic is a position to be prized and protected. Yet the practice of formalism professionalizes the feminist critic and makes her safe for academe. I'm not sure it is worth giving up Procne's Bacchic vine leaves for an academic robe. The writing practice of some new theory is often heavily authoritarian, deliberately difficult, and composed in a pseudo-scientific language which frightens off or intimidates the common reader. If criticism is reading, then contemporary formalists move too aggressively and too fast for "still practice." If we are really worried about how few of our students read, how can we write essays which deny our *own* readers the pleasures of reading? A new feminist alphabet, which we wrest from the text and arrest in our criticism, should not be an imitation of the Greek or Latin by which older generations of critics declared themselves priests of art and culture, superior to the mass of ordinary readers. A demotic female tongue may surely be spelled out in which criticism is conversation as in *A Room of One's Own.* Let yourselves go, feminist critics. Wind Bacchic vine leaves in your hair as Procne did when she went to find her sister. How can we read the message of the tapestry, the words scraped on the sand, if our own tongues practice patriarchal criticism, wars of words? Openness to the text and sharing conversation with our own readers is not as intellectually safe as a formal practice, distanced from the desire Woolf sees embodied in the act of reading. Here is a critic speaking in such a voice, aware of her place in the history of feminist criticism. Intimacy between the woman writer and reader, reproduced by that reader for her reader, is not always easy. The white heterosexual critic often fears such an intimacy with black, Chicana, or lesbian writers, and class can constitute a serious obstacle. It is not surprising that it is in non-academic works where the principle of "still practice" or reading as desire is beautifully practiced, most recently in Rachel Brownstein's *Becoming a Heroine,* Joanna Russ's *How To Suppress Women's Writing* and Alice Walker's *In Search of Our Mothers' Gardens.*[25]

We are now fortunate to have in print, tucked away in the back of her *Collected Poems,* Sylvia Townsend Warner's 1959 Peter Le Neve Foster Lecture delivered to the Royal Society of Arts as a sequel to *A Room of One's Own.* 1959 was a low point for Woolf's reputation and Townsend Warner was reviving a "lost" book by her imitation of it and by asking to have Leonard Woolf introduce her. Sylvia Townsend Warner was a poet, novelist, historian of early music, a lesbian, and a leftist (a long-time member of the Communist party). Her feminist fantasy novel *Lolly Willowes* (1926) is as brilliant as *Orlando* and has had a small but faithful audience of admirers. "Women as Writers" is not a seductive sapphistry like *A Room of One's Own*, but in its own dry, wryly ironic way it continues the work of its predecessor as feminist criticism.[26] It modestly apprentices itself (we might say "daughters itself") to its mother text and brings up to date the history of women writers. Like Woolf, Townsend Warner opens with doubts about the subject chosen for her, a technique which forces the audience to participate in the lecture and makes them responsible for the subject. "Even when people tell me I am a lady novelist, it is the wording of the allegation I take exception to, not the allegation itself. . . . Supposing I had been a man, a gentleman novelist, would I have been asked to lecture on Men as Writers? I thought it improbable." "It would appear," she goes on to say:

> that when a woman writes a book, the action sets up an extraneous vibration. Something happens that must be accounted for. It is the action that does it, not the product. It is only in very rare, and rather non-literary instances, that the product—*Uncle Tom's Cabin*, say, or the *Memoirs of Harriet Wilson*—is the jarring note. It would also appear that this extraneous vibration may be differently received and differently resounded. Some surfaces mute it. Off others, it is violently resonated. It is also subject to the influence of climate, the climate of popular opinion. In a fine dry climate the dissonance caused by a woman writing a book has much less intensity than in a damp foggy one. Overriding these variations due to surface and climate is the fact that the volume increases with the mass—as summarized in MacHeath's Law:

> One wife is too much for most husbands to hear. But two at a time sure no mortal could bear.

> Finally, it would appear that the vibration is not set up until a woman seizes a pen. She may invent, but she may not write down. MacHeath's Law explains why the early women writers caused so little alarm. They only went off one at a time. (265–66)

Townsend Warner adds her own footnotes to *A Room*'s namedropping (the lecture's oblique purpose was to supply students with the names of women writers) from Mother Goose to Lady Murasaki. Her iconoclastic opinions are: "I doubt if Pope would have laid so much stress on Lady Mary Wortley-Montagu being dirty if she had not been inky"; too much is made of Dr. Johnson on women preachers and not enough is made of his support of Fanny Burney; Jane Austen's "immediacy" keeps a bookful of rather "undistinguished characters" alive; George Eliot is a lecturer and an edifier—"it seems to me that George Eliot insisted upon being a superlative Mrs. Trimmer" (270). Like Woolf's socialist insistence on the importance of money and the material circumstances of the artist, Townsend Warner's analysis emphasizes class and economics. She sees the difference between the nineteenth-century writer and the modern writer in terms of the first being hampered by an attribution of moral superiority while the second is hampered by "an attribution of innate physical superiority."

> There is, for instance, bi-location. It is well known that a woman can be in two places at once; at her desk and at her washing-machine. . . . Her mind is so extensive that it can simultaneously follow a train of thought, remember what it was she had to tell the electrician, answer the telephone, keep an eye on the time and not forget about the potatoes. (267–68)

Sylvia Townsend Warner's one positive assertion about women as writers is that they are "obstinate and sly" (267). Her examples of good clear writing are Florence Nightingale's medical reports, a recipe for custard (perhaps in tribute to Woolf's descriptions of the dinners in her lectures), a fifteenth-century letter about apoplexy, a fourteenth-century Norfolk mystic's "I Saw God in a Point," and Frances Cornford's poem describing a Cypriot mother breast-feeding her baby. Obstinate and sly as the writers she discusses, Townsend Warner equates women outsiders with Shakespeare, climbing into the Castle of Literature through the pantry window. "It is a dizzying conclusion, but it must be faced. Women, entering literature, entered it on the same footing as William Shakespeare" (271). That's as daring a rhetorical trick as any Virginia Woolf ever penned. Because they have had no training, women writers share with Shakespeare a "kind of workaday democracy, an ease and appreciativeness in low company," and an ear for common speech. She advocates the Tradesman's Door as an alternate entrance to literature, citing the success of Aphra Behn. Writing is now an acceptable trade except among the upper classes. "Suppose that a royal princess could not tear herself from the third act of her tragedy in order to open a play-centre. People would be gravely put out, especially the men who had been building the play-centre, men who have taught their wives to know their place, and who expect princesses to be equally dutiful" (273).

Since most women writers are middle-class, she says, their writing reflects middle-class virtues. She longs for a woman Clare or Burns or Bunyan. Like Woolf, she urges the working class woman to write: "A working class woman may be as gifted as all the women writers I have spoken of today, all rolled into one; but it is no part of her duty to write a masterpiece." Like Woolf's eloquent peroration to the women absent from her lecture because they are washing up the dishes, Townsend Warner ends with a leap out of the cozy class and cultural world of her audience:

> It may well be that the half has not yet been told us: the unbridled masterpieces, daring innovation, epics, tragedies, works of genial impropriety—all the things that so far women have singly failed to produce—have been socially not sexually

debarred; that at this moment a Joan Milton or a Françoise Rabelais may have
left the washing unironed and the stew uncared for because she can't wait to
begin.

In 25 years feminist critics have shown that indeed the half was not told us
of our heritage in women writers. Princesses are not yet writing plays but the
works of black people and other minorities are being rediscovered, written,
and read. *But Some of Us Are Brave*[27] and the Mexican-American collections
published by Arte Publico Press at the University of Houston make clear that
both artists and critics of subject peoples have voices. Many a stewpot has
burned and many a man has learned to iron or gone unpressed to his job since
then. We all have our own candidates for Joan Milton and Françoise Rabelais.
My Joan Milton is Mary Daly; yours may be the early mystic, Jane Lead. My
candidate for Franço s abela s June Arnold; yours may be Zora Neale Hurston.
As Judith Shakespeare is not only Radclyffe Hall but all the silenced women
of history, the continuing work of the critical task of keeping this heritage alive
and broadening its base across race, class, and national prejudice is part of what
Woolf meant by "thinking back through our mothers."

After Townsend Warner, *A Room* was rewritten and reinterpreted by Mary
Ellmann in *Thinking About Women*, Adrienne Rich in *On Lies, Secrets and
Silence*, Tillie Olsen in *Silences*, Carolyn Heilbrun in *Reinventing Womanhood*,
Lillian Robinson in *Sex, Class and Culture*, Joanna Russ in *How To Suppress
Women's Writing*, and Alice Walker in *In Search of Our Mothers' Gardens*.[28]
These critics consciously paid tribute to Woolf and pushed the barriers further
back to include as many women writers as possible. It was less than a decade
ago that Lillian Robinson read a working woman's diary to an audience of
outraged scholars and called it literature. What these writers have in common
with Woolf and Townsend Warner, as well as with the mute inglorious Joan
Miltons whose writing they value, is obstinacy and slyness. They speak intimately to the reader and they are amusing and witty. One after the other they
have climbed in the pantry window of literary criticism taking note of the muddy
footprints of their predecessors. It is in this way that literary criticism moves
from one generation to the next, affirming its mothers' works and moving them
along.

NOTES

I am grateful to Elizabeth Abel, Judith Kegan Gardiner, Moira Ferguson, Michael
King, and Sandra Shattuck for their helpful comments on drafts of this paper.
    1. I discuss the Procne and Philomel myth in *Between the Acts* in "Liberty, Sorority,

Misogyny" in *The Representation of Women in Fiction*, ed. Carolyn Heilbrun and Margaret Higonnet (Baltimore: Johns Hopkins University Press, 1982), pp. 60–97.

2. "Her Sister's Voice," is part of the argument of my "Taking the Bull by the Udders: Sexual Difference in Virginia Woolf, A Conspiracy Theory," *Virginia Woolf and the Languages of Patriarchy* (Bloomington: Indiana University Press, 1987).

3. Woolf's deconstruction of the lecture form is discussed in "Taking the Bull by the Udders," and the role of Shakespeare is also taken up in "Sapphistry: Narration as Lesbian Seduction in *A Room of One's Own*," ibid.

4. My thanks to Lynda Boose for discussions of *Titus*.

5. Lawrence Lipking, "Aristotle's Sister," *Critical Inquiry*, 10 (September 1983), 61–81. On page 62 Lipking argues that Samuel Butler's *The Authoress of the Odyssey* is regarded as "irredeemably crackpot." For some redeeming features in his "crackpot" theory, see classicist David Grene's introduction to the University of Chicago Press reprint, 1967. Despite my disagreement with Lipking's argument here, I remain grateful for his personal encouragement of my work.

6. Elaine Showalter, "Critical Cross-Dressing: Male Feminists and the Woman of the Year," *Raritan*, 2 (Fall 1983), 130–49.

7. Judith Newton, paper delivered at the 1983 MLA Feminist Criticism session, chaired by Shari Benstock, to which the present essay was also a contribution. Newton's paper is published in this volume.

8. Nina Auerbach, *Woman and the Demon: The Life of a Victorian Myth* (Cambridge, Mass.: Harvard University Press, 1982).

9. *Critical Inquiry*, 10 (September 1983), and Lillian Robinson, "Treason Our Text: Feminist Challenges to the Literary Canon," *Tulsa Studies in Women's Literature*, 2 (Spring, 1983), 83–98. See also Paul Lauter's "Race and Gender in the Shaping of the American Literary Canon: A Case Study from the Twenties," *Feminist Studies*, 9 (Fall 1983), 435–63.

10. Barbara Taylor, *Eve and the New Jerusalem*, (New York: Pantheon, 1983); Marta Wiegle, *Spiders and Spinsters* (Albuquerque: University of New Mexico Press, 1982); *Women Poets of the World*, ed. Joanna Bankier and Dierdre Lashgari (New York: Macmillan, 1983).

11. *Inanna*, ed. Diane Wolkstein and Samuel Noah Kramer (New York: Harper, 1983).

12. Feminists should note the reviews of *Inanna* by Piotr Michalowski in the NYTBR and Harold Bloom in the NYRB (1983). Neither man tells the reader what is in the book. Certainly it appears that much more work must be done on the texts. Michalowski actually declares that Wolkstein "has violated the culture that produced the texts in which Inanna appears," and Harold Bloom writes an essay on contemporary attitudes toward the idea of hell. He is defensive about the Sumerians' primacy as writers and thinkers, and distances them as "alien," thus rejecting this most important text for our culture because it is "mythologically bewildering" to him, "an alien vision that has little in common either with the Bible or with Homer." Bloom is most upset when Inanna sends her husband to take her place in hell and chastizes Wolkstein for praising a goddess "who may not be the best 'role model' for us and our children." He cites this action as "caprice" and "brutality" and urges us to reject Inanna on moral grounds, citing the later patriarchal curse on her in the legend of Gilgamesh.

13. Dale Spender, *Women of Ideas and What Men Have Done To Them* (Boston: Routledge and Kegan Paul, 1982), p. 9.

14. Catherine des Roches (c. 1555–1584). Unpublished translation by Professor Tilde Sankovitch, Northwestern University French Department.

15. Brenda Silver, *Virginia Woolf's Reading Notebooks* (Princeton: Princeton University Press, 1983).

16. See Geoffrey Hartman's talk in *The Challenge of Feminist Criticism*, pamphlet, ed. Joanna Lipking, from the School of Criticism and Theory Symposium, "The Challenge of Feminist Criticism," November 1981, pp. 23–26 (available from The Program on Women, Northwestern University, 617 Noyes St., Evanston, Illinois 60201). My own essay at this symposium, "Gunpowder, Treason and Plot," naively asked male critics to read feminist critics. For what happened when they did, see Elaine Showalter's "Critical Cross-Dressing." See also the papers by Marlene Longenecker and Judith Gardiner in this collection for rejections of formalism and socialist-feminist critiques of contemporary critical discourse and note as well the dialogic interaction of the speakers with each other and with the audience.

17. Shari Benstock, "The Feminist Critique: Mastering our Monstrosity," *Tulsa Studies in Women's Literature*, 2 (Fall 1983), 137–49.

18. *Critical Inquiry*, 8 (Winter 1981), guest edited by Elizabeth Abel.

19. One of the books I questioned was Elaine Showalter's *A Literature of Their Own* (Princeton: Princeton University Press, 1977), arguing that it was not materialist or historical enough. Given the subsequent almost wholesale shift into psychoanalytic theories by feminist critics, her book looks now like a model of materialist scholarly practice.

20. Gayatri Spivak, "Making and Unmaking in *To the Lighthouse*," in *Women and Language in Literature and Society*, eds. Sally McConnell-Ginet, Ruth Borker, and Nelly Furman (New York: Praeger, 1980), pp. 310–27.

21. "Draupadi," *Critical Inquiry*, 8 (Winter 1981), 381–402. It is only in the reading of *To the Lighthouse* that Spivak fails to write theory and practice. See her "Three Feminist Readings" in *Union Seminary Quarterly Review*, 35, nos. 1 and 2 (Fall-Winter 1978–1979), 15–38.

22. Peggy Kamuf, "Penelope at Work: Interruptions in *A Room of One's Own*," *Novel*, 16 (Fall 1982), 5–18.

23. On the footnote, see Shari Benstock's "At the Margin of Discourse," *PMLA*, 98 (March 1983), 204–25. I have remarked in "Storming the Toolshed," *Signs* Feminist Theory Issue, 7 (Spring 1982), 622–40, on the peculiar lack of footnotes to feminist critics whose ideas are used in their essays by male critics. See note 3, pp. 233–34 of J. Hillis Miller's *Fiction and Repetition* (Cambridge, Mass.: Harvard University Press, 1982) for an interesting example of the way in which the critic identifies himself by naming all the critics he wishes to be his brothers and equals. Like some tribal ritual, this incantation places his own work among those he respects; he even names the journals whose views he acknowledges, and throughout the text he refers to the fiction he is writing about as "my seven novels." Does this represent a kind of crisis or anxiety of authorship/critical identity in the establishment? This minimalism in annotation has the political effect of isolating the critic or theorist from scholars and from the history of scholarship. If present practice in footnoting is a legacy of nineteenth-century capitalist recognition of the ownership of ideas, the minimalism of theorists, as opposed to scholars, represents a new economy of critical exchange in which the work of scholars is fair game (like exploitation of third world countries) and the Big White Men only acknowledge each other. Feminist practice continues to acknowledge students, participants in seminars, casual conversations—one scholar recently thanked Ma Bell for enabling her to discuss her work with her colleagues on the telephone. Nina Auerbach goes so far as to say that a whole chapter of *Woman and the Demon* owes its genesis to Martha Vicinus's opening of her files to a sister scholar.

24. Peggy Kamuf, *Fictions of Feminine Desire* (Lincoln: University of Nebraska Press, 1982).

25. Rachel Brownstein, *Becoming a Heroine: Reading About Women in Novels* (New York: Viking, 1982); Joanna Russ, *How to Suppress Women's Writing* (Austin: University of Texas Press, 1983); and Alice Walker, *In Search of Our Mothers' Gardens* (New York: Harcourt Brace Jovanovich, 1983).

26. Sylvia Townsend Warner, "Women as Writers," in *Collected Poems* (New York: Viking, 1983). Viking has also published a selection of Townsend Warner's *Letters*, edited by William Maxwell (1983), and *Scenes of Childhood* (1981) is still in print. There is an Academy/Chicago edition of her brilliant feminist novel *Lolly Willowes* (1926). Virago (London) has reprinted two other novels, *The True Heart* and *Mr. Fortune's Maggot*. Townsend Warner deserves a major revival. I have discussed *Lolly Willowes* in "A Wilderness of One's Own: Feminist Fantasy Novels of the Twenties" in *Women Writers and the City*, ed. Susan Squier, (Knoxville: University of Tennessee Press, 1984) pp. 134–60.

27. *But Some of Us Are Brave*, eds. Gloria Hull, Patricia Bell Scott, Barbara Smith (Old Westbury, N.Y.: The Feminist Press, 1982).

28. Mary Ellmann, *Thinking About Women* (London: Virago, 1982; first published 1968); Adrienne Rich, *On Lies, Secrets and Silence* (New York: Norton, 1979); Tillie Olsen, *Silences* (New York: Dell, 1965); Carolyn Heilbrun, *Reinventing Womanhood* (New York: Norton, 1979); Lillian Robinson, *Sex, Class and Culture* (Bloomington and London: Indiana University Press, 1978).

TOWARD A WOMEN'S POETICS

Josephine Donovan

A recent *New Yorker* cartoon shows a husband returning to the TV set to find the closing credits rolling over the screen. Since he has missed the ending, his wife fills him in: "It came out happily. She shot him." The cartoon suggests that women may evaluate art differently than men. In this rather basic case, the woman viewer's judgment stems from her empathetic identification with the triumphant female character. That woman's victory over the male character is pleasing to the woman viewer. One of the most ancient of critical dicta is that art please its audience (Horace: *aut prodesse aut delectare*). The film pleases this woman because she identifies with women as a class. She might be surprised to learn that her judgment is rooted in a woman-identified epistemology.

The cartoon points to the thesis of this article: women's aesthetic and ethical judgments, when authentic, are rooted in a woman-identified, or woman-centered, epistemology. That epistemology derives from women's cultural experience and practice (praxis). To understand women's art one must have a knowledge of women's experience and practice. A women's poetics will be constructed from comprehensive studies of women's stylistics and thematics, but those studies must be informed by an understanding of women's ways of seeing, a women's epistemology.

A number of feminist critics have started moving in the direction of the formulation of a women's poetics. In 1979 Susan Sniader Lanser and Evelyn Torton Beck urged that "an autonomous woman-centered epistemology" must form the basis of a woman-centered, or gynocentric, criticism.[1] Lanser and Beck deplored "the 'masculinization' of women's minds" that occurs "where men hold power and define women in relation to themselves." Such co-optation means that "androcentric epistemologies" reign supreme and woman-centered modes of perception" are sacrificed (86).

In 1980, Michèle Barrett, in her highly intelligent analysis of Marxist feminism, stated that she believes it "an urgent task" for feminist criticism to take on the problem of aesthetic value "in the context of the female literary tradition."[2] In 1982, Elaine Showalter coined the term "gynocritics" to describe what she saw as the next phase of feminist criticism, that which focuses on "women as *writers* . . . its subjects are the history, styles, themes, genres, and structures of writing by women; the psychodynamics of female creativity; the trajectory of the individual or collective female career; and the evolution or laws of a female literary tradition."[3] One of the obvious tasks of gynocriticism is the formulation of a women's poetics.

The most recent critic to address the issue is Lawrence Lipking, who in 1983 noted, "no established literary theory has yet been devised that builds from the ground up on women's own experience of literature, on women's own ways of thinking." "A classic woman's poetics has yet to be written."[4] Following Virginia Woolf's speculations about the silence of Shakespeare's sister, Judith, Lipking worries about the absence of Aristotle's sister, Arimneste, in the critical canon. "Unlike Shakespeare's sister," he notes, "Aristotle's sister has yet to break her silence" (61). Not only has women's criticism been excluded from the standard critical canon (for there have been a few great women critics), "the classic line of literary theory has hardly acknowledged the existence of two sexes." It goes without saying, therefore, that the male critical establishment has never entertained the possibility "that women might read and interpret literature in some way of their own" (62).

Lipking suggests that while gynocriticism lacks a tradition of its own, it should resist the temptation to build "on masculine modes" (63). Rather, "the outline of a woman's poetics is traced in poems and novels and plays, in essays and pamphlets and letters and diaries, and even in records of conversation" (63). In other words, it is to be found in the cultural and social expressions of women speaking about their experience and practice, in a woman-grounded epistemology.

Lipking goes on to develop his theory of women's literature, which he calls "a poetics of abandonment" (75). This theory, while interesting, depends largely on Madame de Staël's analysis of the classics of the European sentimentalist tradition—*The Portuguese Letters, Heloise to Abelard, The New Heloise* and *The Sorrows of Werther*—most of which follow what Nancy K. Miller has labeled the "heroine's text."[5] The fundamental plot-pattern in such works involves the seduction and abandonment of an innocent young woman. Lipking argues that the phenomenon of abandonment may be an archetypal female experience and provide the basis for an understanding of female creativity, and therefore, of female metaphor, symbolism, and imagery.

Lipking's theory may help to interpret one kind of literature that concerns women, but I would resist universalizing it as *the* "woman's poetics." First, it derives in part from texts written by men. A women's poetics must be wholly grounded in works by women. Second, I urge that we seek to construct a "women's poetics" in the plural rather than a "woman's poetics." I believe that there are common denominators that unify women's experience (as I explore below), but we must be aware of the diversity of women's histories and cultures and try to incorporate that diversity into our theory. A black women's poetics must be rooted in black women's experience and practice, as a lesbian poetics must be grounded in lesbian culture. Similarly, a working women's epistemology is specific, as are the female cultures of various ethnic groups.

A feminist critical theory that is focused on women's art and toward the development of a women's poetics—in other words, gynocriticism—is rooted in a feminist theory that may be labeled "cultural feminism."[6] This particular branch of feminist theory, which has a long history, stresses the identification of women as a separate community, a separate culture, with its own customs, its own epistemology, and, once articulated, its own aesthetics and ethics. Many of the great feminist theorists of the nineteenth century, including Margaret Fuller and Charlotte Perkins Gilman, subscribed to this theory. Not surprisingly, Fuller and Gilman are among the great women critics of the past, a select group that includes Virginia Woolf and Madame de Staël, all cultural feminists.

Contemporary cultural feminist theory has provided important theses that help to identify a woman-centered epistemology. In the remainder of this essay I plan to draw upon these theories to delineate six structural conditions that appear to have shaped traditional women's experience and practice in the past and in nearly all cultures—conditions that have, in short, shaped women's world-views.[7] Finally, I intend to indicate briefly how a knowledge of this epistemology may help us to interpret women's art, to recognize what Alice Walker has called "our mothers' gardens," to establish some foundation for a women's poetics.

1) Women, whether in community or in isolation, share a condition of oppression, or otherness, that is imposed by governing patriarchal or androcentric ideologies. Women as a group, therefore, share certain awarenesses that are common to oppressed groups. There is a psychology of oppression, of colonization, that may be found in works as diverse as Edith Wharton's *Ethan Frome* (1911), Franz Kafka's *Letter to His Father* (1919), Radclyffe Hall's *The Well of Loneliness* (1928), Ralph Ellison's *Invisible Man* (1952), and Sylvia Plath's *The Bell Jar* (1963).

Aspects of the colonized mentality have been described by a number of theorists, notably Franz Fanon, and a thorough discussion of the phenomenon is not possible here. Suffice it to note that one of its most important manifestations is the "internalization of otherness," a psychic alienation that is fundamentally schizophrenic. One common experience that illustrates the imposition of otherness, or objectness, upon women is the catcall. In the early 1970s Meredith Tax analyzed the phenomenon as follows: "What [catcallers] do is *impinge* upon [a woman]. They will demand that her thoughts be focused on them. They will use her body with their eyes. . . . Above all, they will make her feel like a *thing*."[8]

The harassed woman is forced into a schizophrenic response: either she can remain identified with her body which has been objectified as a tool for male purposes, in which case she denies her mind and her spiritual self; or she can deny the body and consider the mind the real self. The latter entails an autistic withdrawal from the everyday public world, a silent living within.

To an extent this schizophrenia parallels the dilemma all would-be women artists must face. To enter the public realm of history—what the French Lacanian feminists call the realm of the Symbolic—means in a sense to capitulate to male domination. But to remain in the pre-literate, pre-Oedipal realm of the Mother, of female dominance and authenticity, means to remain silent.[9]

This is not because the public world of discourse is irretrievably phallic, as the French feminists seem to imply, but because the "social construction of reality" has been done by males, and that construction has cast women in the role of other and seen their experience as deviant, or has not seen it at all. Like the catcall, this process has caused women to withdraw, not to name, to be silent. "To internalize Otherness is almost definitionally to be unable to speak in the language of the self. . . . To experience being an Other is often to feel so schizophrenically torn, that not even a clandestinely authentic 'I' dares to speak."[10]

For the silenced Other to begin to speak, to create art, she must be in communication with others of her group in order that a collective "social construction of reality" be articulated. Other social witnesses from the oppressed group must express their views, to validate one's own truth, that one may name it. This is the process of coming to consciousness described by Paulo Freire and others, a form of praxis as revolutionary activity that leads to social transformation.

Women's art must be understood in the social and political context of oppression in which it is created. The construction of a women's poetics must be seen as part of the "conscientization" process, and gynocriticism as a form of revolutionary praxis.

2) The second structure of experience that seems nearly universal is that women have been confined/consigned to the domestic or private sphere. An important determinant of traditional women's consciousness has been the practice of domestic labor or housework. An essential component of this labor is that it is non-progressive, repetitive, and static.

Kathryn Allen Rabuzzi argues that the Aristotelian notion of plot as a progressive movement from beginning to middle to end is at odds with the traditional woman's fundamentally repetitive or cyclic existence (163–67). A women's poetics, therefore, may have to reconceive the notion of plot as a fundamental aesthetic category so that it may be grounded in an idea of temporal order more appropriate to the cyclic experience of women's lives (see below for an application of this idea).

Another aspect of the domestic woman's work experience is its fundamental "interruptibility."[11] Just as women's colonized lives are fundamentally invadable, so is women's work perceived as interruptible. Others' projects (her husband's, her children's) in the household have a priority. This phenomenon contributes to the structure of women's artistic labor just as it does to their household labor, and it also contributes to a consciousness that is aware of contingency, that perceives itself bound to chance, not in total control. Such an awareness has obvious ethical and aesthetic implications.

3) In the household women have historically created objects for use rather than for exchange. Karen Sacks and more recently Nancy C. M. Hartsock have applied this important Marxist notion to an analysis of traditional women's praxis.[12] Production for use means creation of material that is consumed by the immediate family and not sold off or exchanged. It is material that is valued for itself, for its immediate physical and qualitative worth, and not for its abstract quantitative monetary or exchange value.

The household thus remains the site of essentially pre-industrial production and of relatively unalienated labor. It is so because, unlike the factory worker, the housewife has a measure of creative control over her time and over the design and execution of her products. As Angela Davis noted of the black slave woman's domestic labor, its products are the only ones that are not expropriated by the slaveowner/capitalist. Davis argues that this praxis contributed to the construction of the black woman's critical consciousness.[13] And some of the domestic woman's work—cooking, knitting, sewing, gardening—can be seen as truly creative, indeed a form of art, as Alice Walker has suggested.[14]

The housewife is immersed in the daily world of concrete realities in a way that most men are not, and the qualitative nature of her products—that they have been personalized by her touch—gives women an avenue to the sacred that most men, immersed as they are in the profane, alienated world of exchange or commodity production, do not have. As Hartsock notes, a capitalist male "lives a life structured completely by commodity exchange and not at all by production, and at the farthest distance from contact with concrete material life."[15] Such widely different daily practices have resulted in widely different epistemologies, Hartsock convincingly argues.

4) Women share certain physiological experiences, the most universal of which is menstruation. A great number of women also share the experiences of childbirth and breast-feeding. All of these, too, contribute to a sense of being

bound to physical events beyond the self, and in the case of menstruation to a consciousness of repetition and of the interuptibility of one's projects.

5) Almost all cultures have assigned the childrearing role to women. Even women who do not rear children have been socialized to the caretaker's role, and many have filled roles that are essentially maternal. Sara Ruddick's "Maternal Thinking" is the most important analysis of how the practice of mothering engenders a certain consciousness. Ruddick states, "I am increasingly convinced that there are female traditions and practices out of which a distinctive kind of thinking has developed."[16] Ruddick relies, therefore, on the notion that thinking and consciousness arise out of social practice.

Ruddick draws attention to ways in which maternal thinking differs from the archetypal thought-practice of the public patriarchal world, the scientific. The mother, for whom the preservation and growth of the child is a paramount concern, develops an attitude of what Ruddick calls "holding." Holding is an essentially preservative attitude of "keeping" rather than "acquiring," "of conserving the fragile, of maintaining whatever is at hand and necessary to the child's life" (350). "The recognition of the priority of holding over acquiring . . . distinguishes maternal from scientific thought, as well as from the instrumentalism of technocratic capitalism" (350).

Maternal practice recognizes "excessive control as a liability," in sharp distinction from scientific practice (351). The maternal ethic involves a kind of reverential respect for the process of life and a realization that much is beyond one's control. Following Iris Murdoch (and before her Simone Weil) Ruddick calls this an ethic of humility. It is an attitude that "accepts not only the facts of damage and death, but also the facts of the independent and uncontrollable, developing and increasingly separate existences of the lives it seeks to preserve" (351).

Ruddick decides that "attentive love," an idea derived from Murdoch and Weil, is what describes maternal practice. It is a love that is grounded in daily reality, that is relatively free of fantasy, and that is able to accept the existence of an entity different from oneself.

As I have indicated in another article, I believe that Weil's/Murdoch's/Ruddick's notion of reverential attention provides the basis not only for an ethic, but for a feminist critique of androcentric literature that is distinguished by the absence of attentive love for women.[17]

Kathryn Rabuzzi has also identified a "holding" attitude as an aspect of the traditional woman's experience. Labeling it a "waiting" modality, Rabuzzi contrasts this archetypal experience of the homebound woman to the primary male mode of questing. Rabuzzi notes that a dominant plot in masculine literature is that of the quest. From such a perspective, stasis is the worst of evils, and "entrapment by a woman . . . [becomes] a living death" (147). Rabuzzi, however, suggests that "the static waiting pattern" of women need not necessarily be seen negatively; rather "it is simply another mode of being." "It may imply rootedness of a positive . . . sort. As such it is a condition essential for growth" (151).

Rabuzzi concludes that "both history and story, traditionally so full of quests as to be virtually synonymous with them, may not be formally appropriate to express traditional feminine experience" (153). "If," she wonders, "stories of . . . Hestia, or housewives were to be told, what might they be like?" (155). As I suggest below we already have stories of Hestia, but we have yet to identify their formal patterns; we have yet to establish their poetics.

6) Finally, thanks to Freudian feminists like Nancy Chodorow, we have come to realize that the psychological maturation process in girls and boys is quite different. Chodorow's thesis in *The Reproduction of Mothering* is by now so well known that I will only briefly summarize it here. It must be noted, however, that like all Freudian theory, Chodorow's seems largely relevant to the white, Western, middle-class experience.

Chodorow argues that gender personality is shaped within the psychodynamics of the mother-child relationship. These gender personality traits—independence and relatively affectless behavior in men and interdependency and emotional intensity in women—prepare people for their respective roles in society and in the economy. Men's traits enable them to function in the capitalist world of production; women's prepare them for their place in the world of reproduction, particularly the reproduction of mothering.

> As long as women mother, we can expect that a girl's pre-Oedipal period will be longer than that of a boy and that women, more than men, will be more open to and preoccupied with those very relational issues that go into mothering—feelings of identification, lack of separateness or differentiation, ego and body-ego boundary issues and primary love not under the sway of the reality principle . . . .
> Girls emerge . . . with a basis for "empathy" built into their primary definition of self in a way that boys do not. Girls emerge with a stronger basis for experiencing another's needs or feelings as one's own . . . girls come to experience themselves as less differentiated than boys, as more continuous with and related to the external object-world.[18]

Carol Gilligan relies in part on Chodorow to explain the differences she discovered in moral reasoning in men and women. Not surprisingly, she found that women's thought processes are more contextually-oriented, less concerned with an abstract balancing of rights and more with discriminating among "conflicting responsibilities."[19] Women's "mode of thinking . . . is contextual and narrative rather than formal and abstract" (19).

The men's "morality of rights" tends to emphasize "separation rather than connection" and "a consideration of the individual rather than the relationship as primary" (19). For women "morality and the preservation of life are contingent upon sustaining connection, seeing the consequences of action by keeping the web of relationships intact" (59). Gilligan concludes that the images of hierarchy and web represent the basic differences in the male and female modes of knowledge (33).

As an example of how critics may begin to develop a women's poetics that is grounded in an understanding of women's attentive and contextual epistemology, and how they may apply these ideas to literary works, I am going to return to Sarah Orne Jewett's *Country of the Pointed Firs* (1896). This work has always been something of a puzzle to scholars because it does not fit into traditional (masculine) notions of genre or plot.

Two recent articles by feminist scholars (or gynocritical scholars), Elizabeth Ammons and myself, have addressed the problem of the work's alleged "plotlessness" by suggesting that the work's ordering or structural principle is one that is derived from women's culture and women's epistemology. Ammons uses Gilligan to suggest that the work is indeed structured upon the pattern of a web. Unlike the traditional masculine or Aristotelian narrative structure which is linear and progressive, the structure of *Pointed Firs* is "webbed, net-worked. Instead of being linear, it is nuclear: the narrative moves out from one base to a given point and back again, out to another point, and back again, out again, back again, and so forth, like arteries on a spider's web."[20]

In "Sarah Orne Jewett's Critical Theory: Notes Toward a Feminine Literary Mode," I argue among other things that Jewett's "plotless" structure in *Pointed Firs* and other works is an essentially feminine literary mode that expresses an inductive, contextual sensitivity. Using Rabuzzi's notion that the traditional woman's sense of time is repetitive or cyclic rather than linear (the time of the quest), I suggest that Jewett's plots be understood as reflective of the traditional woman's consciousness. Ultimately, I argue, Jewett's greatest works concern an escape from the androcentric time of history into transcending gynocentric space.[21]

One final issue I would like to introduce (or reintroduce) here is the question of what gynocritical methodologies should entail. Several contributors to a recent volume, *Theories of Women's Studies*, have attempted to suggest ideas on what should constitute a feminist methodology (primarily in the social sciences).[22] Rejecting the quantitative, positivist, "value-neutral" methodology of traditional scholarship, these theorists urge with Lipking that a gynocritical methodology not be built upon masculine modes, for, as Audre Lorde once put it rather succinctly: "the master's tools will never dismantle the master's house."[23]

In an essay in *Theories of Women's Studies*, Renate Duelli Klein rejects the idea of simply "adding on" knowledge about women without changing the way such knowledge is obtained. "Such thinking represents an 'equal-rights-philosophy' . . . [in which] answers from and about women are evaluated against *male* standards. Such research perpetuates a view of women from an androcentric perspective."[24]

Klein further rejects the notion of the researcher as "distant 'expert' who investigates a certain . . . variable out of 'objective' interest." Such "context-stripping" methods have no place in feminist research. Maria Mies in the same volume also rejects the idea of research as "value-free, neutral, uninvolved . . . [and] of a hierarchical, non-reciprocal relationship between research subject and research object." Such an approach forces the woman researcher into the schizophrenic position of being the elevated male scientist on the one hand, studying, on the other, the oppressed, objectified female research material.[25]

Barbara Du Bois urges that "the central agenda for feminist social science and scholarship" is "to address women's lives and experience *in their own terms*, to create theory grounded in the actual experience and language of women."[26] She suggests further that "to see, name and describe the experience and realities of women," we must see it "*complexly*, contextually" (110) and "*within its matrix*," which "includes the knower" (111). "To be open to this complexity and to see things in context means to move out of the realms of discourse and logic that rely on linear and hierarchical conceptions of reality, on dualistic models . . . on dichotomous modes of thought" (110).

In applying all this to literary critical methodology it is interesting to note that René Wellek rejected Madame de Staël's approach to literature as too personal. He wrote, "Her discussion of Greek literature is almost grotesque . . . . The main offense of the Greeks is the low status granted to women: Telemachus ordering Penelope to be silent must have conjured the vision of some man giving the same order to Madame de Staël."[27] One can almost hear the old boys chuckling. Wellek would, of course, have critics be objective and unmoved by such adventitious matters as women's status in society.

A feminist critic is not only moved by such matters but makes them her point of departure. Such a premise necessarily questions the nature of the "objectivity" posed by androcentric critics. For this reason, as Lipking suggests (70), the notion of aesthetic distance is the first concept eliminated from a gynocritical methodology.

The dissection of literature as if it were an aesthetic machine made up of paradoxes, images, symbols, etc., as so many nuts and bolts easily disintegrated from the whole must be rejected in gynocriticism. Literature must not be seen in the dichotomous view of the male scientist as an "it" opposed to the "I" of the analyst. Nor must literature be seen as a transcendent string of disembodied masterpieces that are disconnected from their specific historical sociocultural locale. Literature, communities, critics, and authors must be seen as bound up in a relational network. Just as modern physics recognizes that reality is contingent upon the positional relativity of the observer, so must modern criticism reject the Newtonian notion of critical objectivity. A women's epistemology, as identified by modern theorists, is appropriately contextual and relational. Gynocriticism must be similarly focused.

Finally, Lipking suggests that "a woman's poetics must begin . . . with a fact that few male theorists have ever had to confront: the possibility of never having been empowered to speak" (67). Gynocriticism is a part of the process, of the praxis, through which the voices of the silenced are becoming heard. Not only is gynocriticism naming and identifying what has never been named or even seen before, it is also providing a validating social witness that will enable women today and in the future to see, to express, to name, their own truths.

NOTES

1. Susan Sniader Lanser and Evelyn Torton Beck, "[Why] Are There No Great Women Critics? And What Difference Does It Make?" in *The Prism of Sex: Essays in the Sociology of Knowledge*, eds. Julia A. Sherman and Evelyn Torton Beck (Madison: University of Wisconsin Press, 1979), p. 86. Subsequent references are cited parenthetically in the text.

2. Michèle Barrett, *Women's Oppression Today: Problems in Marxist Feminist Analysis* (London: Verso, 1980), p. 105.

3. Elaine Showalter, "Feminist Criticism in the Wilderness," in *Writing and Sexual Difference*, ed. Elizabeth Abel (Chicago: University of Chicago Press, 1982), pp. 14–15. Other articles that have broached the subject of a women's poetics include: Julia Penelope Stanley and Susan J. Wolfe (Robbins), "Toward a Feminist Aesthetic," *Chrysalis*, 6 (1978), 57–71; Elaine Showalter, "Towards a Feminist Poetics," in *Women Writing and Writing about Women*, ed. Mary Jacobus (New York: Barnes & Noble, 1979), pp. 22–41; Sandra Gilbert and Susan Gubar, "Toward A Feminist Poetics," in *The Madwoman in the Attic: The Woman Writer and the Nineteenth-Century Imagination* (New Haven: Yale University Press, 1979), pp. 3–104; Nancy K. Miller, "Emphasis Added: Plots and Plausibilities in Women's Fiction," *PMLA*, 96 (January 1981), 36–48; and the articles by Barbara Smith, Lorraine Bethel, and Mary Helen Washington in *But Some of Us Are Brave: Black Women's Studies*, eds. Gloria T. Hull, Patricia Bell Scott, and Barbara Smith (Old Westbury, N.Y.: Feminist Press, 1982). This list is by no means complete.

4. Lawrence Lipking, "Aristotle's Sister: A Poetics of Abandonment" *Critical Inquiry*, 10 (September 1983), 63. Subsequent references are cited parenthetically in the text.

5. Nancy K. Miller, *The Heroine's Text: Readings in the French and English Novel 1722–1782* (New York: Columbia University Press, 1980). Madame de Staël's analysis is in "Essay on Fiction" in *Madame de Staël on Politics, Literature, and National Character*, trans. Monroe Berger (Garden City, N.J.: Doubleday, 1964), pp. 257–65.

6. See Josephine Donovan, *Feminist Theory: The Intellectual Traditions of American Feminism* (New York: Ungar, 1985), especially chapters 2 and 7.

7. An earlier version of this thesis appeared in my "A New Direction," in *Feminist Literary Criticism* (Research Triangle Park, N. C.: National Humanities Center, 1981), pp. 83–99, and a similar statement appears in *Feminist Theory*, ch. 7.

8. Meredith Tax, "Woman and Her Mind: the Story of an Everyday Life," in *Notes From the Second Year* (New York: Notes From the Second Year, 1970), p. 12.

9. See Hélène Cixous, "Castration or Decapitation?" *Signs*, 7 (Autumn 1981), 41–55; and Xavière Gauthier, "Is There Such A Thing As Women's Writing?" in *New French Feminisms, An Anthology*, eds. Elaine Marks and Isabelle de Courtivron (New York: Schocken, 1980), pp. 162–63. Also, Mary Jacobus, "The Difference of View," in *Women Writing and Writing About Women*, ed. Mary Jacobus (New York: Barnes & Noble, 1979), pp. 42–60.

10. Kathryn Allen Rabuzzi, *The Sacred and the Feminine: Toward a Theology of Housework* (New York: Seabury, 1982), p. 176. Subsequent references are cited parenthetically in the text.

11. Michelle Cliff, "The Resonance of Interruption," *Chrysalis*, 8 (Summer 1979), 29–37.

12. Karen Sacks, "Engels Revisited: Women, the Organization of Production, and Private Property," in *Towards an Anthropology of Women*, ed. Rayna Reiter (New York: Monthly Review Press, 1975), pp. 211–34; and Nancy C.M. Hartsock, "The Feminist Standpoint: Developing the Ground for A Specifically Feminist Historical Materialism," in *Discovering Reality: Feminist Perspectives on Epistemology, Metaphysics, Methodology, and Philosophy of Science*, eds. Sandra Harding and Merrill B. Hintikka (Dordrecht, Holland: Reidel, 1983), pp. 283–310.

13. Angela Davis, "Reflections on the Black Woman's Role in the Community of Slaves," *Black Scholar*, 3 (December 1971), 7. See also Lise Vogel, "The Earthly Family," *Radical America*, 7 (July-October 1973), 26.

14. Alice Walker, "In Search of Our Mothers' Gardens," *Ms.*, 2, no. 11 (May 1974), 64–70, 105. Marjorie Pryse interprets housework as art in "An Uncloistered 'New England Nun,' " *Studies in Short Fiction*, 20 (Fall 1983), 289–95.

15. Hartsock, p. 292.

16. Sara Ruddick, "Maternal Thinking," *Feminist Studies*, 6 (Summer 1980), 346. Subsequent references are cited parenthetically in the text.

17. Josephine Donovan, "Beyond the Net: Feminist Criticism as a Moral Criticism," *Denver Quarterly*, 17 (Winter 1983), 40–57.

18. Nancy Chodorow, *The Reproduction of Mothering: Psychoanalysis and the Sociology of Gender* (Berkeley and Los Angeles: University of California Press, 1978), pp. 110, 167.

19. Carol Gilligan, *In A Different Voice: Psychological Theory and Women's Development* (Cambridge, Mass.: Harvard University Press, 1982), p. 19. Subsequent references are cited parenthetically in the text.

20. Elizabeth Ammons, "Going in Circles: The Female Geography of Jewett's *Country of the Pointed Firs*," *Studies in the Literary Imagination*, 16 (Fall 1983), 85.

21. Josephine Donovan, "Sarah Orne Jewett's Critical Theory: Notes Toward a Feminine Literary Mode," in *Critical Essays on Sarah Orne Jewett*, ed. Gwen L. Nagel (Boston: G. K. Hall, 1984).

22. Gloria Bowles and Renate Duelli Klein, eds. *Theories of Women's Studies* (London: Routledge and Kegan Paul, 1983).

23. Audre Lord, "The Master's Tools Will Never Dismantle the Master's House," in *This Bridge Called My Back, Writings by Radical Women of Color*, eds. Cherríe Moraga and Gloria Anzaldúa (Watertown, Mass.: Persephone, 1981), p. 99.

24. Renate Duelli Klein, "How to Do What We Want to Do," in *Theories of Women's Studies*, p. 90.

25. Maria Mies, "Toward a Methodology of Feminist Research," in *Theories of Women's Studies*, pp. 120–21. The extent to which classical scientific methodology follows a sado-masochistic model might be a topic for further exploration: the scientist as doer; the research object as done-to. Carolyn Merchant has analogized the experimental method to "torture" in *The Death of Nature, Women, Ecology, and the Scientific Revolution* (New York: Harper, 1980), p. 172.

26. Barbara DuBois, "Passionate Scholarship: Notes on Values, Knowing and Method in Feminist Social Science," in *Theories of Women's Studies*, pp. 105–16. Subsequent references are cited parenthetically in the text.

27. René Wellek, *A History of Modern Criticism: 1750–1950*, 4 vols. (New Haven: Yale University Press, 1955), 2:221–22, as cited in Lipking, 67. The passage referred to in *The Odyssey* is I: 337–55. Of course, I. A. Richards' *Practical Criticism* (1929) is the classic effort to purge readers of such "irrelevant associations" as Madame de Staël's in order to establish some sort of "objective" response.

GENDER, VALUES, AND LESSING'S CATS

Judith Kegan Gardiner

Two disparate conversations in which I recently took part spurred me to think about values and gender. In the first talk, a male colleague who teaches a course on Charlotte Brontë stopped by my office to ask me why there is no feminist literary theory. In preparing for his course, he had read much feminist criticism, including Gilbert and Gubar's *The Madwoman in the Attic* and Abel's *Writing and Sexual Difference*.[1] He assured me that although this reading was very interesting, it was sociology, not literary theory. The second conversation dealt with the weightier topic of nuclear disarmament, and in it my interlocutor insisted that my arguments against our current weapons systems were idealistic and misguided because the Russians can only understand a "two-by-four across the forehead." He thought that women and other liberals were too soft to recognize such political realities.

Both of these examples raised for me, from very different directions, questions about values in relation to both gender and literature. Feminist literary criticism asks two main questions: how is gender inscribed in culture, and what characterizes writing by women. These questions overlap but are asymmetrical, and they often draw their answers from differing theoretical realms. Recently Margaret Homans has taken up the notion put forth by Rachel Blau DuPlessis that women's "(ambiguously) non-hegemonic" status answers both these questions; it explains women's relation to culture and defines the characteristics of women's writings.[2] In this essay I explore some of this theory's results for literature. In particular, I modify the concept of "hegemony" from one unified state of patriarchy and suggest instead that many intellectual structures have been regnant at different periods of history and that differing ideologies compete for allegiance within the same culture. So far all such ideologies have been male dominant, but not in the same ways. I argue that different values belong to different ideologies; that, in fact, ideologies are systems or models that simultaneously claim to describe reality and to represent reality in evaluative terms. Each "hegemonic" ideology encodes its own set of values, and each devalues women, though in differing ways. After considering some dominant ideological models pertinent to modern fiction, I explore one influential new "non-hegemonic" model that claims to value women's experience more justly— the "mothering" theory developed by psychoanalytic feminists. This theory revises the gender-coded evaluations of dominant systems in order to explain women's psychology and writings. I will look at some uses and limitations of this theory for literature, taking my sample texts from the work of Doris Lessing, a prolific and important writer who broadcasts her ideological shifts and who illustrates the problems that arise from separating empathy and history.

Let me return briefly to those two conversations I spoke of, from which I deduced that I perceived things differently from my male colleagues. In the first case, I think that what sounded to me like literary theory did not to him because for him the notion of theory is invested with values antithetical to those of feminist criticism. In conformity with the elite Western tradition in which he is trained, my colleague values the individual instance and the universal abstraction, but he is uncomfortable with anything in between. Thus he likes literary theories that uphold transcendent truths—like the deceptiveness of appearances—and that are capable of virtuoso performance by the individual theorist. In contrast, everything that pertains to women applies only to a social sub-group and is therefore "sociology": there is the human spirit, and then there are "special interest groups," like women. Having said this, however, I recognize one valid reason for my colleague's inability to grasp feminist literary theory as theory. Over the last fifteen years, the women's liberation movement and feminist scholarship have dramatically altered our ideas about men and women. They have not so altered our ideas about literature. Hence the man whose experiences and whose understanding of gender have not changed may not believe that literature changes because our understanding of gender changes, and thus he may not see that feminists have developed an enormously exciting new perspective on literature.

About my second conversation, a frustrating exchange concerning the nuclear freeze movement, I need not go into detail. What is pertinent in it for this train of thought was my realization that he and I meant very different things by words like "freedom" and "security." It was not that I was embedded too exclusively in female networks or concrete specifics to use abstractions, but that these abstractions were labels attached to differing ideological models for the two of us.

The first stage in my quest to disentangle ideologies and their meaning for women is the insight that virtually all the big, value-laden abstractions by which we evaluate specific events in our lives have different meanings for men and for women. Let us start with the Beautiful, the True, and the Good. The beautiful shows its gender-coded difference most obviously: it must mean some- thing different to the person who has all her life been taught to consider whether

or not she is a beautiful object than it does to someone who has always occupied
the position of an observer or even possessor of another's beauty.[3] Sexual de-
sirability to men defines women's beauty, and sexual fidelity to men defines
women's truth. When not assured of possessing women's truth, men have believed women deceitful, changeable, and unreliable.[4] Similarly, women's goodness fits a narrow box. A good man can possess many virtues, but a good woman
must be sexually faithful and altruistically giving, an idealized wife and mother.
Thus for women sexual fidelity and maternal nurture collapse the categories of
truth, honor, and goodness into one another.

What about other abstractions? I thought of love, freedom, and justice.
Surely love means something different to men and to women. Supposedly it
is the center of a woman's life, her joy, her vocation, and her duty; for men,
it is either a fringe benefit to or a noble distraction from a full and accomplished
life.[5] Freedom and justice. Do women think that "freedom's just another word
for nothing left to lose"? In her recent book, *Intimate Strangers*, sociologist
Lillian Rubin reports that when asked their associations with the word "independence," men spoke enthusiastically about work and adventure. In contrast, women replied ambivalently, often with the word "divorce."[6] Concerning
justice, perhaps the most influential statement of a difference between male
and female values is Freud's comment in "Some Psychical Consequences of
the Anatomical Distinction between the Sexes" (1925):

> I cannot evade the notion . . . that for women the level of what is ethically normal
> is different from what it is in men. . . . Character traits which critics of every
> epoch have brought up against women—that they show less sense of justice than
> men . . . would be amply accounted for by the modification in the formation of
> their superego which we have inferred above. We must not allow ourselves to
> be deflected from such conclusions by the denials of the feminists, who are anxious
> to force us to regard the two sexes as completely equal in position and worth.[7]

Feminist theorists Juliet Mitchell and Carol Gilligan accept Freud's description
of female morality as different from men's, while denying that it is necessarily
inferior.[8]

Women's position has always been dual, both outside of dominant values and
inside the society that lives by them. Often enough women have been complicit
with dominant values, and women's culture exists as a "muted" subculture at
the margins of the dominant culture.[9] The analysis of woman's position as "(ambiguously) non-hegemonic" is more subtle than that of woman as simply Other
or Outsider.[10] However, like the analysis of woman as Other, it, too, generalizes
woman's position to a single stance. In this structuralist view the position of
woman is like that of some other colonized groups, for example, like that of
upper-class Africans within French culture. However, we do not need to take
an essentialist view of women's nature to insist that what is distinctive about

women is not merely women's ambiguously insider/outsider position in culture, but the fact that women are women, a unique biological group assigned nearly universal social tasks. To say that women are women is always true but not always useful, and I will attempt, therefore, to carry our quest for a model of women's situation one step further by suggesting that women's "(ambiguously) non-hegemonic" position shifts as ideological hegemonies shift.

Moral abstractions mean different things for men and for women in part because they are embedded in larger ideological systems that are asymmetrically constructed according to gender. Let us look at these ideological systems more closely. I argue that women are faced with various hegemonic ideologies, all of which are male dominant. However, each of these systems positions women differently. This multiplicity of systems confuses our discourse about values, including the discourse of literary criticism. Thus I think the view that women have a distinctive moral voice parallel to men's is too simple.[11]

What are these "hegemonic" ideologies? In Western culture for the past millenium, the hegemonic moral system has been Christianity, and it still is. For the past few hundred years, the hegemonic political ideology has been that of bourgeois liberalism, with its high evaluation of individual effort and universal truth, the values that I encountered in the talk with my first colleague mentioned earlier. Some of the values implied by these two systems contradict one another—for example, Christian self-sacrifice and bourgeois self-aggrandizement. Such contradictions may lead to cultural rebalancings of gender roles. The Victorian doctrine of separate spheres, for instance, let men compete in the public market while women selflessly tended those at home. Though both are sexist, the two systems are not entirely synchronized: the Christian dualism of soul and flesh dichotomizes women as good and evil, whereas bourgeois liberal rationality tends to exclude women rather than exalt or vilify them. Within each system, moreover, recessive egalitarian values like the spiritual equality of all souls or the democratic rhetoric of full citizenship sometimes subvert dominant sexist values. But the hegemonic form of both systems is clearly sexist, so that feminist rebellion in the nineteenth century often took the form of contesting these dominant social values: Emily Dickinson defies the patriarchal God; Charlotte Brontë bursts into anger and Emily Brontë into passion in ways their contemporaries thought unchristian and unladylike.

In the nineteenth and twentieth centuries, new ideologies, such as Marxism and Freudian psychoanalysis, arose to challenge both bourgeois liberalism and Christianity. Marxism disputes bourgeois liberalism's economic analyses and political values. It insists that competing class interests, based on people's relations to the means of production, mediate between the individual and the society as a whole. Classical Marxism recognizes women as exploited and oppressed in the workforce, in the division of labor within the family, and in the operation of the sexual double standard, and it therefore attracts some feminists, even though its analysis marginalizes women as a subset of the working class and its practice often relapses into sexism.

Freudian psychoanalysis, like Marxism, contests the otherworldly imprimatur of Christianity, but it operates less in direct competition to it and more by dividing off a new ideological bailiwick, separating psychology from morality and claiming to describe the operations of the mind, the formation of personality, and the importance of sexuality to both of the above. Its revaluation of sexuality and aggression provides women with images of liberation even though it is radically demeaning in assessing women as inferior to men by virtue of nature, training, and character.

At present, all these systems may be hegemonic. Politically, we value freedom—which we may understand in bourgeois liberal or in Marxist terms. Morally, even for atheists, Christian concepts of goodness prevail. In the psychological sphere, our vocabulary and assumptions are primarily Freudian; we accept as realities the concepts of the unconscious and repression, and we value maturity and integration. For aesthetics, there is no agreed-upon standard of the beautiful, no hegemonic ideology by which to evaluate works of art or literature. This conceptual vacuum validates the established canon and leads to profound conservative distress when feminists challenge the canon because the values of an aesthetic canon are self-referential and self-reinforcing, a touchstone system. We know a poem is good because it resembles one by Donne or Keats, which we have already decided is good. Challenges to the canon provoke anxiety since there is no standard for its revision: any question may topple the whole edifice. Because there is no accepted aesthetic, other ideologies may impose their standards on literature: for example, Christina Froula demonstrates how patriarchal Christian readings overlay literary ones throughout the history of the Western literary canon.[12]

How do these disparate hegemonic value systems function together? We are all capable of holding multiple and contradictory ideas at the same time. Many systems in which we believe confuse us by claiming that they are not judgmental. Moral systems openly divide the good from the evil, but Freudian, Marxist, and other ideologies often claim to be amorally objective. Despite these disclaimers, they encode certain values, like respect for psychological maturity or hatred for capitalist exploitation. Moreover, we are accustomed to switches between these systems, as in the song, "Gee, Officer Krupke!" from *West Side Story* where the same idle youth is decried as disturbed, deprived, or depraved: "this boy needs"—a job, a doctor, a social worker, or "a year in the pen." The argument that a killer is not evil but sick depends on our familiarity with such ideological switches. Furthermore, the various ideologies may gauge the same atrribute very differently. For instance, a Christian might repent anger as a deadly sin, while a Freudian rejoices at expressing repressed hostility and a Marxist incites anger as a step towards political action. Feminists, too, often value anger: Virginia Woolf snubbed Charlotte Brontë's raw fury while striking her own flint against the patriarchy, and Gilbert and Gubar claim that nineteenth-century women writers wore repressed rage as close as their corsets.[13]

To summarize this argument so far, then, we understand different aspects of experience through different ideological models. These models are contradictory in some of their values. They have variously contradictory applications to women, and our value-laden abstractions mean different things to men and to women. Each of these competing ideologies has its own history, yet the same people may believe them at the same time, despite their intertwining contradictions.

Literature creates its own world, we have been told, but never from the whole cloth. The writer makes a world to alter or reproduce the one we inhabit as we understand it through our ideological constructions. When Sir Philip Sidney defended fiction as more just than reality, he upheld ideology over observation. One cannot imagine everything from scratch; one must talk about humans based on some preconceptions about what humans are like, how they think and feel, what social structures they design, and so on. Even the most brilliant and original novelist must rely on assumptions from one set of paradigms while revising or moving on to others. Precisely because novelists can make their own worlds to fit their own values, the novel provides a privileged arena for moral analysis. Women writers, in particular, wield fiction to analyze what society means for women. In so doing, their way is both helped and hindered by the contradictory ideological models available to them. Feminist literary criticism explicates the values of these ideologies and is often caught between them.

Carol Gilligan describes female morality as narrative and contextual, and novels obviously provide an admirable ground on which to construct systems that are narrative and contextual. Gilbert and Gubar describe women's literature as palimpsestic, hiding coded women's meanings beneath superficial patriarchal conventions. But such layers, I suggest, do not lie neatly awaiting our excavation. Instead of lying flat on its foundations, a work may be built on restlessly bubbling ideologies, from which the critic extracts her own favorite brew. That is, many feminist critical controversies debate whether a woman writer breaks traditional paradigms in ways that the critic approves. Thus some readers dislike Kate Chopin's *The Awakening* because its hero weakly commits suicide rather than face social ostracism; whereas other critics praise the novel for demonstrating that a patriarchal society offers no place for the awakened woman.

Doris Lessing, who has taken all of modern Western culture and its future as her province, illustrates the ways that women's ideologies and values collide in fiction. Her work is ambitious and eminent, and she explicitly defends her shifting ideological investments. Her characters frequently appear clipping newspapers, trying to piece together what the twentieth century means. Many readers value *The Golden Notebook* for representing this common bewilderment as individuals try to understand modern societies through various ideologies. Thus the red notebook records Anna's effort to see the world through the red-tinted glasses of Marxism, while the blue notebook focuses on her psychological perceptions, although none of these efforts is consistent or self-enclosed. As readers we empathize with the fragmentation that results from trying to fit these disparate ideologies together to portray a woman's experience of the twentieth century. As feminist readers we may applaud the novel when it transforms traditional paradigms that oppress women and condemn it when it fails our "liberated" values. For example, many women cheered when Anna menstruated in print, meditated about her sanitary precautions, and speculated about her moods. Since menstruating is a nearly universal and emotional female experience, its exclusion from literature demonstrates misogynistic cultural attitudes. Those readers who praise *The Golden Notebook* for breaking this literary taboo, however, may condemn Anna's raptures about vaginal orgasms as a test of true love. In this case Lessing makes her character's sexual experience accord with a Freudian paradigm so powerful that it may create a non-existent physiological distinction. [14]

To cite a later Lessing text, *The Memoirs of a Survivor* describes a disintegrating society from which its narrator escapes by way of "memories" of a repressed girl's past and fantasies of an impersonal future. Each of these three realms—present, past, and future—obeys different laws, laws based on differing paradigms. Anarchy, class division, and bad technology destroy the current public society; the Freudian personal past circles endlessly from repressive mother to denigrated daughter; liberation lies ahead in another dimension, through Sufi transcendence of individuality. The values of these realms also contradict one another. The present public world suffers from irresponsibility and inconsequence, an anarchy so total that it destroys people's consciences and allows abandoned children to survive through heedless cannibalism. On the other hand, the narrator abhors the past's stuffy, intense familial socialization that created consciences. And, yet more confusingly, though the present suffers from irresponsibility, it is not at all clear that personal responsibility can do anything to save it for the future. [15]

I am not trying to blame Lessing for a universal failure—the failure to invent a psychology and a politics that are both consistent and adequate to account for the experience of women. However, the novel does record a healing and

mirroring relationship between the middle-aged female narrator and an abandoned girl who blur into one another, gradually evolving into one complete
female soul and transcending the rifts between past, present, and future. This
female bonding is central to the novel, although neither post-Marxist politics
nor Freudian psychology explains it. The theory that best illuminates this relationship is known as "mothering theory," a feminist reformulation of object
relations psychoanalysis principally developed by Nancy Chodorow, Dorothy
Dinnerstein, and Adrienne Rich.[16]

This aspect of Lessing's work drew my attention because I already knew the
new paradigm. It is not yet hegemonic, though it is very influential, and it
purports to be a model of human psychology that is truer to women's experience
than its orthodox Freudian predecessor. Chodorow's theory specifies that wom-
en's personalities develop in identification and symbiosis with their mothers
through early bonds that are so strong and fluid, and whose pleasures are so
compelling, that women for the rest of their lives will yearn for maternal nurturance and learn to give it to children, men, and other women. Empathic and
comfortably intimate with others, women are so profoundly interdependent
with one another, especially their mothers and their daughters, that their identities may seem to merge into one another. In stressing positive aspects of
empathy and interdependence, this theory revalues the Freudian paradigm as
well as correcting its picture of female psychological development. Moreover,
it has important ramifications for literary criticism. It claims that the intense
infantile bonds that daughters develop with their mothers will shape their
fantasies, needs, and dispositions, and hence the ways that women write and
read.[17]

Although this theory is very influential, it has also drawn significant criticism.
Some feminists fear that it accepts too much of its Freudian fathering, over-
emphasizing fantasy and infantile experience while slighting real events and
adult development; others deplore its heterosexist bias.[18] As an analytic tool
for the literary critic, however, I think the chief defect of mother-daughter
theory is that it separates empathy from history according to conventional
stereotypes: women become their mothers; whereas men go off to conquer the
world. By this division, women are comic; men are tragic.[19] Women peddle
along their natural cycles; men climb to peaks of individual autonomy, or dy-
namite the mountains. Dinnerstein blames mother-dominated child-rearing for
male technological attitudes that irreparably exploit nature and other people.
According to this theory, empathy belongs to women, history to men.

Now let us return to Lessing, tracking empathy and history in her texts while
testing the uses and limitations of mothering theory to her work. I start with
the short story "Our Friend Judith," a frequent anthology favorite. Published
in 1960 before the re-emergence of feminism, the story questions dominant

assumptions about gender roles. Its narrator introduces us to "our friend Judith," a middle-aged unmarried woman who lives alone, writes poetry, and adores cats. On a continental trip to research the Borgias, she succumbs to an Italian barber in a short affair that crosses class, national, and religious lines. If this information leads us to believe that Judith is a pitiable old maid, however, the story confutes this deduction. In fact, it opens by satirizing just this misrecognition: "I stopped inviting Judith to meet people when a Canadian woman remarked, with the satisfied fervour of one who has at last pinned a label on a rare specimen: " 'she is, of course, one of your typical English spinsters.' "[20] The narrator soon reminds us, "that one's pitying admiration for women who have supported manless and uncomforted lives needs a certain modification" (189). But Judith is not "manless"; she has adoring lovers whom she will not marry. Thus she resembles ancient models of the virgin goddess as integrated female power, not as sexless being. In a borrowed green dress, for instance, she "could . . . evoke nothing but classical images. Diana, perhaps, back from the hunt" (190).[21]

Judith's awesome integrity separates her from both men and women, and most of the story consists of vignettes designed to reveal her character to us. Several of these incidents involve cats. In one, Judith kills her boisterous tomcat rather than allowing it to be castrated. She cries about it but does not consider compromising. Later she explains the sudden rupture of her affair with the Italian barber as due to another incident with a cat. The essence of the situation, she says, was that she "had the wrong attitude to that cat. Cats are supposed to be independent" (205). The cat in question was too young to have kittens, but pregnant nonetheless. Judith assists at its painful delivery:

> There were two paws sticking out of the cat's back end. The kitten was the wrong way round. It was stuck. I held the cat down with one hand and I pulled the kitten out with the other. . . . It was a nice fat black kitten. It must have hurt her. But she suddenly bit out. . . . It died. . . . She was its mother, but she killed it. (206)

The Italian lover kills the lone surviving kitten before its mother does, and Judith leaves him, feeling a "complete gulf in understanding" between them (204).

At first the story seems a simple rebuttal of sexist condescension to unmarried women. However, if we look at it through the perspective of mothering theory, we see it in a different light. For one thing, this theory about the permeability of female ego boundaries helps us to understand the blurry frame of the story in which the narrator has no character of her own but sometimes identifies with Judith and sometimes blends into Betty, a shadowy third character, a typical wife and mother, who exists solely to talk about Judith to the narrator. Implausibly, both Betty and the narrator follow Judith to Italy to find out what she did there. The story does not devalue Judith for being unmarried; rather, it shows her as an admirable new woman. However, its attitudes to motherhood are ambivalent. When asked about having children, Judith replies it is too bad "one couldn't have everything," but she sounds completely satisfied with her life as it stands (205). However, the incident of the cat who killed her kitten exposes Judith's thwarted maternity as the essence of her character. Only in attending the birthing cat does she experience empathy and vulnerability, and only in this episode does she evoke our sympathy. But the incident closes when Judith rejects submerging herself in "somebody else" and returns to lonely integrity (205). The story separates this austere autonomy from both empathy and history. We, the motherly, understand people as do the narrator and her friend Betty. Judith does not: "I don't understand human behavior," she says, "and I'm not particularly interested" (203). Because she does not understand people, she cannot understand history either. She must give up researching the Borgias because she can't figure out "what made those people tick" (199). As she explains to the narrator, she thinks "one surely ought to stay in character" (190). That is, since she cannot understand others, she is doomed to remain a fictional character, not a motherly creator.

My conviction about the importance of "mothering" theory to explicating "Our Friend Judith" receives support from one of Lessing's lesser-known books, *Particularly Cats*, a volume for petlovers puffed by its publishers for avoiding "those anthropomorphic touches that make you want to throw a can of tuna at people," and apparently written as a potboiler in the years when Lessing was finishing her ambitious novel, *The Four-Gated City*.[22] In *Particularly Cats*, Lessing tells the cat incidents of the Judith story as her own experiences. For example, her black and white cat kittened too young, and the birth was difficult: "At last the first kitten appeared, but it was the wrong way. . . . It came out, but the head got stuck. The cat bit and scratched and yelled. . . . That cat . . . killed the first-born kitten in each litter, because she had such pain with it" (27).

Judith thought spaying a cat destroyed its identity. Lessing has a cat "fixed" and bemoans the results, curiously using the very sexist stereotypes that her story effectively debunks: after the operation, she says, her cat's "shape changed . . . she coarsened everywhere. . . . A strident note entered her character. . . . She was spiteful. . . . In short, she had turned into a spinster cat" (61). Talking of cats, it seems, Lessing allows herself to slip into careless conventions that she otherwise examines more scrupulously. This carelessness helps the critic, because it means that here Lessing leaves unprocessed chunks of ideology lying exposed in her prose. For example, the cat book clarifies one essential contradiction of Judith's story: maternity both defines a female's identity and separates one from one's true nature. Time and time again, Lessing judges her cats by how well they mother their kittens. Yet when her black cat "dozes off, eyes half-closed," Lessing comments that then she shows us "what she really is, her real self, when not tugged into fussy devotion by motherhood" (128).[23]

In fact, the whole cat book reveals Lessing's difficult and contradictory attitudes toward motherhood. The book begins with reminiscences of her African childhood. Her mother loved and tended the farm cats, but it was also her job to kill the excess kittens. One year she refuses this task, and hordes of crippled, hideous cats overrun the farm. Finally, her father rounds them up and shoots them in a sickening slaughter, a "holocaust of cats" for which Lessing angrily holds her mother responsible (19). If the mother refuses to play the goddess of nature, giving and taking life, it seems, then men are forced to extreme acts of violence. Lessing was completing her *Children of Violence* novels at this time, and the word "holocaust" must have been peculiarly charged for her.

The mother's role in the cat book extends from Lessing's mother to Lessing as mother of the next generation. It is the only one of her books dedicated to the daughter she left behind in Africa when she moved to England with her young son. In this light, the book's many incidents in which Lessing faithfully feeds and nurses sick cats appear as covert proofs that she is really a good mother after all. The book thus becomes a plea for the possible coexistence of empathy and history: she can be a better mother than her mother was. Female life need not be merely reduplicative; generational change, even progress, is possible.

My last Lessing text drops cats but retains a lesson about empathy and history, although, alas, a far more pessimistic one than earlier. In the past few years Lessing has been writing—at a pace only slightly less rapid than some of us can read—angry and urgent speculative fictions which warn us that doom is near. *The Making of the Representative for Planet Eight*, the fourth novel in her *Canopos in Argos* series, concerns cosmic justice; it describes an ice age that destroys a whole planet. One hundred pages of ice bored me, but I thawed to read the volume's fascinating afterword in which Lessing explains how she first became interested in the British expeditions to the Antarctic led by Robert Falcon Scott between 1901 and 1913, expeditions that exemplified heroism and personal transcendence, but also class discrimination, gender discrimination, imperialist arrogance, and a great deal of freezing to death. Lessing writes:

> I first heard of Scott and his band of heroes thus. It was in the middle of Africa
> . . . on my father's farm. . . . There, most vividly in my memory, is my mother,
> standing head back, hands out, in a posture of dramatic identification. . . . My
> mother, choked with emotion, and radiant, for she enjoyed these moments, is
> saying, "and when I think of Captain Oates going off alone to die in the blizzard—
> oh, he was a most gallant gentleman!" and I then, with the raucous bray of the

adolescent: "but what else could he have done? and anyway, they were all in the dying business." I regret the bray, but not the sentiment; in fact, it seems to me that I was as clear-sighted then as I have been since, and I envy the way that hard girl bulldozed her way through pieties and humbug, for there is no doubt life softens you up: tolerance makes nougat of us all.[24]

In this passage, Lessing scorns her mother for identifying with the men who go "off alone to die in the blizzards," although exactly this "dramatic identification" seems to be the source of her own fiction: we have just read a hundred pages about gallant beings who freeze to death. In her sixties, Lessing still rejects her mother and applauds her own adolescent harshness, as if she now denies the cat book's middle-aged optimism that generations can learn from one another.

This despair continues in the afterword as she digresses into an essay on history, denouncing all of us for not having listened to her clear-sighted and, we must agree, correct denunciations of southern Africa and other "criminally oppressive tyrannies" (127). "But it seems that the repetitiveness of historical, of sociological processes is not even noticed," she laments, while history seems to her nothing else than this blind repetition (127). She continues:

> I could fill pages, volumes, with facts illustrating this theme, that the heresies of one year are the pieties of the next. . . . but for some reason we cannot apply the obvious lessons of history to ourselves. Why? Is it possible that we could learn not to impose on each other these sacred necessities, in the name of some dogma or other, with results that inevitably within a decade will be dismissed with: *We make mistakes.* It is only too easy to imagine The Spirit of History . . . a blowzy but complacent female, wearing the mask of the relevant ruler or satrap: "dearie me!" she smiles, "but I have made a mistake again!" and into the dustbin go holocausts, famines, wars, and the occupants of a million prisons and torture chambers. (127)

This is an astonishing, even shocking passage. Lessing personifies history as the goddess Fortuna, throwing people into the trash—that is, as an enormous bad mother, an exaggeration of her own mother in the cat book whose irresponsibility caused the "holocaust of cats." We know that in fact women have perpetrated rather few of the holocausts, wars, prisons, and torture chambers of history, yet this sexist stereotype blames the "blowzy but complacent female," just as Lessing blames her mother for the Scott expedition's sentimental imperialism.

Blaming mother, I think, causes Lessing's despair at human endeavor in these last works. History is like mother: if we don't understand her, we are doomed to repeat her, as Lessing both identifies with her mother and repudiates her about the Scott expedition. In "Our Friend Judith," Lessing included history within empathy and connected both to maternal care rather than to spinsterly autonomy. *Particularly Cats* covertly argues that both empathy and history are possible for women: women can understand their mothers and change to become better mothers than their own mothers were. In these last speculative fictions, Lessing despairs of both empathy and history. And this returns us to the importance of the paradigms through which we understand our world. If we do not incorporate gender into our model of history, we may relapse into the sexism that blames the "blowzy but complacent female." But if, on the other hand, we feminists do not incorporate history into our model of gender, we are doomed to simple repetition—while, perhaps, as Lessing warns us, the world perishes.

NOTES

I thank Elizabeth Abel, Richard Gardiner, John Huntington, and Linda Williams, as well as audiences at Brown, Dartmouth, Stanford, and the Universities of Chicago and New Hampshire for their comments on various versions of these ideas.

1. Sandra M. Gilbert and Susan Gubar, *The Madwoman in the Attic: The Woman Writer and the Nineteenth-Century Imagination* (New Haven: Yale University Press, 1979); Elizabeth Abel, ed., *Writing and Sexual Difference* (Chicago: University of Chicago Press, 1982).

2. Margaret Homans, " 'Her Very own Howl': The Ambiguities of Representation in Recent Women's Fiction," *Signs*, 9 (Winter 1983), 186–205, citing Rachel Blau DuPlessis and Members of Workshop 9; "For the Etruscans: Sexual Difference and Artistic Production—the Debate over a Female Aesthetic," in *The Future of Difference*, eds. Hester Eisenstein and Alice Jardine (Boston: G.K. Hall & Co., 1980), pp. 128–56.

3. See John Berger, *Ways of Seeing* (Middlesex, England: Penguin, 1972).

4. For the related idea that women are associated with natural change, see Sherry B. Ortner, "Is Female to Male as Nature Is to Culture?" in *Woman, Culture, and Society*, eds. Michelle Zimbalist Rosaldo and Louise Lamphere (Stanford, Calif.: Stanford University Press, 1974), pp. 67–87; and Dorothy Dinnerstein, *The Mermaid and the Minotaur: Sexual Arrangements and Human Malaise* (New York: Harper and Row, 1976).

5. See Simone de Beauvoir, *The Second Sex* (New York: Vintage, 1974); and Germaine Greer, *The Female Eunuch* (New York: McGraw-Hill, 1971).

6. Lillian B. Rubin, *Intimate Strangers: Men and Women Together* (New York: Harper and Row, 1983), pp. 120–21.

7. Sigmund Freud, "Some Psychical Consequences of the Anatomical Distinction Between the Sexes," in *The Standard Edition of the Complete Psychological Works of Sigmund Freud*, 19, trans. and ed. James Strachey (London: The Hogarth Press, 1961), pp. 243–58.

8. Juliet Mitchell, *Psychoanalysis and Feminism* (New York: Random House, 1974); Carol Gilligan, *In a Different Voice: Psychological Theory and Women's Development* (Cambridge, Mass.: Harvard University Press, 1982).

9. Elaine Showalter, "Feminist Criticism in the Wilderness," in Abel, pp. 9–35.

10. Simone de Beauvoir popularized the idea of Woman as Other.

11. For the contrary view, see Gilligan.

12. Christine Froula, "When Eve Reads Milton: Undoing the Canonical Economy,"

Critical Inquiry, 10 (December 1983), 321–47; also see Barbara Herrnstein Smith, "Contingencies of Value," *Critical Inquiry*, 10 (September 1983), 1–35.

13. Virginia Woolf, *A Room of One's Own* (New York: Harcourt Brace Jovanovich, 1957); Gilbert and Gubar, *The Madwoman in the Attic*. On this issue, also see Jane Marcus, "Art and Anger," *Feminist Studies*, 4 (1978), 69–98.

14. Doris Lessing, *The Golden Notebook* (New York: Bantam, 1973). For reactions to reading Lessing, see Jenny Taylor, ed., *Notebooks/Memoirs/Archives: Reading and Rereading Doris Lessing* (Boston: Routledge & Kegan Paul, 1982).

15. Doris Lessing, *The Memoirs of a Survivor* (New York: Bantam Books, 1976). I write about this novel at more length in "Evil, Apocalypse, and Feminist Fiction," *Frontiers*, 7 (1983), 74–80.

16. Nancy Chodorow, *The Reproduction of Mothering: Psychoanalysis and the Sociology of Gender* (Berkeley and Los Angeles: University of California Press, 1978); Dorothy Dinnerstein, *The Mermaid and the Minotaur*; Adrienne Rich, *Of Woman Born* (New York: Norton, 1976).

17. For one application of the theory to literary criticism, see Judith Kegan Gardiner, "On Female Identity and Writing by Women," in Abel, pp. 177–92.

18. The criticism against heterosexism applies to Chodorow and Dinnerstein, not Rich. See Janice Haaken, "Freudian Theory Revised: A Critique of Rich, Chodorow, and Dinnerstein," *Women's Studies Quarterly*, 11 (Winter 1983), 12–16.

19. Linda Bamber applies these terms to Shakespeare in *Comic Women, Tragic Men* (Stanford, Calif.: Stanford University Press, 1982).

20. Doris Lessing, "Our Friend Judith," in *A Man and Two Women* (New York: Popular Library, 1963), pp. 188–208. Page references to this story follow in the text.

21. In Italy, she is more like Venus as she "strolls into the sea and vanishes into the foam" (198).

22. Doris Lessing, *Particularly Cats* (New York: Simon and Schuster, 1978). The book was first published in 1967, two years before *The Four-Gated City*. The tuna blurb on the back jacket is quoted from *Harper's*. Page references follow in the text.

23. In one pertinent passage, for example, Lessing discusses a cat who became neurotic in her eating habits because "she was taken away from her mother too young. . . . And she shares another characteristic with people who have not had enough mother-warmth. . . . Kittens who are left with their mother seven or eight weeks eat easily, and they have confidence. But of course, they are not as interesting" (39).

24. Doris Lessing, *The Making of the Representative for Planet Eight* (New York: Alfred A. Knopf, 1982), pp. 124–25. Page references follow in the text.

MAKING—AND REMAKING—HISTORY
Another Look at "Patriarchy"

Judith Newton

Lillian Robinson once said that the most important question we can ask ourselves as feminist critics is the question "so what?" and implied by that question
is a view of feminist criticism that I think we all share—that the point of it is
to change the world. But to begin with the question "so what?" is to be put to
the task of asking other questions as well—like what is the relation of literature,
and therefore of literary criticism, to the real conditions of our lives? For feminist critics who work within a central insight of the women's movement—that
gender is socially constructed—it is a natural step to the assumption that forms
of consciousness, like literature, literary criticism, and thought itself are socially
constructed too. It is a natural step to the assumption that we make our own
knowledge and are constantly remaking it in the terms that history provides,
and that in making knowledge we act upon the power relations in our lives.

As feminist critics we speak of making our knowledge of history, choosing to
see in it not a tale of individual and inevitable suffering, signifying nothing,
but a story of struggle and relations of power. We speak of making our notion
of literary texts, choosing to read them not as meditations upon themselves but
as gestures toward history and gestures with political effect. Finally, we speak
of making our model of literary criticism, choosing to see in it not an ostensibly
objective reading of a text but an act of political intervention, a mode of shaping
the cultural use to which women's writing and men's will be put.[1]

This reconstruction of our knowledge, however, has been a form of struggle,
a political action upon our culture and ourselves, for in reconstructing history,
literature, and literary criticism we have implicitly committed ourselves to resist
the ways in which many of us, as literary critics, have been trained. We have
implicitly committed ourselves to resist English Department formalism—the
view that literature and literary critics are divorced from history—a view still
perpetuated, despite their air of currency and French fashionableness, by the
forms of criticism now dominant in Britain and the United States.[2] We have

also implicitly committed ourselves to resist a view of history once beloved by English Departments throughout the land, the view that history is the essentially tragic and timeless story of individual suffering, a suffering most often universalized and guaranteed permanency as part of the human condition.

Given that knowledge is constructed and reconstructed inside of history and that remaking knowledge is a form of struggle against our culture and ourselves, it is not surprising that we should still be immersed in critical practices which it is against our interests to maintain or that our theoretical commitments and our practice have not always developed hand in hand. Thus—as many of the essays received by feminist journals would testify and as I will later explore— much of the feminist criticism we write has little explicit history at all, while its implicit history tends unwittingly to recapitulate the politics of the English Departments and culture in which we were trained.[3] Much feminist criticism, although it assumes the existence of unequal gender-based relations of power, implicitly constructs those relations in such a way as to render them tragic— unchanging, universal, and monolithically imposed.

Despite the fact that we often refer to such constructions of history as "patriarchy," insofar as they obscure historical alteration, cultural complexity, and women's agency, our own constructions of history might themselves be called patriarchal. Insofar as our constructions of history suggest that gender relations do not change, they distance us from a sense of their social construction and return us to a sense of their inevitability and tragic essentiality. Insofar as our constructions of history see gender relations as discreet or disconnected from other relations of power and as universally the same, they simplify what we are up against, simplify the way we construct the gestures and politics of women writers and of men, and simplify our own political intervention as critics. Insofar as our constructions of history suggest a monolithic male hegemony, they rob women of a sense of agency and quite simply give men too much "credit."

This tendency in feminist criticism toward tragic essentialism in regard to male domination is part of a larger tendency in feminist theory and politics generally where, one might argue, it has sometimes contributed to an evasion of analysis in regard to relations of domination.[4] This tragic essentialism in regard to male domination, moreover, has gone hand in hand with an inclination to comedic essentialism on the other side of the equation. I am thinking here of the proposal that promoting women's nurturing and connecting qualities is somehow a cure for male domination, a proposal which in some of its manifestations roots us once again in the essential and the unchanging.[5]

There have been important counters to this polarization and reification of male domination and female virtue. Theories of gender construction advanced by feminist theorists like Nancy Chodorow, Dorothy Dinnerstein, and Jane Flax have re-emphasized the idea that gender identity and ideologies of gender, as one part of a sex-gender system, are socially constructed and relational, that is, created by women as well as men, despite women's lesser access to cultural power.[6] Feminist history by historians like Mary Ryan and Judith Walkowitz, meanwhile, has countered the ahistorical quality of much feminist psychoanalytic theory by illuminating the ways in which constructions of gender and sexuality have changed with changing historical situations and have related to other categories of analysis such as that of class.[7] Together these developments in feminist theory and feminist history, with their emphasis on social construction, change, relationality, and women's participation, provide a more adequate and helpful model for our continuing construction of feminist history and feminist literary criticism than our current implicit focus on the unchanging, the universal, and the monolithic.

As an illustration of what difference these two models of gender relations might make to a feminist literary critic, I would now like to deconstruct, or reconstruct, a reference to patriarchal tradition taken from *The Madwoman in the Attic*, one of the most insightful, complex, and fruitful analyses of women writers to be published in the last few years.[8] I do this not as a means of criticizing this particular book, but as a means of suggesting how even in our most nimble constructions of women's writings our production of history as context might be opened out and up. The reference here is to Wordsworth's "Tintern Abbey" and to Arnold's "A Buried Life" and within these poems to the "tradition Arnold inherits from Wordsworth, for both poets seek to escape from the dreary intercourse of daily life through the intercession of a girl, image and source of the poet's faith . . . emblems of the calm and peace that nature brings.[9]

The ideologies of gender that are reflected in Wordsworth's and Arnold's desire to make women useful in these two poems do indeed suggest a continuing tradition of male domination and female subordination, but it is important, I think, to begin with the observation that what might at first appear as an unchanging patriarchal tradition is actually a changing one, for there are radical differences in what Wordsworth and Arnold think women are useful for. If at the end of "Tintern Abbey," for example, Wordsworth regains a sense of his own youthful pleasures in nature from Dorothy's "wild eyes," it is finally Wordsworth and not Dorothy who is an emblem of "calm peace" and of refuge from the "dreary intercourse of daily life."[10] It is Dorothy's memories of Wordsworth that will bring her "healing thoughts of tender joy" in the hours of "solitude, or fear, or pain, or grief" which Wordsworth generously imagines for her (lines 144–45). Dorothy is less useful as a refuge for William than as confirmation of his own continuing capacity to create refuge for himself.

That is 1798. The situation is different in 1852 where at the end of "A Buried Life" Arnold drops the fiction that both men and women, the "we" of the early stanzas, find "rest" and "anodyne" by gazing into each other's eyes. The "we" of the final stanzas refers to men who do indeed find refuge in women, who feel a lull in the "hot race," who feel a "lost pulse of feeling stir," who feel an "unwonted calm" when a beloved female hand is laid in theirs and when "our eyes can in another's eyes read clear."[11] In 1852 women may indeed provide men of the literary elite with a sense of refuge and restoration, for fifty-four years of economic and social development have seen shifts in the construction of class relations and gender identity as well. The "dreary intercourse of daily life" is drearier, is dominated by class relations that are more suppressive of human connection than in 1798. Classical liberal ideology with its emphasis on material production and the unrestricted pursuit of private profit is more dominant, and so is its construction of middle-class masculine experience as acquisition, competition, rationality, self-dependence, and hard work. Thus, Wordsworth may feel that the "fretful stir unprofitable, and the fever of the world" hang upon "the beatings of my heart" (lines 53–54), but Arnold feels benumbed by the same forces. In "Tintern Abbey," therefore, Dorothy can be seen as useful to William because she reminds him of his capacity to heal himself and her, while the beloved woman in Arnold's poem is useful because she, not the poet, is a source of healing.

Arnold's beloved woman is more necessary than Wordsworth's and so it is more necessary to contain and control her, a recognition perhaps that accounts for the greater tone of command in Arnold's poem: "Give me thy hand, and hush awhile, and turn those limpid eyes on mine" (line 10). But the use to which Arnold's beloved woman is put, and his need to control the resources she provides, cannot be seen as an example of a purely male-created tradition, even of a changing male-created tradition. The notion that women provide refuge for men is central to the ideology of woman's proper sphere, an ideology that was largely reconstructed in the 1830s and the 1840s by middle-class women for each other.

This reconstruction of womanhood, moreover, was not a matter of gender relations alone, as so many of our references to patriarchal traditions suggest, but was closely related to class identity. On one level this reconstruction of ideology reflects middle-class women's appropriation of the class identity of middle-class men. For as middle-class men gained new access to economic, social, and political power with the development of industrial capitalist society, middle-class women suffered a loss of recognized economic value and perhaps a loss of social status as well.[12] It was apparently in reconstructing the ideology of woman's sphere that middle-class women extended to themselves the sense of meaningful work, social significance, and social power which were increasingly part of the class and gender identity of middle-class men. Thus the popular manual writer Sarah Ellis praises the "habits of industry and personal exertion" found in women of the past while another writer, Sarah Lewis, promises that "women have a mission! aye, even a political mission of immense importance!" Woman "is the regulating power of the great social machine."[13]

Although middle-class women were not to achieve social importance through the self-advancing powers of men—the powers of economic achievement or political control—they participated in a shared class strategy. On the one hand they reconfirmed the value of work and industry, but on the other they moderated the value of both by promising to facilitate, through enlarging men's capacity to feel, a sense of community and a greater social concern in middle-class men—a sense of community and a concern which a reformulation of classical liberal and masculine ideology itself called for. Classical liberal and middle-class masculine ideology were undergoing a shift in the 1840s when a series of booms and depressions sharpened the edge of class conflict and drew attention to perceptions entirely alien to the bourgeois world view, namely that systematic inequities might be increased rather than lessened by capitalist free enterprise. One response to these perceptions was the subtle reformulation of classical liberal ideology itself, a reformulation in which private property, free enterprise, and profit were preserved but in which the liberal concept of self-interest was broadened to include concern over housing, sanitation, and public service; and a new sense of community based on voluntary social regulation and reform was super-imposed on the free market.[14] This shift in liberal ideology also represented a shift in male gender identity towards greater concern for others.

It is in part this shift in class and gender identity for middle-class men that female writers of women's manuals responded to when they defined middle-class women's role in life as the exertion upon men of moral influence, an influence meant to counter the dehumanizing force of market relations and meant to restore men, in the words of Sarah Ellis, to their "wiser and better selves," to a capacity once again for "poetry and nature" (49). As in classical liberal and masculine ideology, this evocation of greater feeling was not to change but to soften class relations, for like bourgeois leaders, female writers of women's manuals usually defended the principle of class hierarchy. Thus Sarah Ellis praises the "order and symmetry" of England's three classes which she sees as a column, the upper class being "the rich and highly ornamental capital" and the base "the important class of the laborious poor" (49), while the author of *Woman's Rights and Duties* maintains that "inequality is the condition of existence" and that "the superior has the same right to every advantage he can secure without robbing others."[15]

The ideology of woman's proper sphere, therefore, helped, on one level, to consolidate a larger class strategy, a strategy according to which class division, profit, and free enterprise were to be maintained while class conflict was softened by the creation of a more communal order. The ideology of woman's sphere, in effect, helped to forge a class compact between women and men, a compact whereby bourgeois men ran the world for their own profit—a profit in which their wives and daughters shared—and middle-class women acted as the necessary and tension-relieving voice of conscience.[16] The reasoning that justified class division, moreover, was used to justify gender relations as well, the author of *Women's Rights* arguing that "as it is chiefly by the male sex collectively taken that the property of society is both created and defended it is very clear that their interests have the first claim to consideration" and that they have "the best right to control" (233–34). The ideology of woman's influence, therefore, as formulated in manuals written by women, re-enforced a class and gender compact between middle-class women and men, an indication surely that feminine values—nurturance and feeling—are not automatically antagonistic to the status quo.

If gender ideology with its emphasis on women's virtues helped to consolidate class and gender alliance, it appeared to generate class and gender conflict as well, and in this way it suggests a more complex social agency on the part of middle-class women. The very linchpin of feminine ideology, for example, was self-sacrifice, a virtue directly antagonistic to the masculine ideology of self-interest and self-advancement. The prescriptive manuals for women published in the 1830s and 1840s, although officially accepting the doctrine of male superiority and male rule, often pointedly criticized the behavior of men. In another work Sarah Ellis wrote, "men in general are more apt than women, to think as if they were created to exist of, and by, themselves." Indeed, when one considers "how little cultivation of the heart is blended with what is popularly called the best education, the wonder should be that men are not more selfish still."[17] Male selfishness and lack of feeling, moreover, are identified as a primary cause of problems in class and gender relations. In the public world of man, according to Sarah Ellis, "there is no union in the great field of action in which he is engaged; but envy, and hatred and opposition, to the close of the day,—every man's hand against his brother, and each struggling to exalt himself" while in the private world "every morning brings the same hurried and indifferent parting; every evening the same jaded, speechless, welcomeless return—until we almost fail to recognize the man, in the machine" (*Women of England*, 46, 49).

Manual writers also inevitably praised women's nature and often asserted that women had greater social impact than men: "power exerted principally in the shape of authority is limited in its sphere of action" but "influence has its source in human sympathy and is boundless in its operation" (*Woman's Mission*, 13). In another work, Lewis wrote: "the whole life of woman is but one chain of anxieties, to promote the happiness of all the objects of her heart; surely this attribute overmatches the gigantic energies of ambition and courage of man."[18] Indeed, if female manual writers identified men as the problem, they offered middle-class women as the solution, not merely in the private sphere but in the public as well and not merely through their influence on men but through their benevolent intervention on behalf of the suffering poor: the vice and misery of the working class, according to the author of *Woman's Rights and Duties*, speak to the hearts of women (157).

Thus, despite their class and gender collaboration, the writers of women's manuals, in their tendency to place men at the bottom of industrial capitalist and domestic ills and in their tendency to isolate women like themselves as social heroes, challenged the power relations of their world and in the process entertained a view of mid-nineteenth-century society which middle-class men, by and large, did not share. It is not surprising, perhaps, that when Sarah Ellis imagines men gazing into women's eyes, the dynamics are significantly different from those in Arnold's poem: "How often," she proclaims in 1839, "has man stood corrected before the clear eye of woman" (*Women of England*, 46). The image of woman as moral influence, far from being simply male-imposed, becomes in its own way a source of challenge for men and a shaping force upon their gender identification, a suggestion that the creation of gender systems is a more reciprocal process than we have sometimes believed.

If on one level the ideology of woman's sphere found widespread cultural acceptance among men of the intellectual elite, on another it appears to have generated not only cultural tension but sexual horror. The degree of cultural tension, for example, may be partially gauged by conservative and liberal male reviewers of women's manuals, who tended to ignore or in some cases condemn women's claims to a far-reaching influence and to focus instead on why women ought not to vote or to hold public office.[19] Few reviewers went so far as the author of *Woman: As She Is and As She Should Be*, who complains that a "love of power would seem almost part and parcel of woman's composition" and that women's influence has produced "effeminacy," "supine and excessive softness of manners" in men and is "an unsuspected leprosy at the heart of nearly all our social evil."[20] But many male reviewers of female texts, while assuring readers that women do not want and ought not to have political power, are also uneasy about women's influence. Thus one reviewer argues against the extension of suffrage on the grounds that the addition of "direct influence" will only make the "temptation to exercise indirect influence much stronger."[21]

It would seem that female writers of women's manuals and male reviewers of their texts tended to take different views of women's influence, women making large claims for its social importance and men either dismissing those claims or expressing uneasiness in relation to them. Implicit in this disparity were different views of industrial capitalist society itself, of who or what lay at the bottom of its excesses, of who or what it would take to cure its ills, and of who were to be the social heroes.[22] This conflict over influence and power, for example, and the cultural disquietude that it produced rumble in the sea depth of Dickens's *Dombey and Son*, from the gloom of Dombey's sea bottom office where he enlists his manager to command the submission of his wife, to the snug back parlor of Sol's ships' instrument shop from whence Captain Cuttle exercises surveillance of enemy bonnets, to the salt drenched pillow of Dombey's sick bed where, as Julian Moynahan puts it, Florence Dombey finally drowns her father in "a dissolving love."[23]

On one level, of course, *Dombey and Son* appears, like "The Buried Life," to celebrate the power of women's influence, for the novel is structured by a shift in Dombey's assessment of Florence, from the "wrong" assessment that, as a female, she is so much "base coin," "a bad boy—nothing more" to the "right" assessment of her as a "household spirit" full of feeling and moral influence. In this sense, the novel reproduces that shift in ideology represented by the expansion in the 1830s and 1840s of the ideology of woman's sphere. But if "The Buried Life" suggests the degree to which the ideology found cultural acceptance among middle-class literary men, *Dombey and Son* suggests the degree to which this same ideology produced sexual horror; it suggests, indeed, how deeply fear of women's power shaped the culture we refer to as simply patriarchal or male-dominated, and for this reason I wish to examine it in some detail.

Dombey and Son, of course, also suggests how differently the ideology of woman's influence was produced by middle-class literary men as opposed to middle-class literary women like Sarah Ellis. To Ellis, the difference between women and men in terms of their ability to feel is more apparent than actual. Man may put on a "hard surface" but underneath "he has a heart as true to the kindly affections of our nature, as that of woman—as true, though not as suddenly awakened to every passing call" (*Women of England*, 50). When men come under women's influence, then, they are open to its operation:

> [H]ow often has man returned to his home with a mind confused by the many voices, which in the mart, the exchange, the public assembly, have addressed themselves to his inborn selfishness or his worldly pride; and while his integrity was shaken . . . he has stood corrected before the clear eye of woman, as it looked directly to the naked truth, and detected the lurking evil of the specious act he was about to commit. (*Women of England*, 46)

"Nay, so potent" is this "secret influence," Ellis continues, that it changes men's behavior in the marketplace itself, for it becomes "a kind of second conscience, for mental reference, and spiritual counsel, in moments of trial" (*Women of England*, 46).

To Dickens, however, the hearts of men like Dombey are not at all like the

hearts of middle-class women, as the multiple antitheses between Florence
and Dombey testify. If Dombey is stiff, Florence is fluid; if Dombey thinks of
profit, Florence thinks of love.[24] After the first few pages of the novel, the real
problem with Florence from Dombey's perspective is not that she is "base coin"
at all but that she is a tintype of the woman who feels.[25] This exercise of women's
feeling has nothing to do with the world of economic affairs, for Dombey, in
all his guilt, never feels that Florence stands between him and the pursuit of
profit. (If he feels something like that once when the image of Florence blends
with the defeat and persecution of the slums, Dickens raps his knuckles and
tells him he is wrong.) Florence, far from requiring Dombey to feel more for
the poor—or for his "weaker brothers" whom Ellis imagines fainting by the
businessman's side or being "borne down by numbers, hurried over and forgotten" (*Women of England*, 46)—requires Dombey to feel more for *herself*.
Women's influence is represented as entirely self-referential, and for this reason
as unheroic, enclosed, and threatening as well.

Since Dombey embodies a split in the novel, and perhaps in the culture at
large, between the celebration of women's influence and feeling on the one
hand, and horror at them on the other, his response to the demand is complex.
Dombey feels jealous of Florence, Edith, and Mrs. Dombey for their capacity
to feel, and having never made a friend himself, he has a "dull perception of
his alienation from all hearts" (583). Indeed, his sense of separation from the
affection between women is poignantly expressed:

> the last time he had seen his slighted child, there had been that in the sad
> embrace between her and her dying mother which was at once a revelation and
> a reproach to him. . . . He could not forget that he had had no part in it. That,
> at the bottom of its clear depths of tenderness and truth, lay those two figures
> clasped in each other's arms, while he stood on the bank above them, looking
> down a mere spectator—not a sharer with them—quite shut out. (41)[26]

But if Dombey expresses some "vague yearning for what he had all his life
repelled" (583), what he feels more deeply than that is reproach and rage, and
his resistance, far from proving a mere "hard surface," might be more aptly
termed hard core. What appears in *Women of England* as a bracing stand before
the bar of woman's "clear" and correcting eye appears in *Dombey and Son* as
the maddening experience of being secretly accused and silently surveilled:
Florence "watched and distrusted him. As if she held the clue to something
secret in his breast, of the nature of which he had hardly informed himself"
(41), while her "speaking eyes, more earnest and pathetic in their voiceless
speech than all the orators of all the world" impeached him "more nearly in
their mute address" (524). What is worst of all, of course, is that Dombey feels
guilty as charged: "had he begun to feel her disregarded claims and did they
touch him home at last, and waken him to some sense of his cruel injustice?"

(524). No wonder the "tearful blessing" of this passive/aggressive prosecutor seems "heavier on him than a curse" (523).

Still, Dombey's rage at Florence is accompanied by a sense of impotence against her—she thrives without him, blooming in his deserted house "like the king's fair daughter in the story" (338). Florence, indeed, has an awful inevitability, a hold upon Dombey which is, I would suggest, the hold of cultural ideals upon Dombey and Dickens both.[27] It is the hold of the ideology of woman's influence, according to which a highly sensitive and moralizing female is the "household spirit" of a "happy home"—never mind that this "household spirit" may be experienced as a reproachful, guilt-inducing judge and that a "happy" home life may appear more nearly to resemble a life sentence at feeling guilty: "he cannot bear to see a cloud upon her face. He cannot bear to see her sit apart. He fancies that she feels a slight when there is none" (903).

The emotional cost of embracing this "household spirit" is suggested in the novel by the fact that Dombey's reconciliation with Florence does not take place until his previous identity is catastrophically destroyed. It is only when Dombey is ruined, deserted by friends and on the point of suicide, a "spectral haggard, wasted likeness of himself" (866) that Florence magically reappears and exerts her influence, and "magically" is the controlling word.[28] Once he embraces woman's influence, Dombey enters the kind of fairy tale reality which has been associated with Florence throughout the novel. Dombey becomes the "king's fair daughter" immersed in her empty castle while Florence becomes the rescuing prince whom Dombey follows out with "docile submission" (869). Ultimately, cut off from the world of action and of men, Dombey enters a life of permanent enchantment in which guilt, fears, and attendance on female feeling become the whole content of his autumnal existence.[29]

It is not surprising, given this, for the most part covert, rendering of women's debilitating power, that Dickens's solution to the problems of industrial capitalist society as presented in this novel is not female influence. Dickens's solution, indeed, is represented by a group of economically marginal, poetically sensitive, "old-fashioned" men—another version of the sensitive male novelist multiplied. Dombey's "ship," which has foundered from having been strained so hard against the storm, is to be taken over by those old survivors of shipwreck, Solomon Gills, an unsuccessful tradesman dealing in ships' instruments; his nephew Walter, a junior clerk in Dombey's shipping firm; and, as symbolic partner, Captain Cuttle, a retired sea pilot and privateer. Thus at the end of the novel, mysterious, "old investments" on the part of Gills suddenly materialize, and he begins to assist Walter in "mounting up the ladder with the greatest expedition"(899), laying the foundation for a new Dombey and Son "perhaps to equal perhaps to excel" the old (901).

Dickens, in place of a newly expanded female influence, offers "old-fash-

ioned" men, offers a benign male capitalism in which the men who run the
world also save it and in which female influence is itself outmoded. For Dickens's "old-fashioned" men are characterized less by the masculine values of
consuming and taking than by the feminine values of giving and feeding—Sol
and Cuttle, indeed, being rather astonishing cooks. All three men are non-
competitive or at least too marginal to feel personally committed to the capitalist
race. They are also great weepers, sure signs that they are men of feeling; they
are linked with stormy seas, hence with nature that is undominated; they are
respectful of working-class characters, and they value Florence, Cuttle's "heart's
delight."

They value Florence but they scarcely need her, and Dickens's official tribute
to her moral influence—Walter sees her image "restraining him like an angel's
hand" (233)—is belied by the fact that Walter is already perfect and by the
equally important fact that the real moral influences on his life have been male.
Solomon Gills, in a fantasy of the family totally masculinized, has been both
mother and father to Walter while Walter has been both child and wife to him:
"I could never have been fonder of her than I am of you" says Sol of the wife
Walter wishes he had been (128). In a world where male capitalists cook, weep,
sympathize, and form families together, womanly influence and womanly skills
have little place.[30]

This fantasy of domesticated and feeling men, which also appears in Kingsley
and Carlyle,[31] is one expression of an ideological power struggle between middle-class women and middle-class men, a struggle in which middle-class women
were not merely victims of men's domination, but in which women had a
shaping and a defining hand and in which men's fear of women's power played
a central part.[32] But once again patriarchal tradition, which turns out to be
matriarchal, at least in part, does not stand still, and a very different formulation
of this struggle appears to emerge in the 1860s and 1870s in the shape of
masculine ideals which emphasize separation from women rather than appropriation of their virtues, which devalue feeling and domesticity and valorize
"manliness" defined as "anti-effeminacy, stiff-upper-lippery, and physical hardness."[33]

This apparent shift in gender identity was part of a shift in class identity as
well, a process whereby middle-class men further abandoned the liberal values
of work, inventiveness, and making money for the adoption of values associated
with men of the upper class: leisure, style, and public service.[34] For according
to Martin Wiener, among others, Britain's essentially capitalist ruling class
became richer and more self confident with the industrial Revolution, and this
"rentier aristocracy succeeded to a large extent in maintaining . . . cultural
hegemony and consequently . . . in reshaping the industrial bourgeoisie in its
own image" (*English Culture*, 8). The central institution of this consolidation

was the public boys' school, which first expanded its population base in the 1840s and 1850s and which, in the last three decades of the century, forged a new cross-class elite, "a community of men who recognized in each other a similarity of outlook, values, and code of honour because they shared a similar type of boyhood experience in what was becoming in effect a community of schools" (*TBU*, 228).

To some degree the public school facilitated the upward mobility of middle-class boys and in this sense expressed a form of family consciousness and ambition. But on another level the public school became an alternative to the Victorian family and a locus of conflicting loyalties and values (*TBU*, 208, 157). Specifically, the Victorian public boys' school, while officially endorsing contemporary ideologies about moral womanhood, imposed a separation from women and women's values and in particular from the "mollycoddling influence" of women (*TBU*, 223). At some schools, for example, home, mothers, and sisters became taboo subjects, and even the display of their photographs in boys' rooms might be forbidden by school custom (*TBU*, 223). At the same time, passionate friendships between boys, common in the schools of the 1830s and 1840s, became suspect in the 1850s and 1860s,[35] and homosexuality became for the first time an obsessive concern (*TBU*, 194; *Godliness*, 43–45). Ultimately suppression of feeling itself became a masculine goal as manhood, defined in opposition to childhood in the 1830s, came to be defined in opposition to effeminacy (*Godliness*, 196–97).

The cultural dominance of "manliness," was also reflected in the hardening regimes of public schools with their emphasis on fresh air, cold baths or no baths at all, insufficient heat and starvation diets. At Winchester in the 1870s, for example, breakfast, held after two hours of chapel and lessons, might consist of tea, bread, and butter (*TBU*, 215), a long way surely from the luxurious repasts, the "fried sole with a prospect of steak to follow" served by Uncle Sol (47). Games were also important to the development of "manliness," and an emphasis on athletics, already noticeable at universities in the 1850s, reached public schools in the 1860s. By 1880, when athletics had become compulsory as well, games had in effect become a kind of work (*TBU*, 110, 114; *Godliness*, 222).

But games were also important because they encouraged team building and the consolidation of a male community. Indeed, emotions which had gone into passionate friendships in mid-century were now channeled into loyalty to a community of old boys, a loyalty underscored by the development of organized games, a house system, school songs, and by the isolation of school buildings themselves (*TBU*, 193, 153, 142). To some extent the development of the new male elite with its emphasis on group loyalty was a response to the demands of carving out and maintaining an imperialist empire, for "a world becoming

smaller put a premium on shared values, predictable social and political behavior" (*TBU*, 226; *Godliness*, 200–01). But the creation of this new elite, with
its devaluation of the feminine and of feminine values, may also be seen as a
response to the cultural power of the ideology of woman's sphere and hence
to middle-class women's self-identification, to the new exertion of women's
influence in relation to children and men, to the construction of a mother-
dominated family,[36] which the ideology of woman's influence promoted and
helped to sustain, and to the extension of women's influence into the public
sphere. The agency of middle-class women helped produce "manliness," as a
counterpoint to woman's influence and to the emerging sisterhood that shared
identification was to create.

It is perhaps this new ideology of "manliness" that we see at work in Ten-
nyson's "Maud," where the over-sensitive hero, in contrast to the feminized
heroes of *Dombey* and "A Buried Life," longs to become a "new" kind of man,
a "still strong man who can rule and dares not lie."[37] This hero, in further
contrast to the sensitive heroes who have gone before, abandons the woman
"whose gentle will . . . made my life a perfumed altar-flame" and throws himself into an all male community, not of cooking and weeping capitalists, but of
imperialist warriors. In the end, woman's influence accedes to a male God's
"just" purpose while her violet blue eyes, the traditional emblems of life, refuge,
and feeling, are supplanted by "the blood-red blossom of war."[38]

Thus what we have sometimes imagined as an unbroken patriarchal tradition—the appropriation of women as refuge—would appear to be a changing,
indeed, a broken one. What we have sometimes assumed to be the construction
of male energies and male power alone appears also to be the creation of female
energies and female influence. What we have often referred to as a matter of
gender would appear also to be a matter of class, and what we have sometimes,
overhastily, celebrated as socially progressive—women's capacity for nurturing
and feeling—would appear to have challenged male values, to have provoked
male fear and resistance, while at the same time representing an investment
in the status quo. History, that is, appears less straightforward, less tragically
unchanging, less univocal than we have made it—all of which is an argument
for further remaking it to better suit our sense of complexity and our goals.

NOTES

1. See, for example, Lillian Robinson, *Sex, Class and Culture* (Bloomington: Indiana
University Press, 1978); Annette Kolodny, "Dancing Through the Minefield: Some Ob-

servations on the Theory, Practice, and Politics of a Feminist Literary Criticism," *Feminist Studies*, 6 (Spring 1980), 1–25; Kate Belsey, *Critical Practice* (London: Methuen, 1979); Dale Spender, "Introduction," in *Men's Studies Modified: The Impact of Feminism in the Academic Disciplines*, ed. Dale Spender (Oxford: Pergamon Press, 1981), pp. 1–9. For similar formulations of history, literature, and literary criticism see Tony Bennett, *Formalism and Marxism* (London: Methuen, 1979); Fredric Jameson, *The Political Unconscious: Narrative as a Socially Symbolic Act* (Ithaca, N.Y.: Cornell University Press, 1981); Michael Ryan, *Marxism and Deconstruction: A Critical Articulation* (Baltimore: Johns Hopkins University Press, 1982); Terry Eagleton, *Literary Theory: An Introduction* (Minneapolis: University of Minnesota Press, 1983).

2. For two excellent articulations of this view see Frank Lentricchia, *After the New Criticism* (Chicago: University of Chicago Press, 1980) and Michael Ryan, *Marxism and Deconstruction*.

3. I base this observation on my own six years as editor in literature and culture for *Feminist Studies*, on the experience of my sister editors at the same journal, and on the experience of women who edit feminist work for journals that are not explicitly feminist.

4. Kate Ellis sees this trend among theorists of the antipornography movement, theorists who, she argues, "surround us with a monolithic world 'out there,' a patriarchal system of which all the parts are equally developed and fit perfectly together." Such theorists, she continues, "despair" of the process of "finding fissures and weak points in the armor of patriarchy." "I'm Black and Blue from the Rolling Stones and I'm Not Sure How I Feel About It: Pornography and the Feminist Imagination," *Socialist Review*, 75/76 (May-August 1984), 115. The same trend is apparent in some sectors of the peace movement. See, for example, Donna Warnock, "Patriarchy is a Killer: What People Concerned about Peace and Justice Should Know," in *Reweaving the Web of Life: Feminism and Nonviolence*, ed. Pam McAllister (Philadelphia: New Society Publishers, 1982), pp. 20–29. It is also in part this tragic view of men and masculinity that Barbara Haber sees behind the "evasiveness" of many heterosexual feminists "in confronting critically the nuclear family and female/male relationships in particular." Among several other factors, such as the difficulty of conducting sexual politics and the failure to build alternative communities, Haber feels that it was "the dismissal [as opposed to the critique] of heterosexuality [that] caused heterosexual women to withdraw from radical feminism and from dialogue with lesbians. Having discovered that smashing monogamy and heterosexuality were inadequate programs for their lives, women who were committed to their sexual preference for men and unwilling to write off family life became defensive and eventually (more or less) silent on sexual and family issues." "Is Personal Life Still a Political Issue?" *Feminist Studies*, 5 (Fall 1979), 421–22.

5. See Alice Echols on this tendency among members of the antipornography movement: "if the source of the world's many problems can be traced to the dominance of the male principle, its solution can be found in the reassertion of the female principle." "The New Feminism of Yin and Yang," in *Powers of Desire: The Politics of Sexuality*, eds. Ann Snitow, Christine Stansell, and Sharon Thompson (New York: Monthly Review Press, 1983), p.442. See Karen Rosenberg on this same tendency among members of the peace movement: "the (gender) gap has been taken as evidence that women are inherently more benevolent and caring than men, and even as heralding the long-awaited appearance of a force large enough to form a major peace movement." "Peaceniks and Soldier Girls," *The Nation*, April 14, 1984, p. 453. See also Judith Stacey on the "New Conservative Feminism" of Betty Friedan and Jean Elshtain, among others: "Despite a few rather vague affirmations of sexual equality neither identifies male domination as a problem requiring political, or any other attention. Friedan wants us to shift to concern for 'human' problems; Elshtain asks us to elevate female-identified virtues. Neither supports direct efforts to confront the domination of women by men." "The New

Conservative Feminism," *Feminist Studies*, 9 (Fall 1983), 569–70. Nancy Chodorow, finally, sees this celebration of female virtues as one consequence of a feminist essentialist position on gender difference: "an alternate sexual politics and analysis of sexual inequality has tended toward an essentialist position, posing male-female difference as innate. Not the degendering of society, but its appropriation by women, with women's virtues is seen as the solution to male dominance. . . . In this view, women are intrinsically better than men and their virtues are not available to men." "Gender, Relation, and Difference in Psychoanalytic Perspective," in *The Future of Difference*, eds. Hester Eisenstein and Alice Jardine (Boston: G.K. Hall, 1980), p. 3.

6. Dorothy Dinnerstein, *The Mermaid and the Minotaur: Sexual Arrangements and Human Malaise* (New York: Harper and Row, 1976); Nancy Chodorow, *The Reproduction of Mothering: Psychoanalysis and the Sociology of Gender* (Berkeley and Los Angeles: University of California Press, 1978); Jane Flax, "The Conflict Between Nurturance and Autonomy in Mother-Daughter Relationships and Within Feminism," *Feminist Studies*, 4 (June 1978), 171–91.

7. Mary Ryan, *Cradle of the Middle Class: The Family in Oneida County New York, 1790–1865* (Cambridge: Cambridge University Press, 1981); Judith R. Walkowitz, *Prostitution and Victorian Society: Women, Class, and the State* (Cambridge: Cambridge University Press, 1980). See also Jeffrey Weeks, *Sex, Politics, and Society: The Regulation of Sexuality Since 1800* (London: Longmans, 1981). See the following for a critique of the ahistorical tendencies of Chodorow and Dinnerstein: Judy Housman, "Mothering, the Unconscious, and Feminism," *Radical America*, 16 (Nov./Dec. 1982), 47–62.

8. Sandra M. Gilbert and Susan Gubar, *The Madwoman in the Attic: The Woman Writer and the Nineteenth-Century Imagination* (New Haven: Yale University Press, 1979).

9. Gilbert and Gubar, 402.

10. "Lines Composed a Few Miles Above Tintern Abbey on Revisiting the Banks of the Wye During a Tour, July 13, 1798," lines 158, 148.

11. "The Buried Life," lines 7–8, 91, 85, 95, 82.

12. For a fuller articulation of this process see the introduction to my *Women, Power, and Subversion: Social Strategies in British Fiction 1780–1860* (Athens: University of Georgia Press, 1981).

13. Sarah Ellis, *The Women of England, Their Social Duties, and Domestic Habits* (New York: D. Appleton and Co. 1839), p. 20; Sarah Lewis, *Woman's Mission*, 2nd ed. (London: John W. Parker, 1839), p. 46. Subsequent references are cited parenthetically in the text.

14. See Ted Koditschek, "Class Formation and the Bradford Bourgeoisie," (Diss., Princeton University 1981), pp. 837–40.

15. Anon. ("By A Woman"), *Woman's Rights and Duties: Considered with Relation to Their Influence on Society and on Her Own Condition, By a Woman*, 2 vols. (London: John W. Parker, 1840), pp. 203–04. Subsequent references are cited parenthetically in the text.

16. Barbara Taylor makes a similar point about the ideology of women's influence although she speaks of it here as male imposed: "A morality more convenient and yet more contradictory would be hard to imagine. Having confined all those virtues inappropriate within the stock market or the boardroom to the hearts of their womenfolk, middle-class men were then left free to indulge in all those unfortunate vices necessary for successful bourgeois enterprise." *Eve and the New Jerusalem: Socialism and Feminism in the Nineteenth Century* (New York: Pantheon Books, 1983), p. 126. See Dorothy Dinnerstein, however, for an (ahistorical but provocative) articulation of the psychoanalytic basis for what I have interpreted as male-female collaboration: "in leaving to man the enactment through compulsive public enterprise of our counter-assertion to

carnal morality, woman makes it possible for him to do what both neurotically need to have done; and . . . in taking upon himself the responsibility to do it, inside an arena fenced around with 'men only' signs, man makes it possible for woman to express something that both neurotically need to have expressed outside, not inside, this fence: the feeling that there is something trivial and empty, ugly and sad, in what he does" (216).

17. Sarah Ellis, "The Wives of England: Their Relative Duties, Domestic Influence and Social Obligations," in *The Family Monitor and Domestic Guide* (New York: E. Walker, nd). pp. 26, 25.

18. Anon. *Woman: Her Character and Vicissitudes* (London: Davis and Co., 1845), p. 56.

19. The doctrine of women's moral superiority, of course, while it justified women's immersion in the home, was to become justification for many non-domestic activities as well, from female volunteer work to female suffrage. In some feminist writers of the 1840s this argument was already being made. See, for example, Mrs. Hugo Reid, *A Plea for Woman: Being a Vindication of the Importance and Extent of Her Natural Sphere of Action; with Remarks on Her Recent Words on the Subject* (Edinburgh: William Tart, 1843), p. 27. Reid argues that it has not been shown that "the proposed enlargement of woman's sphere is incompatible with the spirit of self-renunciation; . . . the wider the sphere of action, the wider also is the field for self-renunciation."

20. Anon., *Woman: As She Is and As She Should Be* (London: James Cochrane and Co., 1835), pp. 14, 20, 28.

21. T. H. Lister, "Rights and Conditions of Women," *Edinburgh Review*, 73 (April 1841), 203.

22. Where Sarah Ellis imagines middle-class women counteracting the evils of competition by "calling back the attention of man to those sunnier spots in his existence, by which the growth of his moral feelings have been encouraged, and his heart improved" (*Women of England*, 49), Carlyle calls upon male industrialists themselves to "retire into their own hearts": "Arise, save thyself, be one of those that save thy country." Thomas Carlyle, *Past and Present* (1843; rpt. Boston: Houghton and Mifflin, 1965), pp. 268–69.

23. Charles Dickens, *Dombey and Son* (1846–1848; rpt. New York: New American Library, 1964), pp. 616, 381, 884. Subsequent references are cited parenthetically in the text. Julian Moynahan, "Dealings with the Firm of Dombey and Son: Firmness versus Wetness," in *Dickens in the Twentieth Century*, eds. John Gross and Gabriel Pearson (London: Routledge and Kegan Paul, 1962), p. 126.

24. See Julian Moynahan. See also Nina Auerbach, "Dickens and Dombey: A Daughter After All," in *Dickens Studies Annual 5*, ed. Robert B. Partlow, Jr. (Carbondale: Southern Illinois University Press, 1976), pp. 95–144.

25. Both Moynahan and Auerbach allude to Victorian ideologies of womanhood, but see Louise Yelin, "Strategies for Survival: Florence and Edith in *Dombey and Son*," *Victorian Studies*, 22 (Spring 1979), 297–319, for a more detailed treatment of the connection between Dombey and "the woman question."

26. Michael Slater suggests that Dickens was fascinated by the idea of natural sisterhood between women and that he found in it everything "exciting, lovable, fascinating, admirable, and inspiring in Woman," but he also suggests that in Dickens "woman's apparently endless capacity for devotion to those she loves is made to turn into devotion to revenge, devotion not to life but to death, and she becomes fearful indeed." *Dickens and Women* (Stanford, Calif.: Stanford University Press, 1983), pp. 371, 356.

27. Moynahan and Yelin both notice Florence's enormous power over Dombey.

28. Yelin sees this fairy tale quality as an evocation of woman as "other," "the only constant in a world of change, exempt—as opposed to excluded—from history" (304).

29. Moynahan is particularly acute about this: "Dombey moves from hardness through debility to a maundering, guilt-ridden submission to feminine softness" (130).

30. Moynahan, Auerbach, and Yelin, among others, see feminine qualities as triumphant at the end of the novel, but the feminine qualities in Dickens's men actually make feminine qualities in women and women's feminizing influence over men seem less necessary and less potentially powerful. Dombey is perhaps a warning to those men who ignore Carlyle's injunction to "save themselves."

31. When Carlyle imagines social relations in familial terms, the terms are entirely male: "without father, without child, without brother, Man knows no sadder destiny," (*Past and Present*, p. 271). In *Alton Locke* (1850; rpt. Garden City, N.Y.: Doubleday, 1961), which draws on the work of Carlyle, happy domestic relations are also imagined as male.

32. Although she does not explore a struggle between middle-class women and men over their relative power and over the identity of social heroes, Nina Auerbach does suggest that myths about male social heroism had less life than mythic constructions of women's power, that myths of women's power had different impact, and that "the social restrictions that crippled women's lives, the physical weaknesses wished on them, were fearful attempts to exorcise a mysterious strength." *Woman and the Demon: The Life of a Victorian Myth* (Cambridge, Mass: Harvard University Press, 1982), pp. 11, 8.

33. J. R. De S. Honey, *Tom Brown's Universe: The Development of the Victorian Public School* (London: Millington Books, 1977), p. 209. Subsequent references are cited parenthetically in the text as *TBU*.

34. Martin J. Wiener, *English Culture and the Decline of the Industrial Spirit, 1850–1980* (Cambridge: Cambridge University Press, 1981), p. 13. Subsequent references are cited parenthetically in the text.

35. *Tom Brown's Universe*, 191. See also David Newsome, *Godliness and Good Learning: Four Studies in a Victorian Ideal* (London: John Murray, 1961), p. 88. Subsequent references are cited parenthetically in the text.

36. See for example, Mary Ryan on Victorian America: "Well before mid-century it was clear that the mother's control over the socialization of infants and children had been expanded and extended," pp. 157–58. For a similar point about the family in Victorian Britain, see Mark Poster, *Critical Theory of the Family* (New York: The Seabury Press, 1978), p. 170.

37. "Maud; A Monodrama," I, lines 392–95.

38. "Maud: A Monodrama," I, lines 621–22; III, line 45; I, line 890; III, line 53.

FEMINIST CRITICISM
How Do We Know When We've Won?

Lillian S. Robinson

The specific question we have been invited to address here appears, as initially stated, to be either ingenuous to a fault or impossible to answer. This is not a comfortable dilemma to sit on the horns of. Yet, when asked whether it is essential that scholarship on women writers operate within feminist assumptions and with a feminist orientation, one hesitates over the appropriate response. On the one hand, I am committed to an almost reflexive "Yes, of course," that seeks to place the issue beyond discussion. On the other hand, I catch myself saying things like "on the other hand," attempting to redefine the terms of the question and its possible applications for both feminist and literary theory.

Is there a place for research—criticism and scholarship—on women's literature that, while not being explicitly anti-feminist, nonetheless is not explicitly feminist either? What sort of place? And what work (or whose, as we might more candidly express our uneasiness) may properly be characterized as "merely work on women" but not feminist work? Once these matters have been responsibly dealt with, I am afraid my own answer to the original question comes out a far from resounding "Yes, but. . . . " Rather than being as absolute as one—as I—might wish it to be, that answer starts with a limiting case and approaches what I believe to be most necessary in feminist literary scholarship only by a succession of increasingly closer approximations.

For the limiting case, I give you my nephew who, at age fourteen, pronounced his considered opinion that a neighbor's intellectual work was of little interest. Why was that? "Oh, she's just writing a book about women in the French Revolution." It sounded like an important subject to *me*, wrapped up as I am in women and revolutions, so I asked the kid why he was so dismissive. "Well," he replied, "it can't be very important, can it? I mean, *I* never heard of any women in the French Revolution!"

I found myself explaining at the top of my voice that it was precisely because he felt free to declare his ignorance so confidently that such research was of value. And so do we all find ourselves shouting, at some time or another, at departmental colleagues or university administrators, more's the pity, more often than at teenage nephews. Of *course* there have been enough important women writers—or enough before 1800 or in this national tradition or that, enough black or Chicana writers, enough dramatists or poets—to justify the study and teaching of this material. If feminist literary scholarship has not yet eliminated all declarations that (aside from the names that are household words) there really are no women writers to speak of, it has made serious inroads into the complacency with which that absence is asserted.

And that is one of the primary and legitimate tasks of such scholarship: simply to make it impossible to ignore women's contribution to both our common and our distinct literary heritages. The principal locus for the debate, of course, is not the face-to-face polemic, however frustrating, enervating, and necessary it may be, but the larger processes of canon formation, critical attention, and curricular reform. The significance of the limiting case, it seems to me, lies in the conclusions that are automatically drawn from the absence of women in the canon or the syllabus typically based on it. If an undergraduate is required to take one course on the Great Books and they all turn out to have been produced by Great Men, that student will very likely also take it as a given that no woman writer is considered to be suitably Great. Worse, the student will probably not give any thought to the matter. If the American literature survey these days includes a few white women, it is not surprising for the student to conclude that black women have failed to wield the pen to any good literary purpose. (The same conclusion is likely to be reached, of course, about a lily-white syllabus purporting to explore *"women's* literature.")

Considering the negative consequences of the absence of women—negative both intellectually and politically—I would conclude from my limiting case that, by contrast, any work that places the study of women writers at the center has an objectively feminist effect. Extending the female canon lengthwise, back into the centuries before the Industrial Revolution, or laterally, to include writers of color, working-class writers, writers of popular "women's fiction," has a feminist effect almost regardless of the nature of the arguments and connections that are made or ignored about the work itself.

Now, there is a name for the theoretical stance that informs the position I am taking here, and it is a pejorative one. Welcoming all such studies, however limited their contribution to an overall feminist analysis or interpretation, on the grounds that they do add something to What We Know, to the (quantitative or factual) truth, is called empiricism. As one is permitted to do in traffic court, I plead "guilty with an explanation." For the empiricism I am espousing is not vulgar empiricism, increasing the Body-of-Knowledge stuff, but, if you will, an enlightened empiricism, originating in and sustained by the conviction that every piece of something that is provided is better than nothing.

But "Better than Nothing" is a most depressing banner to be carrying through the streets in a feminist demonstration. (The only worse one I can think of, in fact, would read "Lesser of Two Evils.") Moreover, it is a particularly incongruous one for me to seem to be lugging since, from my earliest published work, I have been vocal in challenging feminists to create a criticism qualitatively different from the received tradition. Thirteen years ago, I was saying that feminist critics must not remain "bourgeois critics in drag." Seven years ago, I was saying that working-class women needed no outside apologists to make and justify their literature for them. Four years ago, I was applauding Jane Marcus's trenchant aphorism (wishing I had said it first) about how it is far more important to be Shakespeare's sisters than Bloom's daughters.[1] So am I not contradicting my own most cherished principles in admitting the Better than Nothing position? I hope not, for while including as much work as possible under the potentially feminist rubric, I nonetheless believe that, once the outer limits are defined, there are those successively closer approximations to the *best* work feminists need to do.

On the one hand, as you will not fail to observe, I am still convinced that I know what "the best" feminist work would be. On the other, I am by no means prepared to dismiss all the other work as not feminist. This inclusive imperative derives from my experience as one of five collaborators on a forthcoming study of feminist scholarship in its first decade.[2] My co-authors are an anthropologist, a historian, a philosopher, and a specialist in comparative education. One of the issues we originally planned to address in our book was the distinction between feminist scholarship in our respective disciplines (*our* side) and research in those fields that was "merely" work on women (the opposition, obviously).

In literary studies, such a distinction lies ready to hand and distinctly prior to any invidious discriminations among structuralist, Lacanian, Derridean, Marxist, reader-responding, or eclectic approaches to the issues raised by women's writing. There are women authors, and much of the scholarship and criticism devoted to them—and to the best known of them in particular—concentrates on aspects of their work unrelated to their own gender or to questions of gender in their writing. There is certainly a feminist way—or rather several—of understanding Jane Austen's irony or George Eliot's religion or Virginia Woolf's metaphors. But the vast bulk of critical prose annually devoted to such topics tends, more often than not, to do the thing "straight," that is, gender-blind. There might not even be anything necessarily wrong with that. This vast bulk constitutes the literary equivalent of social science work that makes women the object rather than the subject of, say, some series of statistical observations. Discussing it would, I thought, be my contribution to our collective analysis of feminist scholarship versus work on women. From there it could be readily determined which of these categories was appropriate for the scholarship chiefly devoted to recovering the work of lost women writers of the past.

But as this section of our book progressed, we discovered, painfully and at length, that although we all still had firm ideas about what was and was not a genuinely feminist endeavor in the areas we knew best, we could articulate no standards that really worked, particularly across disciplinary lines. The criteria we established were either so narrow as to exclude work we otherwise accepted as feminist or so broad as to include precisely that which we had considered most questionably so. We were forced to the conclusion that the intellectual challenge posed by the women's movement in general and by women's studies in particular is so potent, even where unacknowledged, that at the present time it creates the historical context within which all discourse on women occurs.

For instance, each of us had also done a statistical analysis of journal articles, dissertation abstracts, and presentations at scholarly conventions. In literary studies, I had unsurprisingly concluded that far more of these various types of scholarly contributions were devoted to women writers in 1980, the last year in the survey, than in 1965. Much of this material was in the "merely on women" category. But the sheer increase in volume is a by-product of the existence of feminist criticism, both in general and as addressed to these particular writers. Women writers are now more acceptable as thesis subjects, in a situation where a graduate student must seek and obtain approval of the topic. It is likelier nowadays that the centennial or other anniversary of the birth or death of a major woman writer will be marked by a special journal issue or a conference. And even when we are properly infuriated that such a special issue or confabulation has not even solicited a feminist contribution, we can take a certain amount of credit, cold comfort though it may be, from the realization that our work in the aggregate made it happen. Experiences like this, as well as those trickier cases where commentators who remain well outside the feminist frame of reference or discourse nonetheless reflect some small gleaning from our bountiful harvest, giving some indication that we are not speaking always and only to ourselves, were common to all five of us. Hence, as I say, we were forced to the conclusion that, at the present moment, feminism provides the locus and the context even for work on women that does not bear a directly feminist stamp. I say "forced" advisedly, yet it may not really be such a bad place to find ourselves. For the time being.

Still, still I do worry. Although I am prepared to define the limits so inclusively, I also have a sense of priorities that speaks to me—and, I believe, to us—in the imperative mood. There is an insistence, even an urgency, underlying my sense of what is to be done—along with a terrible fear that that is increasingly what is not being done. I start from the premise that "woman" as a category defined by gender alone and, hence, in contradistinction to the other category so defined, that is, to "man," does have a historical specificity, a different experience or set of experiences, as well as a different consciousness and a different perspective on those experiences that the two sexes share. Empiricism, the inclusion of women in hypothetical canon or pragmatic curriculum, is not enough. A populist insistence on representing all aspects of our culture in canon and curriculum, without admitting the controversies and contradictions aroused by such representation, is not enough. Inclusion of women should radically and fundamentally alter our sense—everyone's sense—of what the overall canon or curriculum is and what it says. All our generalizations about, say, "the" seventeenth century or "the" American national character have to be re-examined in the light of what women's contributions to making up the literature of the various centuries and nations tells us.

The nature and direction of these changes depend on a prior issue, however: the extent to which challenges to the male-dominated canon also entail challenges to the dominant stylistic, thematic, and aesthetic norms. As the archaeological aspect of feminist scholarship is pursued to good purpose, the academic world in general is increasingly likely to admit to us that, yes, after all, there were some women writing in the seventeenth century. But how many of them, we will be asked, we will ask ourselves, were any good? How many of them are good enough to deserve a place in an honest "coed" canon? How many are good enough to deserve to (deep breath) displace some gentleman on "the" syllabus for seventeenth-century literature? These are by no means rhetorical questions; their answers are not obvious. It all depends on what we mean by "good," on how far scholarship alone, simply uncovering the lost or never-heard voices of women of past centuries, suggests or even dictates a new set of aesthetic principles. How do we know that it is as good? Do we leave the definitions untouched and demonstrate—as is clearly possible in certain cases—that a given woman meets all the existing criteria for goodness? Or do we explicitly or implicitly modify the aesthetic compact? Which: explicitly or implicitly? And according to what criteria?[3]

To undertake investigation of the earlier history of women writers without considering the criteria *other than gender* for inclusion in the canon (and hence for these writers' exclusion) is to walk headlong into an elitist quagmire. It may also mean ignoring some of the richest sources of female expressive tradition, as well as all the further implications of that or any tradition. What, for instance, if it turned out that the Countess of Pembroke really wrote *The Countess of*

Pembroke's Arcadia? After all, if Shakespeare's sister was an exemplary myth, Sidney's sister was a living reality, a highly cultivated woman, a patroness, and a writer. There is, as far as I know, not a shred of evidence that she wrote the *Arcadia.* But what if...? One for our side and a terrific one—but so what? What would it tell us about women or even about women writing? No special case would have to be made to include Mary Sidney's *Arcadia* in the canon—not now. And the gentlemanly study of gentlemanly texts would recover from the shock absolutely unscathed, particularly if Mary Sidney's *Arcadia* were to be subjected, even by feminists, to the currently fashionable approaches of the responding—or anguished or deconstructing—reader; but not if it were to be subjected to an approach that notices phenomena of class and race, as well as gender.

When it is a question of broadening the canon to include popular literature written by and about women for an overwhelmingly female audience, it is well, once again, to be clear about the reasons for proposing *this* material as literature and for placing it beside the traditional (and traditionally male-authored) monuments hallowed by literary history. Is the argument here to be based on representation? Or is our common definition of literary excellence due for an overhaul?

Although I spoke earlier and temporarily of woman as a category defined by gender alone, such a definition is a sort of mathematical abstraction; the problem is further compounded when we recognize that the difference of gender is not the only one that subsists among writers or the people they write about. It may not always be the major one. Women differ from one another by race, by ethnicity, by sexual orientation, and by class. Each of these contributes its historic specificity to social conditions and to the destiny and consciousness of individual women. Moreover, these differences are not simply or even primarily individual attributes. They are *social* definitions, based on the existence and the interaction of groups of people and of historical forces. As scholarship— itself primarily or secondarily feminist—reveals the existence of a black female tradition or a working-class women's literature, it is insufficient simply to tack these works onto the existing canon, even the emerging women's canon. Once again, every generalization about women's writing that was derived from surveying only relatively privileged white writers is called into question by looking at writers who are not middle class and white. It may be that some of these generalizations will hold. My suspicion is, however, that most do not. This is even more likely when, say, black women's literature is assimilated into a *general* American canon that was hitherto predominantly white and male. The addition not only enriches the canon, it changes our sense of what the canon is and what it is about.

Here again, the aesthetic issues are at the forefront. In order to add black women's literature to an all white—much less an all white and all male—canon, certain judgments will have had to be made. On what basis are they to be made? Does the received idea of what is "good" literature have to change and how do we get it to do so? Or is "representativeness" of all available voices in the culture to become the only aesthetic?

At present, it seems to me that a curious double standard is in effect whereby only the women's literature produced by middle-class white women is subjected to the full range of critical and analytic apparatus, including all the currently fashionable linguistic and psychological modalities. Literature by women of color and, perhaps, even by working-class white women may be granted some modicum of critical and (even likelier) pedagogical attention, but it is rarely, if ever, included in general discussions of the female tradition, and it is almost never read according to the modish new ways of reading. Instead it is read as social document. As you can imagine, I have no objection to this unless it ignores the fact and the consequences of the fact that non-elite women's writing is nonetheless fiction or poetry or drama or narrative—that it is, in fact, *literature*. And I have no objection to this unless it gives such unexamined primacy to the author's race or class that it fails to observe any other aspect of her experience or her expression.[4]

But what bothers me even more is the implication that only women of color possess a racial identity that has to be understood by the critic, that only working-class women possess a class identity whose consequences need to be studied. In fact, in a society divided not only by racial differences but by racism, all writers have a significant racial identity. In a society wracked by class tensions—acknowledged or not—all have a class identity. Hence it is my contention that all women's literature deserves to be considered in the light of its full range of social, as well as individual, connotations.

Take, for example, the Countess of Pembroke, to whose career I gave a hearty, if fanciful, boost a few paragraphs back. If it were established that the *Arcadia* was not written by her brother to amuse her but by the Countess to amuse *herself*, then how do we read the book? If the many emendations she made from his notes and known intentions were as much her own invention as the older, simpler text onto which they were grafted; if, in short, it had always been her book, in fact as in name, how do we read it? It seems to me obviously absurd to maintain that interpretation of this text could be altered only by the fact of gender rather than by the interlocking facts of *class* and gender.

That Mary Sidney was a woman of wealth, standing, and some political influence, that she was a patroness of (male) writers, as well as the wife and the mother of great patrons, has to be taken into consideration in apprehending the works she did leave us. All this becomes even more significant if that slender *oeuvre* were to be enriched by the addition of a long prose romance. The *Arcadia* embodies the ideology of a powerful class striving for further self-definition and social domination, ideology that involves ethical and political constructs, as well as those specifically regulating the character and relations of the two sexes. In this way, text and author participate in history, and one function of criticism is to situate and understand them there.

It is true that the archaeological work on the female canon excites me rather less than it might because so much of it—necessarily, inevitably—involves digging up the literary remains of the Honourable Miss This and the Countess of That and the (recusant, secretly Jacobite) Lady The-Other. I confess a general preference for Jacobins over Jacobites, whatever their gender. But when it comes to the newly uncovered literature, a large part of my impatience is owing to the bland assumption on the part of scholars that the combined operations of class and gender have no literary consequences worth bothering about. Now, if Lady Pembroke's *maid* had written the *Arcadia* . . . or something.[5] Well, what? Yes, frankly, it would interest me as an expression of the mass female voice, of someone living through class as well as sex oppression, but chiefly because everyone *else* would also be forced to look at its class dimensions. The maid, you see, has a class identity. The Countess and her knightly brother are treated as belonging to the world of literature and hence, in the peculiar late twentieth-century perception, do not. They are "normal"—that is, they possess a brain and a pen and no history. Indeed, the social exception, the individual of leisure and privilege, *becomes* the literary norm. Surely such madness is only enhanced as we accord to women writers, as well as their brothers, a reading that ignores the material and ideological meaning of class.

I am very much disheartened by increasingly hegemonic, essentialist tendencies in feminist scholarship and criticism. Day by day, even that scholarship that is "merely about women" is providing fundamental links in the chain of knowledge, revealing the existence of a wealth of hitherto unknown, unrecognized, or unremembered literature. Our task, the *feminist* task, is to know what to do with that treasure now that, increasingly, it is in our hands.

NOTES

1. The two pieces of my own referred to here are "Dwelling in Decencies: Radical Criticism and the Feminist Perspective," *College English*, 32 (1971), 879–89, based on a paper delivered at the December 1970 Annual Meeting of MLA, and "Working/ Women/Writing," in my *Sex, Class, and Culture* (Bloomington: Indiana University Press, 1978), pp. 223–53, based on a paper delivered at the Annual Meeting of MLA

in December 1976; Jane Marcus's remarks were part of a personal communication in the fall of 1979.

2. Ellen Carol DuBois, Gail Paradise Kelly, Elizabeth Lapovsky Kennedy, Carolyn W. Korsmeyer, and Lillian S. Robinson, *Feminist Scholarship: Kindling in the Groves of Academe* (Urbana: University of Illinois Press, 1986).

3. On this point, see Myra Jehlen, "Archimedes and the Paradox of Feminist Criticism," *Signs*, 6 (1981), 575–601.

4. Mary Helen Washington discusses the disastrous effects of mechanically dividing a syllabus into white and black women authors, turning each one into an implicit representative or spokeswoman for her race alone, in her article, "How Racial Differences Helped Us Discover Our Sameness," *Ms.*, 10 (September 1981), 60–62, 76.

5. If my fantasy about Sidney's sister owes its existence and shape to Virginia Woolf's creation of Shakespeare's sister, my thinking about Sidney's sister's *maid* is informed by Woolf's discussion of Mercy Harvey in *The Common Reader: Second Series* (1932; rpt. London: Hogarth Press, 1959).

ENGORGING THE PATRIARCHY

Nina Auerbach

Too often, when I am invited to represent Women's Studies, I am praised on behalf of us all for the "ideological purity" of feminist criticism. I find this odd, because I have always seen myself as defiantly impure. As a writer and as a member of the academic community, I take strength from my sense of impurity—my own and the world's. Scholars of women's history are seismographs of taint, pointing their readers to the lie within the label, the aggression within the altruism, the murder within the marriage, the dark questions within the sleek answers. As a representative of purity, moral, ideological, intellectual, or anything else, I am a walking lie. My own work and that of the women I admire gives its allegiance to the messiness of experience.

I have an uneasy feeling that we whose vision was once seen as dangerous are now authenticated because, like the Victorian woman, we are perceived as being beyond culture. The perceptions that once were taboo have become purifying and exemplary. "Reading as a woman" is currently an ennobling activity, exuding the sanctity of marginality. The ostracism and enforced self-discovery that taught us each, in our varied ways, to see as we do beckons those in power to learn our language, crack our codes, adopt our ways.

A few years ago, when we began to be feminist critics, it was fun to be a demon, and now—for all of us, I think—it is amusing being an angel. But there is a danger in our believing our own mythology too ardently. History and taste change so rapidly and so irrationally that we all may be disenfranchised at any time, abandoned to the quaintness of yesterday's iconography and the purity of yesterday's ideology. It is salutary to remember that I and my community are impurely human, and that our diverse ideologies have been soaked from the beginning in the impurities of experience. For each of us, I think, there was an epiphany, an era in our lives when we realized that our experience of the world had to pit us against that world as we experienced it, and then, to oversimplify, we became feminists. I should like to go back to some of those moments in our differing lives, in order to find the source of the kind of reading and writing we do. I hope to present these as powerful and durable as well as pure, because they are rooted in the mixed and changing conditions of the history that is our lives.

Since its genesis in the late 1960s, feminist criticism has absorbed effusions of Lacanianism, institutionalized anxiety, Marxist mentoring, and reader response theory. At heart, though, I think we are still engaged in "Life Studies," as Sandra Gilbert beautifully and simply dubbed our work in 1979. We are not criticizing life with Arnoldian detachment; we are bringing its inequities and perplexities to the bland restricting formulas that have told us what to be. An early anthology of feminist criticism was called *The Authority of Experience;*[1] this authority taught us texts and readings the academy ignored, taught us to live lives whose dimensions we had not learned, and I think it will shape our varied ideologies as these mutate into the future. Since the authority of experience first let us see as we do, we should remain true to it. In tribute to its authority, I want to return to two sorts of formative experiences and the ideologies they shaped. The first is not my own; the second is.

Sandra M. Gilbert's "Life Studies" describes her conversion to feminist criticism in rapturous religious language. Elaine Showalter's dissertation, which would become *A Literature of Their Own*, shook the scales from her eyes: "I had awakened, my consciousness had soared, all was changed, changed utterly: I was a born again feminist." Years of good studentship fall away as she awakes to the primary authority of her female life: "Most feminist critics speak—at least from time to time—like people who must bear witness, people who must enact and express in their own lives and words the re-visionary sense of transformation that seems inevitably to attend the apparently simple discovery that the experiences of women in and with literature are different from those of men."[2] The books we need convert us to their source in experience, an experience our tasks as good women had up to then taught us to betray and deny.

For Gilbert's autobiography gives her ideology its life. She begins as a good daughter of the patriarchy: she is a student while her husband teaches, and she is writing about D. H. Lawrence, that seductive guru of our generation, who told us in the lushest language what to be and not be. With dreadful psychic logic Gilbert moves from writing about Lawrence to studying death, but that saving dissertation intervenes, redeeming her from the drift toward death to the study of life. She is saved from the deathwish of obedience by a female authority that permits undiluted and unmediated speech. Elaine Showalter's reclamation of woman writers galvanized Gilbert to reclaim her own writing life.

This interchange of lives and books continues. Elaine Showalter's talk at the 1983 English Institute was a happy footnote to "Life Studies."[3] In it, Showalter describes her own conversion from obedient good woman to enraptured feminist critic. As a caretaking faculty wife, she doubted whether she would finish the dissertation that was to illuminate Sandra Gilbert; she describes her own conversion to "born again feminism" in Gilbert's language. In this community, lives are exchanged as freely as books and ideas, for feminist ideology is inseparable from the lived knowledge of subordination, just as reading and writing are part of our continual self-authorization and self-authentication. An unexpected substitution at the English Institute dramatized this interweaving of life studies with feminist criticism, as it did the communality of our lives: Elaine Showalter was ill, and so another feminist critic, Nancy K. Miller, read her paper. The easy conviction with which Miller wove Gilbert's words into Showalter's life epitomizes the choric, even boundaryless, quality of feminist criticism as a school. Lives are our medium of exchange. Books are inseparable from the private experiences that authorized them, while these experiences take on the semi-public and shared quality of our books. Finally, this conjunction is the only gospel we trust.

I emphasize the boundarylessness that joins our lives to our books, making experience our most avidly shared text, to demonstrate our mistrust of precept, of rule, of an abstraction not proved upon our pulses. Our ideology, if we have one, is fluid, mutable, continually taking on the shifting dimensions of our continually shifting lives. Gilbert and Showalter's "born again feminism," their conversions from good womanhood, shape their ideological method: though both welcome men, with some apprehension, into women's studies,[4] and though both have written incisively about male texts, their dominant allegiance is to gynocriticism, which, as Elaine Showalter defines it, asks the following question: "How can we constitute women as a distinct literary group? What is *the difference* of women's writing?"[5]

Gynocritics is a quest for woman's "precious specialty," as George Eliot somewhat gushingly called it, distinguishing women as a group. It is not a biological inheritance, but a cultural creation, endowing us with distinction through subordination. This is the quest of women who redeemed their own authority, who reclaimed their writing selves, by differentiating themselves from their culture. The study of woman's distinctiveness converts oppression into a saving creed. Gynocritics is probably the must influential and productive school of feminist criticism, but, because my own experience differs from theirs, it is not my method or my ideology. At the cost of admitting my complicity in a fallen world, I shun my "precious specialty" and seek access to the larger, if tarnished, culture that dictates our own and others' differences.

When I think back to the origins of my own feminism, I cannot remember a moment of conversion, because I cannot remember ever having believed what I was told to be. I was always sardonically resisting. I enjoyed thinking of myself as a bad woman; never, until recently, did I admit that it was never "bad" to refuse to be "good" in the self-mutilating way young women were raised to be in the 1950s. I never wanted to be a caretaker; I never saw myself as a wife or a mother, and I never was one; nor, as I remember, did I see myself as a man. As a sheltered graduate student, I did assume that I would write my dissertation on Jane Austen and George Eliot, and that I would be a faculty member rather than a faculty wife. These things did happen, but few such confident shelters survive growing up. Unlike Sandra Gilbert's, my conversions were generally Carlylean unconversions from a grandiose sense of possibilities. My experience did not redeem my life; instead, it made me question the ego I imagined I had, the reception I imagined I would receive, the disinterestedness of the community I was eager to enter. My feminism, then, is less a quest for my own saving difference from powerful men than it is a compromise with my idealism about the male-dominated community, which looked to me like Camelot.

I never cared about being a good woman, but when I moved from New York to Los Angeles to become an assistant professor at California State College, I was fueled by belief in myself as a good pilgrim. Looking back to that sprawling, car-choked school between two freeways on the fringe of the barrio, I am abashed at my own expectations for it. Cal State was then, and I think still is, a university for the unacknowledged people of this very urban city. Our students were blue collar workers, blacks, Chicanos, foreigners, and housewives; many of them drove fifty miles across spirals of freeways to make their early morning or late afternoon classes without jeopardizing their jobs. At that time, 1970, their average age was twenty-seven, my own age. For a large percent of them, men and women, college was stigmatizing. Their families resented their new, forbidden dreams of professions instead of jobs, choices instead of routines, anger instead of acquiescence. In their dangerous illumination, I saw my own. Teaching *Great Expectations* at Cal State transformed it from the boring little homily I had always privately thought it to a celebration of—just what its title says. The great expectations came alive, the cautionary moral, which only the privileged accept, receded. The bullied poor boy, hungry for glorification, whom my present middle-class students condemn with sanctimonious ease, was heard by his own. Perhaps Jonathan Culler would call the passion with which class after class adopted *Great Expectations* reading as a woman, but I doubt whether you have to be a woman to read that way. All you have to be is despised.

No doubt all beginning teachers identify with their students rather than with their colleagues, and I did too. Trying to negotiate the den of vipers, which the Cal State English Department looked like to me at that time, I saw myself in my students, and I saw myself for the first time. In general, my colleagues approved neither of challenging teaching nor of any kind of scholarship; there were hidden rewards for mediocrity, suppressed sanctions against ambition. The most aspiring students, male and female, were put down when they tried to learn too much, see too far. Original work was punished by derision and bad grades; mindless work was rewarded by comradely smiles and by A's. Like my students, I tried to learn to be blandly affable and to keep my mind in the closet, my unorthodox scholarly writing a secret. My disdain for good womanhood had carried me to a place where I was made to behave like a good woman at last. I was converted into subservience.

The bad climate of Cal State was largely a seepage from California's political climate. The administration of then-Governor Reagan had programmed the state colleges to be drearily functional and nothing more: our administrators feared retaliation if we overweened intellectually. The California state system as a whole was suffering backlash from the Berkeley, San Francisco State, and UCLA uprisings. We had our unspoken mandate: to educate our streetwise students with great expectations into a self-contempt that would keep them in their place. No individual was at fault for the servility that pervaded our classes and strangled our most energetic faculty and students. Like patriarchy, it was the air we breathed, a fear that became an article of faith.

No doubt people breathe more freely now at Cal State than they did in those revolutionary years, and no doubt I was a thin-skinned pilgrim who saw sharper moral contrasts than I might find now; but my two years there were a political baptism. Books would never be transcendent again, nor would I be able to escape into them: they were only vehicles of oppression or the fight against oppression, as they had been for my students and my studentized self. When Kate Millett claimed in *Sexual Politics* that the western cultural tradition was a weapon against women, the indictment that shocked so many people seemed to me tame and limited compared to the weapons I was living with at Cal State.

My conversion, then, is not Sandra Gilbert's. For one thing, I was un-converted into a loss of faith, forced to see (and sometimes to implement) the ways in which books betrayed experience. Moreover, though my un-conversion illuminated my later work as a feminist critic, it was only tangentially related to my life as a woman. My first job was a lesson in feminist methodology: there is no haven of the mind, no art is pure of ideology and politics, books are powerful weapons because they transform our sense of reality, how we read is a political self-declaration. But I did not learn these things in relation to women alone.

I became a feminist critic at the University of Pennsylvania because my department assumed I already was one. A predominantly male university was being forced to mend its ways; in 1972, a burgeoning women's program was bringing feisty life to the faculty of Arts and Sciences. My un-conversion from eastern loftiness, my new awareness of culture as a battleground, literature as torn with this battle, all made feminist reading and writing my natural medium. But unlike my feminist colleagues, I embraced this discipline obliquely. Putting

aside my private, lifelong and often enjoyable rebellion, I accepted my oppression as a woman after living with a racist and a class oppression that included
men as well. I recognized myself as a victim when I saw others victimized. In
the best female, caretaking tradition, I learned to fight for myself by fighting
for others.

My experience as good pilgrim rather than good woman shaped an ideology
that differs from gynocriticism. I do not look for, or see, *"the difference* in
women's writing; I hear no *"different voice,"* in Carol Gilligan's resonant phrase;
I do not observe a female morality that is more humane, less abstract, than
that of men, as Gilligan does.[6] I may be blind to these differences because I
did not find feminism through my uniquely female experience, but through a
broader experience of injustice that helped me see injustice to women. Oppression has made the women I know and study resilient rather than discrete;
my emphasis in *Woman and the Demon* on a disruptive, mutable female force,
and my present research on the power of actresses, spring from my awareness
that victims learn to assume many selves. I do not think oppression has given
us a sole self, however humane we claim we all are; it has given us instead a
variety of personae with which to blend into a society that threatens us. The
resilience of the oppressed strikes me, not her or his uniformity; it is those in
power whom I hear speaking in the same different voice.

Extravagantly as I admire the work it has produced, then, I find I must avoid
gynocriticism for myself. My interest lies less in the muted culture of women
than in woman's mutable role in the history of the main culture as a vehicle of
disruptive, dispossessed energy. When I write about it, that energy is female,
but it could stand for *all* "hunger, rebellion, and rage."[7] Such energy has no
"precious specialty," but only its own, self-generated power. All the voices of
the outcast energize my concern for women.

My feminism is equally diluted by a dangerous nostalgia for the gorgeousness
that has traditionally been part of our oppression. This nostalgia for the victimization we study so assiduously is one of the many impurities in feminist criticism
as a whole: if all our battles were won, where would the female tradition be?
Unlike some recent feminist theorists, though, I have no nostalgia whatever
for woman's separate sphere.[8] Feminism has traditionally tended to attract
advocates of a self-glorifying separatism so extreme that it meets the extremes
of patriarchy, purging women of all violence and ego until we become a gush
of sheer nurturance in an angry world. This sort of sentimental hygenic myth-
making is a dangerous strategy, apart from being false to all human women.
Its removal of woman from the rapacious, morally complex human species
bestows on men a power that was never theirs. When a woman attributes all
aggression, all thrust for power, to men alone, she gives her own potential
violence to her oppressor, making him more loomingly omnipotent than any

actual man ever was. Such self-denying feminists create a gargantuan oppressor who never existed in life. It seems wisest for women to forfeit dreams of purity—which are generally patriarchal in origin—in order to gain for ourselves the best possible lives in an imperfect world.

We early feminist critics in the academic world invested men with just this mythic, dehumanizing power. Our first impulse toward separatism would lead, we feared, to patriarchal apocalypse, revolution, repression, some sort of fire from heaven. The last thing we expected from men was their envy. Recently, though, powerful men have yearned to speak in what they conceive as our voice: the compromised conditions of the 1980s have brought them to women, no longer as angels or whores, but as vessels of a lost integrity. Jonathan Culler has devoted a key chapter of his *On Deconstruction* to the art of "reading as a woman"—that is, with all the skeptical purity of an outcast from culture.[9] In our student days, male professors forbade us to read "as women," that is, as they called it then, "subjectively." Lee R. Edwards's eloquent essay on *Middlemarch* reminds us of the classroom taboos that forbade our despair over Dorothea Brooke's final, married anonymity, which the jargon of that time called "maturity."[10] Now, such luminaries as Jonathan Culler, Jerome McGann, Lawrence Lipking, Wayne Booth, Terry Eagleon, and J. Hillis Miller laud the ideological purity of feminist reading, but I fear that this acceptance will lead to our being locked into a new prison. If a woman's reading of a novel is perceived as insufficiently "womanly," will her fresh perceptions be tabooed as our feminist ones were in the old days? Separatism is always a double-edged sword; women are praised for having qualities that are then forced on them; and if "reading as a woman" becomes an institutionalized enterprise, I fear that its hegemony will crush our power to read as it has been crushed so often before.

Moreover, vertigo sometimes overwhelms male critics trying to read as women. Some of them do not read as anybody: their scholarly contours dissolve with frightening rapidity, leaving them thrashing around in limbo trying to be virtuous. As I watch this, my early wariness returns, and I fear that the embrace of patriarchy means our own disappearance as well as the man's. My paranoia may be right. Some, though not all, of these men have written of their conversion as if feminism were an act of grace freely given to them: lauding their own illumination, they fail to cite the names of any actual, female feminist critics. This shyness about acknowledging female authority probably springs from an attempt to reproduce the evangelical feminist voice, but when they abandon conventional scholarly decorum to embrace life studies, they abandon the female lives that inspired our writing, and then their own, in the first place. Wayne Booth unreads Rabelais with the same antinomian zeal with which Sandra Gilbert read Elaine Showalter, but Booth's unacknowledged tribute to her method obliterates her authority.[11] Is the wheel coming full circle now that we are being heard? Like those of Dorothy Wordsworth, Zelda Fitzgerald, and other exemplary helpmates, our experiences are continually threatened by absorption in the self-proclamations of male truth. The next generation's Anon. may be ourselves.

As a strategy, the monolithic potential within gynocriticism may make us vulnerable to this sort of invasion. If we turn in on ourselves to isolate "the difference" between our voice and that of supposedly powerful men, our voice will become easy to mimic. Our stress on our uniformity and uniqueness in culture may make us look frailer and more boring than we are. Lawrence Lipking reduces us to a single plaintive note: affirming that women are not "a subspecies of men," he isolates our corporate focus on "love and its discontents," on "needs rather than forms." "Hence," he concludes, "[woman's] poetics obeys another law of nature, the unsatisfied craving of children who cry to be held."[12] Is that really what we've been saying through the ages? It has not felt that way to me, nor have I heard that particular cry in our complex history and varied voices. Lipking is also the author of *The Life of the Poet: Beginning and Ending Poetic Careers,*[13] a rich and moving study of a medley of male lives as these create themselves through poetry. Surely no child's cry could encompass for Lipking the lives of Keats, Dante, Whitman, and the rest: his wonderful book takes its life from the subtle differences among these men as they transfigure themselves into art.

I had always thought our own life studies were about these self-creating differences as well, but I see us increasingly reduced by the tendency to segregate women from the dominant culture—which is construed as relentlessly male—to immure us in a culture and tradition that are solely our own. Our own complicity in this isolation may invite scholars to define us in reductive formulas they do not apply to more intimately known material. Our "precious specialty" may make us feel, and appear, too special for the gross machinery of scholarship. It also may shut us away from the full range of the world. My own sort of writing, at least, requires the flexibility that studying men as well as women allows me. I do not want to give up writers I love because my allegiance to women tells me to do so: we have been told for too long that being a woman means giving things up. I am resigned to giving up the Papacy, but I am not prepared to give up *Moby Dick*—or, for that matter, *The Life of the Poet*—in the name of some greater good. I do not want to abandon the energy, the achievements, of patriarchal culture any more than I want to be abandoned by these things.

Many of us feel the same warm appreciation of the culture that has made us feel outcast, but we justifiably fear its invasion of the sole territory we have made our own. The alternative, of course, is for us to become invaders. This is what I have tried to do in my writing and, in the best of times, in my life. Instead of dwelling on an inviolate female tradition, I have looked at men along with women through a female prism. It may be, as some feminists claim, that writing about men and women as if they were a single species reinforces the patriarchy, but I like to imagine my writing self as well as my living self as a pilgrim in a new country. For me, writing about something is an imperial act: it is my way of claiming power over it. Its magic is dispelled by being understood; it loses its awesome otherness as it is absorbed into the shape of my consciousness and my language. Probably, I share the primitive superstition that by writing about the patriarchy, as by eating it, I engorge its power. Carlyle is my sanction: "to reduce matters to writing means that you shall know them, see them in their origins and sequences, in their essential lineaments, considerably better than you did before."[14] To know and to see are essential steps toward conquest.

In *The Madwoman in the Attic*, Gilbert and Gubar write brilliantly about the anxiety of authorship many woman writers still feel. Their title, and the Gothic thrill that courses through their book, associate this anxiety with pathology. But our anxiety is self-knowing and justified: since writing is an exercise of enormous power, it is not mad but sane to fear an assertion of that power over the decomposed substance to which you have reduced the subject of your book. Whether we are women or men, reading is a similar engorgement and appropriation: an intensely read text circulates through our body and mind. If we make men our property in this way, we can absorb the patriarchy before it embraces—and abandons—us into invisibility.

When I wrote *Communities of Women*, men were the grain of sand in my oyster. I did not know quite what to do with them, but I knew I could not leave them out, and so I included a long chapter on Henry James and George Gissing, which allowed me, through James's *Bostonians*, to confront a venerable tradition of patriarchal criticism. This integration, which was the essence of *Communities of Women*, hints at the impossibility of its own subject, but its method gave me the assurance to write my next book, *Woman and the Demon*, which is my attempt to embrace Victorian patriarchy: I looked into its face and a coldly triumphant mermaid looked back. Under her gaze, *The Madwoman's* pen/penis lost its authority for me. Adopting the mermaid as my totem, I hoped to write the patriarchy in such a way that it would lose its appearance of power. Writing *Woman and the Demon* exorcised my sense of the otherness of "high" culture. No longer did I, as a Victorian scholar, inhabit a world that was noble, humanistic, central—and barred to my marginal self.

I began by affirming our impurity because the best of our writing is entangled in the messiness of our experience. I conclude by suggesting that the varied ideologies we evolve arise in large part from the imperial experience of writing.

Dispossessed women throughout history have used writing to possess forbidden experiences, forbidden knowledge, forbidden powers. Writing for us expresses not so much "the unsatisfied craving of children who cry to be held" as the will-to-satisfaction of adults who refuse to be held, and who try to swallow the world that holds us. The evangelical voice that announced women's life studies echoes now in literary prophecy and in the prophetic visions of science fiction. Women's new visionary literature aims to transfuse an oppressive world into its own myth-making substance, creating spaces large enough to fit our dreams of invasion.

Writing suffused in experience and literary visions suffused in the expansive experience of writing may not compose a pure ideology, but they do, I hope, compose one that is durable, able to demystify, diminish, and finally engorge the power that subordinated us; and what is most important, able to change each time our experience changes. For women's ideologies, like men's, have always been less pure than passionate because they reflect the humiliations and the compromised victories of all of our lives.

NOTES

1. *The Authority of Experience: Essays in Feminist Criticism*, ed. Arlyn Diamond and Lee R. Edwards (Amherst: University of Massachusetts Press, 1977).

2. Sandra M. Gilbert, "Life Studies, or, Speech After Long Silence: Feminist Critics Today," *College English* 40 (April, 1979), 850.

3. Elaine Showalter, "Women's Time, Women's Space: Writing the History of Feminist Criticism," The English Institute, 1983, included in this volume.

4. See "Life Studies," 864–65, and Elaine Showalter, "Critical Cross-Dressing: Male Feminists and the Woman of the Year," *Raritan: A Quarterly Review* (Fall 1983), 130–49.

5. Elaine Showalter, "Feminist Criticism in the Wilderness," *Critical Inquiry* 8 (Winter 1981), 185.

6. Carol Gilligan, *In a Different Voice* (Cambridge, Mass.: Harvard University Press, 1981).

7. This is the suggestive phrase Matthew Arnold used to denounce Charlotte Brontë's *Villette*. See his letter to Mrs. Forster, April 14, 1853, in *Letters of Matthew Arnold*, collected and arranged by George W. E. Russell, 2 vols. (New York and London: Macmillan, 1895), I: 33–34.

8. Susan Gubar dignoses this nostalgia shrewdly in *The New York Times Book Review*, February 19, 1984, p. 26.

9. Jonathan Culler, *On Deconstruction: Theory and Criticism After Structuralism* (Ithaca, N. Y.: Cornell University Press, 1982).

10. Lee R. Edwards, "Women, Energy, and *Middlemarch*," *The Massachusetts Review; Woman: An Issue*, ed. Lee R. Edwards, Mary Heath, and Lisa Baskin (Boston and Toronto: Little, Brown & Co., 1972), pp. 223–38.

11. Wayne Booth, "Freedom of Interpretation: Bakhtin and the Challenge of Feminist Criticism," *Critical Inquiry* 9 (Sept. 1982), 45–76.

12. Lawrence Lipking, "Aristotle's Sister: A Poetics of Abandonment," *Critical Inquiry* 10 (Sept. 1983) 62, 76, 78.

13. (Chicago: University of Chicago Press, 1981).

14. Quoted in Fred Kaplan, *Thomas Carlyle: A Biography* (Ithaca, N. Y.: Cornell University Press, 1983), p. 486.

TO WRITE MY SELF
The Autobiographies of Afro-American Women

Elizabeth Fox-Genovese

Autobiographies of black women, each of which is necessarily personal and unique, constitute a running commentary on the collective experience of black women in the United States. These writings are inescapably grounded in the experience of slavery and the literary tradition of the slave narratives. Their common denominator, which establishes their integrity as a sub-genre, derives not from the general categories of race or sex, but from the historical experience of being black and female in a specific society at a specific moment and over succeeding generations. Black women's "autobiographies," as used here, includes some autobiographical fiction as well as formal autobiographies, both streams of which have sources in a rich oral Afro-American culture. Black women's autobiography resists reduction to either political or critical pieties and resists even more firmly reduction to mindless empiricism. In short, it commands an attention to theory and method that respects its distinctiveness as a discourse.

"The autobiographies of Afro-American women": each word invites a theoretical and practical battle. So does the concept itself. Why should the autobiographies of black women not be lumped with those of black men or those of white women? Politics justifies the differentiation, but its introduction challenges what some would see as the self-referential nature of the autobiographical text. To categorize autobiographies according to the race and gender of those who write them is to acknowledge some relation, however problematical, between the text and its author and, more, between the text and its author's experience. To acknowledge this relation is to challenge the prevailing theories of the multiple deaths of the subject, the self, and the author. Much contemporary theory has found the relations between politics—understood broadly as collective human experience—and the text difficult. These autobiographies defy any apolitical reading of texts, even, perhaps especially, when they seem to invite it.

To accept the ruling pieties about double oppression will not do. Simple addition does not add up to a new theoretical category. Sex assigns black women to the same category as white women; race assigns them to the same category as black men. Both feminist and black-nationalist critics consider their particular claims prior and decisive. Neither group shows much interest in class relations in particular or social relations in general. In all fairness, sex and race more readily lend themselves to symbolization than does class, and thus more readily lend themselves to representation, fabulation, and myth. Sex and race more obviously define what we intuitively perceive ourselves to be: male or female, white or black. But even these basic self-perceptions are socially learned and result from acts of (re)cognition. The question thus remains: why do we find it so much more acceptable to perceive ourselves as members of a sex or a race than as members of a gender or, even more, of a class?

Americans do not, as a people, like fences. Yet we, as a people, have spent most of our history raising them. Our open lands lie carved, parceled, and constructed. Our landscape features barriers. Gender and class transform sex and race into barriers, transform the forms of their exclusion into positive social values. To argue for the centrality of gender and class to any analysis of women's self-representation is not to deny the overpowering force of the racism and sexism that stalk women's experience. It is to argue that if we focus exclusively on sexism and racism we remain mired in the myths we are trying to dissipate.

In theory, it is possible to write about black women's autobiographies as so many discrete cases of the genre "autobiography." Like any other autobiographers, black women construct prose portraits of themselves as histories of their lives or of the salient aspects of their lives. The special relation between the autobiographer and the final text outshines all other considerations, especially referential considerations, and reduces specific aspects of the individual history to accidents. There is no theoretical distinction to be made between Jean Jacques Rousseau's *Confessions* and Zora Neale Hurston's *Dust Tracks on a Road*.[1]

Feminist critics, like critics of Afro-American and third world literature, are beginning to refuse the implied blackmail of Western, white, male criticism. The death of the subject and of the author may accurately reflect the perceived crisis of western culture and the bottomless anxieties of its most privileged subjects—the white male authors who had presumed to define it. Those subjects and those authors may, as it were, be dying. But it remains to be demonstrated that their deaths constitute the collective or generic death of the subject and the author. There remain plenty of subjects and authors who, never having had much opportunity to write in their own names or the names of their kind, much less in the name of the culture as a whole, are eager to seize the abandoned podium. But the white male cultural elite has not, in fact, abandoned the podium. It has merely insisted that the podium cannot be claimed in the name of any particular personal experience. And it has been busily trying to convince the world that intellectual excellence requires depersonalization and abstraction. The virtuosity, born of centuries of privilege, with which these ghosts of authors make their case, demands that others, who have something else to say, meet the ghosts' standards of pyrotechnics.[2]

Rejection of the pyrotechnics does not solve the problem of what to put in their place. The theoretical challenge lies in bringing the most finely honed skills to the service of a politically informed reading of texts. To read well, to read fully, is inescapably to read politically, but to foreground the politics, as if it could somehow be distinguished from the reading itself, is to render the reading suspect. Political and social considerations inform any reading, for all readers are political and social beings. To deny the applicability of political or social considerations is to take a political position. The reading of black women's autobiography forcefully exposes the extent to which the tools of criticism are shaped by the politics that guide them. Wole Soyinka cogently reminds us of the bourgeois character of "culture": its origins, its finality, and its instruments. But he also insists that to dismiss all "culture" because of its bourgeois contamination ends in "the destruction of all discourse."[3]

To discuss black women's autobiography we need a discourse, a way of thinking, that can justify the category.[4] We must begin with classification and then proceed to principles and practice of reading. The classification of black women's autobiography forces careful consideration of extra-textual conditions. Some current critical tendencies reject the relevance of the extra-textual and insist, in a manner reminiscent of what was once the "new criticism," on taking the text on its merits, free of such extraneous influences as the experience of the author. These days, taking the autobiographical text on its merits is further taken to expose as "romanticism" and "humanism" any concern with the "self" as, in some way, prior to the text. These views embody a sharp and understandable reaction against the more sentimental manifestations of bourgeois individualism, but hardly provide adequate critical standards for the classification of black women's autobiography as a distinct sub-genre.

To take the text on its merits legitimates Mattie Griffith's *Autobiography of a Slave Girl* as the autobiography of an Afro-American slave—which it was not.[5] As Robert Stepto has tellingly argued, authentication of the author as author of his or her own text ranked as an important concern for the authors of slave narratives. Stepto proposes a categorization of slave narratives according to the relation between plot or narrative and legitimation in the text as a whole.[6] Although Stepto does not discuss the earliest known prose writings by Afro-

American women, both Harriet Jacobs's *Incidents in the Life of a Slave Girl*
and Harriet Wilson's *Our Nig* contain legitimating documentation that different
readers may perceive as more or less integral parts of the texts. But both Harriet
Jacobs, who wrote under a pseudonym, and Harriet Wilson, who did not, felt
impelled, if not obliged, to provide verification of their being both themselves
and worthy women.[7] These tactical manoeuvres to authenticate the black woman's authorship oblige modern readers to respect these authors' concern for the
relation between their texts and their experience. They do not oblige us to
take any of the history offered in the texts at face value, merely to accept the
text as bearing some (possibly distorted) relation to reality.

The principles of classification must begin with history. Barbara Christian
insists upon the significance of periodization for understanding the development
of black women's fiction during the twentieth century. Gwendolyn Brooks, who
organized her own autobiography around the historical sea change of the emergence of a new form of black consciousness in the 1960s, forcefully emphasizes
the relation between history and consciousness. "There is indeed," she wrote
in 1972, in *Report from Part One*, "a new black today. He is different from
any the world has known. . . . And he is understood by no white." And, she
adds: "I have hopes for myself."[8] For Christian, Brooks, and other critics of
and participants in black women's culture, the relevant history concerns the
coming to consciousness of Afro-Americans during the second half of the twentieth century, and perhaps the growth of American women's coming to consciousness during the same period. The black movement and the feminist
movement, with all their internal currents and tensions, have presided over
the recent developments in Afro-American women's political and self-con-
sciousness. Both have contributed to the growing emphasis on varieties of Pan-
Africanism, including Pan-African feminism, and the repudiation of slavery as
a significant contributor to contemporary black consciousness. In this general
respect, race is taken to transcend class in the forging of Afro-American identities. The debates are long, tempestuous, and not susceptible to easy resolution.
Here, I shall try to cut through them in order to make a specific case about
the autobiographies of black women.

Nikki Giovanni has, with special force, made the case for the relation between
black women's autobiographies and changing political conditions. Responding
to a question from Claudia Tate, she rejected its very premise, saying that
"what was wrong with that question" was its assumption "that the self is not
part of the body politic. There's no separation."[9] For Giovanni, literature, to
be worthy of its claims, must reflect and seek to change reality. And the reality
black people have known has left much to be desired: "It's very difficult to
gauge what we have done as a people when we have been systematically subjected to the whims of other people."[10] For Giovanni, this collective subjection

to the whims of others has resulted in the alienation of black Americans from other Americans. For as black Americans, "living in a foreign nation we are, as the wandering Jew, both myth and reality." Giovanni believes that black Americans will always be "strangers. But our alienation is our greatest strength."[11] She does not believe that the alienation, or the collective history that produced it, makes black experience or writing incomprehensible to others. "I have not created a totally unique, incomprehensible feat. I can understand Milton and T.S. Eliot, so the critic can understand me. That's the critic's job."[12]

Personal experience can and must be understood in social context. The representation of that experience is susceptible to the critic's reading, whether or not the critic shares the personal experience. Giovanni rejects the claim that black writing should be the exclusive preserve of black critics—that it is qualitatively different from white writing, immune to any common principles of analysis, and thus severed from any common discourse. There is no argument about the ways in which the common discourse has treated black writing, especially the writing of black women: shamefully, outrageously, contemptuously, and silently. The argument concerns who can read black texts and concerns the principles of the reading. For as Soyinka said, if the denial of bourgeois culture ends in the destruction of discourse, the refusal of critical distance ends in the acceptance of an exceptionalism that portends extreme political danger. Giovanni explicitly and implicitly makes the main points: the identity of the self remains hostage to the history of the collectivity; the representation of the self in prose or verse invites the critical scrutiny of the culture. Both points undercut the myth of the unique individual and force a fresh look at the autobiographies of black women.

Selwyn R. Cudjoe, writing of Maya Angelou, has insisted that Afro-American autobiography, "as a form tends to be bereft of any *excessive subjectivism* and *mindless* egotism." Rather, Afro-American autobiographies present the experience of the individual "as reflecting a much more *im-personal* condition, the autobiographical subject emerging as an almost random member of the group, selected to tell his/her tale." Accordingly, he views Afro-American autobiography as "a *public* rather than a *private* gesture, *me-ism* gives way to *our-ism* and superficial concerns about *individual subject* usually gives way to the *collective subjection* of the group."[13] For Cudjoe, these characteristics establish black autobiography as objective and realistic. In so arguing, he is extending significantly the tradition of the slave narratives that sought to provide living, first-hand accounts of the evils of "that demon slavery" for a northern audience.[14]

The genre of black autobiography contains an important strand that could be subsumed under the general rubric of "report from the war-zone." Brooks uses "report" in her title. Giovanni's *Gemini* features a rather staccato, journalistic style.[15] Both depict the author's "self" indirectly, obliquely, through reports of actions more than discussions of states of mind. The responsibility to report on experience even more clearly shapes such autobiographies as those of Ida B. Wells and Era Bell Thompson.[16] In these ways, many of the autobiographical writings of black women, like those of many black men, do bear witness to a collective experience—to black powers of survival and creativity as well as to white oppression. Much of the autobiographical writing of black women eschews the confessional mode—the examinations of personal motives, the searchings of the soul—that white women autobiographers so frequently adopt. Black women's autobiographies seem torn between exhibitionism and secrecy, between self-display and self-concealment. The same is true of all autobiographies, but the proportions differ from text to text, perhaps from group to group of autobiographers. And the emotions and events displayed or concealed also differ.

All autobiographers confront the problem of readers, of the audience to whom their self-representation is addressed. Black female autobiographers confront the problem in an especially acute form—or so their texts suggest. Harriet Jacobs and Harriet Wilson both seem to have assumed that most of their readers would be white abolitionists or potential abolitionists. Both, especially Harriet Jacobs, also seem to have addressed themselves especially to white, middle-class women. Neither Jacobs nor Wilson identified with those likely readers, but both sought to interest them. And in both cases, the professed reason for seeking that interest was to instruct white women in the special horrors of slavery for women and to instruct them in the ways in which the tentacles of slavery reached into the interstices of northern society. Both texts reveal that their authors harbored deep bitterness towards northern society in general and northern white women in particular, even though they frequently expressed that bitterness indirectly. And the bitterness inescapably spills over into their imagined relations to their readers, into the ways in which they present themselves and their histories.

There is little evidence that black women autobiographers assumed that any significant number of other black women would read their work. To the extent that they have, until very recently, written for other black women, they seem to have written for younger women, for daughters, for those who would come after. Black women's autobiographies abound with evidence of or references to the love that black female autobiographers felt for and felt from their female elders: mothers, aunts, grandmothers, and, for the most part, those older women are represented as rural in identification and origin, if not always in current location. They tend to be immersed in folk communities, to be deeply religious, and to be the privileged custodians of the values and, especially, of the highest standards of their people. They are not necessarily literate. They are unlikely to spend money on any books except the Bible.

From Harriet Jacobs and Harriet Wilson onward, black female autobiographers wrote to be read by those who might influence the course of public events, might pay money for their book, or might authenticate them as authors. Neither Jacobs nor Wilson wrote primarily, much less exclusively, for members of the slave community. Subsequent black women autobiographers, many of whom have been writers or professional women, have also tended to write as much for white readers, or black male intellectuals, as for other black women. Their focus has been changing recently with the explosion of Afro-American women's fiction in the work of Tony Morrison, Alice Walker, Ntzonge Shange, Gloria Naylor, and many others.[17] But whatever the changes now, it is difficult to find evidence for the emergence of a distinctive Afro-American domestic literary tradition or women's culture during the nineteenth and even the first half of the twentieth century.

Afro-American women have written of themselves as persons and as women under very special conditions of colonization. In this respect, their writings cry out for comparison with those of white women. Prevailing opinion insists upon the special tradition of white American women's writing during the nineteenth and early twentieth centuries. Despite frequently sharp differences among feminist critics, there remains a general consensus that white women, as it were, wrote themselves out of their domestic tradition in both senses of the phrase: they wrote from the experience, and they wrote to subvert the constraints it imposed upon them. It has not been especially fashionable recently to insist upon the colonization of the imagination of white women writers, but it too existed. For white women did suffer exclusion from the dominant cultural traditions and frequently from the educations and careers that provided the institutional foundations for equal participation in those traditions. That is a different problem, but deserves mention as a way of locating the experience of black women in relation to the complex system of American culture in general. It has, in part, been possible for feminist critics to pass briefly over white women's relation to the so-called high culture of their period because of the general agreement about women's identification with literary domesticity. White women largely accepted the limitations of their sphere, which they sometimes turned to advantage, and wrote either as representatives of its values, or for its other members, or both. However one assesses the value of their efforts and of their contributions (neglected, silenced) to American culture, it remains beyond dispute that they self-consciously wrote as women, as the representatives of a gender.[18]

For white American women, the self comes wrapped in gender, or rather, gender constitutes the invisible, seamless wrapping of the self. Such is the point of gender in a stable society. For gender in the sense of society's prescriptions for how to grow up as a man or as a woman is, in stable societies, inculcated in tandem with, indissolubly from, the child's growing sense of "who I am." To be an "I" at all, to be a self, is to belong to a gender. Any society contains individuals who, for whatever reason, find their gender identification problematic. During the nineteenth and twentieth centuries, many American women began to find the attributes of or limitations on their gender problematic. But at least until the Second World War, most white American women apparently accepted their society's view of gender as in some deep way related to whom they perceived themselves to be. For gender, understood as the social construction of sexuality, mediates between sexual identity and social identity— binds the former to the latter, roots the latter in the former.

Under unstable social conditions, it is possible for gender as a normative model of being male or female to come unstuck from sexuality. Once the gaps between sexuality and gender begin to appear, men and women can begin to question whether gender flows naturally from sexuality, whether social demands on the individual are biologically determined. Gender identities derive from a system of gender relations. How to be a woman is defined in relation to how to be a man and the reverse. Neither maleness nor femaleness exists as an absolute.

In a society and culture like those of the American, a dominant gender system or model of gender relations wrestles with various subsystems or alternate systems. But from at least the beginnings of the nineteenth century and the consolidation of the special American version of the ideology of separate spheres, the dominant model of gender relations has exercised a powerful hegemony, in part because off its importance as an alternative to class relations as a system of social classification, and in part because of its invitation to different groups of immigrants who brought with them one or another version of separate male and female spheres and a commitment to one or another form of male dominance. The hegemony of that gender system has powerfully influenced the ways in which most American women have written about themselves and their lives, and has especially influenced their sense of their readers.

The experience and writing of Afro-American women have departed significantly from this model. The experience of Afro-American women has left them simultaneously alienated from and bound to the dominant models in ways that sharply differentiate their experience from that of white women. There is no reason to believe that Afro-American women experienced gender as the seamless wrapping of their selves. Slavery bequeathed to Afro-American women a double view of gender relations that fully exposed the artificial or problematic aspects of gender identification. Slavery stripped black men of the social attributes of manhood in general and fatherhood in particular. As a result, black women had no satisfactory social definition of themselves as women. This social "unmanning" of the men, with its negative consequences for the women, should, however, not be confused with the personal emasculation that some historians have erroneously insisted upon.[19] Sojourner Truth powerfully captured the contradictions in her address "Ar'n't I a Woman?" In effect, Truth was insisting on her own femaleness and then querying the relation between her experience of being female and the white middle-class experience of being a woman. She may not have put it quite that way, and she may not fully have elaborated the depths of the pain and the contradictions, but she exposed the main aspect of the problem: black slave women had suffered the pain of childbirth and the sorrow of losing children and had labored like men. Were they, or were they not women?[20]

Truth's query has been widely recognized as a challenge to the possible self-satisfaction of middle-class men and women with respect to black slave women, who were not normally helped over puddles or wrapped in protective coverings. It has less widely been recognized as a challenge to assumptions about the nature of the links between femaleness and self-perception or identity in Afro-American women. Truth effectively chided white men and women for their racism—for not welcoming black women into the sisterhood of womanhood. But there is more to the story.

Truth counterposed "I"—the self—and "woman" in her hostile challenge to her white audience. Black female autobiographers have done the same, although not always with such open defiance. The tension at the heart of black women's autobiography derives in large part from the chasm between the autobiographer's intuitive sense of herself and her attitude toward her probable readers. Imagined readers shape the ways in which an autobiographer constructs the narrative of her life. Harriet Jacobs, in *Incidents in the Life of a Slave Girl*, left no doubt about whom she thought she was writing for: "O, you happy free women, contrast *your* New Year's day with that of the poor bond-woman!" (14).

Jacobs wrote, at least in part, to introduce the world to the special horrors of slavery for women. To achieve her goal, she sought to touch the hearts of northern white women and, accordingly, wrote to the extent possible in their idiom. She so doggedly followed the tone and model of sentimental domestic fiction, that for a long time it was assumed that her editor, Lydia Maria Child, had written the book. Jacobs's surviving correspondence proves that she, not Child, wrote her own story, as she claimed in its subtitle "written by herself."[21] And Jacobs's text differs significantly in tone and content from other examples of domestic fiction. She casts her withering indictment of slavery as the violation of womanhood. Time and again she asserts and demonstrates that if slavery is bad for men, it is worse for women. Thinking that she understands the northern middle-class female audience, she depicts the horrors of slavery for women as specifically related to the assaults upon female chastity and conjugal domesticity. Linda Brent, Jacobs's self in the narrative, grows up in the shadow of her master's determination to possess her sexually. She claims to fend off his advances as an affront to her chastity. Ultimately, her determination to avoid him leads her, after her master has prohibited her sale and marriage to the free black man she loves, to accept another white man as a lover and to bear him two children. One important strand of her story concerns the ways in which she atones for this "fall" and, especially, regains the respect and love of her own daughter. In some sense, Jacobs attempts to present her resistance to her master as a defense of her virtue, even though that defense leads her into a loss of "virtue" by another route. Jacobs does not fully resolve the contradictions in her behavior and principles at this level of discourse, however hard she tries. Ultimately, she throws herself on the pity—and guilt—of her readers, as she threw herself on the pity of her daughter. But Jacobs's text also invites another reading or, to put it differently, conceals another text.

Jacobs begins her narrative: "I was born a slave; but I never knew it till six years of happy childhood had passed away"(3). The claim not to have recognized one's condition —of race or of enslavement—until six or seven years of age is common among Afro-American authors.[22] For Jacobs, that opening sentence underscores the difference between condition and consciousness and thereby distances the self from the condition. But Jacobs never suggests that the condition does not, in some measure, influence the self. She insists that her father "had more of the feelings of a freeman than is common among slaves," thereby implicitly acknowledging the difference between slavery and freedom in the development of an independent self. In the same passage, she reveals how heavily slavery could weigh upon the slaves' sense of manhood. On one occasion Jacobs's father and mistress both happened to call to her brother at the same moment. The boy, after a moment's hesitation, went to the mistress. The father sharply reproved him: "You are *my* child . . . and when I call you, you should come immediately, if you have to pass through fire and water" (7). The father's desire to command the primary obedience of his own child flows from his feelings of being a free man and contradicts the harshest realities of slavery. Slavery stripped men of fatherhood. Even a free father could not call "his" child by a slave wife his own, for the child, following the condition of the mother, remained a slave. Jacobs is, surely not by accident, depicting a spirit of manliness and an instinctive grasp of the virtues of freedom in her father as the introduction to her own story of resistance.

Jacobs's narrative rests upon every conceivable element of fantasy and ambiguity. If her father had the feelings of a free man, both of her parents were

mulattoes who lived a model of conjugal domesticity, and her maternal grandmother was the daughter of a South Carolina planter who apparently had in-
herited The Chivalry's own sense of honor—more than could be said for her
owners. Jacobs, in other words, endows herself with a pedigree of physical,
mental, and moral comeliness. She is not like the other slaves among whom
she lives. She has the capacity to rise above her condition. Her sense of herself
in relation to the other slaves leaves something to be desired for an opponent
of slavery, or, worse, it reflects either her assimilation of "white" values or her
determination to play to what she takes to be the prejudices of her audience.
Jacobs offers a confused picture of the relation between the identity and behavior of Afro-Americans, including herself, and the effects of slavery. If slavery
is evil, it has evil consequences. If those evil consequences include a breaking
of the spirit of the enslaved, then how can slaves be credited with character
and will? The questions circle on and on, admitting of no easy answers. They
clearly plague Jacobs.

These difficult questions do not seriously cloud Jacobs's sense of her self.
They affect her sense of how best to present that self to others, her sense of
the relation between her self and her gender, her sense of the relation between
self and social condition. The awareness of white readers deeply influences the
ways in which she depicts life under slavery. But under, or woven through,
the discourse for the readers runs a discourse for herself. For Jacobs, the issues
between her and her master did not primarily concern virtue, chastity, sexuality, or any of the rest. They concerned the conflict of two wills. Having
described her master's foul intentions towards her, she adds that he had told
her "I was made for his use, made to obey his command in *every* thing; that
I was nothing but a slave, whose will must and should surrender to his . . . "
(16). The words make her "puny" arm feel stronger than it ever had: "The war
of my life had begun; and though one of God's most powerless creatures, I
resolved never to be conquered. Alas, for me!"(17). The "alas for me" should
not be read as some regret about her determination or any acknowledgement
that such willful feelings might be inappropriate for a woman, but as a confirmation that everything that follows follows directly from her determination not
to be conquered.

Jacobs's narrative of her successful flight from slavery can be read as a journey
or progress from her initial state of innocence through the mires of her struggle
against her social condition, to a prolonged period of ritual, or mythic, concealment, on to the flight itself, and finally to the state of knowledge that
accompanies her ultimate acquisition of freedom. The myth or metaphor of the
journey to selfhood is as old as culture, although it has carried a special resonance for Western Christian, notably Protestant, culture. Jacobs, in some respects like Harriet Wilson, registers the end of the journey as a rather bleak

dawn on a troubled landscape. Here is no pot of gold at the end of the rainbow. The self-knowledge that accrues consists above all in the recognition that there is no resting place for the fugitive. The struggle for the dignity of the self persists. Insult and injury abound in freedom as under slavery, albeit in different forms. Life remains a war. But the focused struggle of wills with the master has given way to a more generalized struggle to affirm the self in a hostile, or indifferent, environment.

Significantly, for Harriet Wilson, whose narrative unfolds entirely in freedom, the primary enemy is a woman rather than a man. To explore the respective cultural roles of men and women as heads of households in slave and free society respectively would take us far afield. But the difference should be noted, not least because that enemy represents the world of female domesticity and, inescapably, underscores the possible adversarial relation between the Afro-American autobiographer and her readers.[23] Wilson's narrative remains even more problematical as autobiography than Jacobs's, for it is cast as a fiction. I can only note in passing that its structure commands close attention, especially Wilson's purpose in beginning with the story of her white mother Mag Smith's marrying the black man who has come to love her as the only alternative to starvation.

Taken together, Jacobs's and Wilson's narratives establish some important characteristics of black women's autobiographical writing. Both work with the metaphor of the journey. Both betray mixed emotions towards their probable and intended (white, female) readers. Both embrace some of the rhetoric and conventions of literary domesticity even as they challenge the reigning pieties of its discourse. Both subvert the candor that they seem to promise those readers.

The problem of readers, of whom one is writing for, persists in the autobiographical writing of black women, although it assumes a variety of forms. Maya Angelou, writing in the late 1960s, noted in an apparent aside in the first volume of her own autobiography: "If you ask a negro where he's been, he'll tell you where he's going."[24] Her observation should be appreciated in the context of Zora Neale Hurston's calling storytelling "lying"—and then offering the world her own, demonstrably inaccurate, autobiography.[25]

Hurston's autobiography poignantly captures the apparent dilemmas of black women autobiographers—or writers or intellectuals—of her generation. *Dust Tracks on a Road* inimitably combines all the best and worst of Hurston's intellect and imagination. Critics and scholars have demonstrated that it does not pass muster as a factual account of her life, beginning with its inaccurate date of birth. Theoretically, for modern critics of the text-in-itself, that mere inaccuracy should not matter: take the text on its merits and to hell with the facts. But Hurston's deceptions in *Dust Tracks* may exceed mere facts. She further decked it out with a series of observations on contemporary politics and race relations that seriously disturbed some of her most devoted would-be admirers. Finally, although Hurston wrote much more in the idiom of Afro-American culture, even folk culture, than Jacobs or Wilson, her text does not inspire confidence about the authenticity of her self-revelation. In most respects, *Dust Tracks* constitutes a marvel of self-concealment. Hurston, like the story-tellers on the porch whom she celebrated in *Mules and Men*, delighted in "lying."[26]

Hurston's autobiography deserves much more detailed attention than can be given here, but, as the single most important link between the different phases in black women's autobiographies, it commands at least a preliminary assessment. Hurston should be understood as a woman who was, so far as her self-representation was concerned, primarily concerned with a "self" unconstrained by gender. She clearly describes her attitude in the autobiography: "I did not know then, as I know now, that people are prone to build a statue of the kind of person that it pleases them to be." Few people, she adds, "want to be forced to ask themselves, 'What if there is no me like my statue?' The thing to do is to grab the broom of anger and drive off the beast of fear"(34). Hurston became an expert on the anger and the fear. Determined to become a person of respect, to become someone, she wrestled, not always gracefully or successfully, with the expectations of those around her. In mediating between the world of Eatonville, from which she came, and the worlds of Baltimore, Washington, D.C., and New York, to which she moved, she functioned as a translator. In fact, Hurston used her acquired skills as anthropologist to describe the world of her childhood. Her uncommon gift for language brought that world to life in her pages, but her obsession with self-concealment led her to veil the nature of her identification with her origins. Hurston's narrator is her statue—the amused observer she wished to become.

Hurston's autobiography singularly lacks any convincing picture of her own feelings. Her little essay on "love," which purports to convey her adult feelings towards men, reads like the amused and balanced memories of a perfectly successful individual. Men are presented as having loved her even more than she loved them. Love is portrayed as having invariably treated her well. No hint of tragedy, longing, or crippling loss. And maybe there was none, although extratextual sources invite skepticism. But the passage itself looks more like a screen than a window. Nothing in *Dust Tracks* suggests that Hurston trusted her readers. Nothing precisely identifies them, although she cultivates an arresting mixture of the urbane intellectual and the *enfant terrible*. Presumably, she expected to be read by New York intellectuals, black and white. And, presumably, she was not about to trust them with her private self.

Hurston does provide clues about where she wants to go, what kind of statue she wants to build. She resoundingly repudiates any possible legacy of slavery for her own life or self-representation. Slavery, however unfortunate, is a thing of the past that has left no relevant legacy: "I have no personal memory of those times, and no responsibility for them" (282). Above all, she fears the debilitating effects of bitterness: to be bitter is to become dependent, crippled, humiliated. She appears to have forgotten her own earlier evocation of the "broom of anger," appears not to want to explore the place in her responses of righteous anger. The broom of anger was to sweep away fear. She is no longer acknowledging fear. By collapsing anger into bitterness and repudiating bitterness as, in some way, an unclean emotion, she is denying the need for anger. Facing the white reader, she prefers to deny the relevance of previous oppression to her sense of herself. Just as clearly as Jacobs, she expects "you"—her reader—to be white: "So I give you all my right hand of fellowship and love . . . In my eyesight, you lose nothing by not looking just like me. . . . Let us all be kissing-friends" (286).

Hurston also refuses to attribute any significance to race. Having been bombarded with the problem of race for years, she saw the light when she "realized that I did not have to consider any racial group as a whole. God made them duck by duck and that was the only way I could see them" (235). She learned that the color of the skin provided no measure of the person inside, even though she bitterly points out that blacks, like whites, rank blacks according to the degree of lightness of their skin. She then reminds her readers that she is of mixed race. Finally, with deep ambiguity, she asserts: "I maintain that I have been a Negro three times—a Negro baby, a Negro girl and a Negro woman." Yet she knows not what "the Negro in America is like " (237). The Negro does not exist. Independent of the political problems—and Hurston's politics were nothing if not complex—this statement casts considerable doubt about Hurston's identification as a woman. If the Negro does not exist, and the only times that she has been a Negro included the times at which she was a girl and a woman, then what? The reader is left to complete the syllogism.

Dust Tracks constitutes only one panel in the triptych of Hurston's autobiography. The second can be found in her extraordinary novel, *Their Eyes Were Watching God*, the third in her collections of black folklore, notably *Mules and Men*. Hurston's collections of folklore provide a way for her to appropriate the collective history of the community to which she belongs. *Their Eyes Were Watching God*, which is widely acknowledged as an autobiographical novel, offers her most sustained attempt to provide some representation of her own emotional life. Here, I can only evoke it as an indispensable counterpoint to *Dust Tracks*, and emphasize one theme. In the novel's most famous phrase, Hurston depicts the protagonist Janie's grandmother as saying: "Honey, de white man is de ruler of everything as fur as Ah been able tuh find out." There may be some place "way off in de ocean" in which the black man rules, "but we don't know nothin' but what we see." The white man throws down his load and forces the black man to pick it up. "He pick it up because he have to, but he don't tote it. He hand it to his womenfolks. De nigger woman is de mule uh de world so fur as Ah can see" (29). Janie's grandmother has been praying for it to be different with her. Hurston portrays the answer to that prayer as Janie's relations with Teacake—mutual delight in shared sexuality.

The world that Hurston depicts in *Their Eyes Were Watching God* closely resembles that of Maya Angelou's Stampes, Arkansas. In *I Know Why the Caged Bird Sings*, Hurston does not emphasize the oppressive weight of the neighboring white community as much as Angelou does. But she does not shy away from its influence on the possible conditions of black lives, even in an entirely black community. Her plot mercilessly reveals the burdens that a legacy of slavery and racism impose on black people. In particular, she subtly, almost deceptively, offers hints of her real feelings about what it means to be a black woman. She reveals the extent to which the black community—or black men— have embraced the gender conventions of white bourgeois society. Black men seek to transfer their burdens to black women by forcing those women into domestic corsets. A woman like Janie resists. She retains her commitment to equality and partnership with the man she loves. She, above all, retains a commitment to the possible joy of love and sexuality. But even at her moment of greatest success, the legacy of the social features of black manhood leads her Teacake into a terrible battle. And at the novel's close, which is also its beginning, she is returning home to other black women alone—and childless. Mules. Metaphors or reality? Mules abound in Hurston's work. Is she inviting us to understand black women like herself as of mixed ancestry and incapable of reproduction? Is she inviting us, as she seems to be, to recognize both the richness and the deadend of black women's own traditions? For me, at least, a clear answer would be premature. But the elements of the puzzle should not be denied.

Hurston provides numerous clues throughout *Dust Tracks* that her primary identification, her primary sense of herself transcends gender. Most dramatically, in a manner reminiscent of other mythic births on mythically stormy nights, she relates that at her birth her mother was taken unawares and without assistance.[27] Fate intervened by sending "a white man of many acres and things" to "granny" for her mother—to fill in for the missing midwife, Aunt Judy. Wonderful reversals: Zora was brought into the world by a man rather than a woman, by a white rather than a black. And she concludes the chapter in which she relates her birth with a passage about her mother's alarm that at an early age Zora manifested a clear tendency to keep on walking towards the horizon. The mother explained this behavior by blaming "a woman who was an enemy

of hers" for sprinkling " 'travel dust' around the doorstep the day I was born."
Zora wonders at her mother's acceptance of such an explanation. "I don't know
why it never occurred to her to connect my tendency with my father, who
didn't have a thing on his mind but this town and the next one." She might
have taken a hint from his wanderlust. "Some children are just bound to take
after their fathers in spite of women's prayers" (32).

Hurston vacillates among sympathy, scorn, and amused tolerance in her
discussion of the women of the black community from which she springs. She
movingly depicts her grief and guilt at her own inability to carry out her dying
mother's instructions because of the opposition of the other members of the
black community. And she clearly links her own departure from the world of
her childhood with her Mother's death. She shows flashes of tenderness. But
her identification of herself with other black women remains shaky. She refuses
the double role of victim and warrior that Jacobs constructs for herself. For
Hurston to admit the conditions or causes of her possible victimization is to
belittle herself. But her goals for herself—her statue—remain shaped by that
refusal: she aspires, in some way, to transcend the constraints of group identification. By insisting on being a self independent of history, race, and gender,
she comes close to insisting on being a self independent of body.

Hurston, writing at a particular moment under the influence of the Harlem
Renaissance and the increasingly successful attempts of Afro-American men to
establish a model of cultural respectability, as well as under the shadow of
emerging professional success for some middle-class white women, sought to
carve a compelling statue for herself. Much like Harriet Jacobs, she saw herself
at war with the world in her attempt to defend her integrity. Much like Harriet
Jacobs, she refused the limitations of gender and cultivated what she took to
be the language of her readers only to subvert—or manipulate—their values.
But where Jacobs warred with slavery, Hurston warred with a dominant bourgeois culture in which she sought acceptance as an equal. No less than Jacobs
did Hurston war with the legacy of slavery for black women. But changing
times had made it difficult for her to name the war. And, unable or unwilling
to name that war, she spun web upon web of deception so that her statue of
herself would appear to be standing in clouds.

Those who came after, especially Angelou, Giovanni, and Brooks, would find
new names for the war and a new acceptance of their own black female bodies.
But they would also benefit from the slow emergence of a black, female read-
ership. And even they would remain at odds with the gender identifications
of white society. The gap between black women and the dominant model of
womanhood continues to provide the richness and the mystery of black women's
writing. The account of origins remains, at least in part, a map of "where I'm
bound." The account of the black woman's self cannot be divorced from the

history of that self or the history of the people among whom it took shape. It also cannot be divorced from the language through which it is represented, or from the readers of other classes and races who not merely lay claim to it but who have helped to shape it. To write the account of one's self is to inscribe it in a culture that for each of us is only partially our own. For black women autobiographers, the gap between the self and the language in which it is inscribed looms especially large and remains fraught with struggle.

Few have written more movingly or with greater anger of the toll extracted by cultural colonization than Frantz Fanon. In particular, he walked the narrow boundary between recording the dreadful impact of specific instances of colonization and raising the concept of colonization to the status of a metaphor for all of our dependent status in a dominant culture. The autobiographies of Afro-American women similarly delineate a specific history of colonization and offer a compelling metaphor for the dependency of the human spirit on the communities and forms of expression to which it belongs. Black women like Jacobs and Wilson insisted on their right to an independent self under conditions in which they could counterpoise the self to enslavement. Since emancipation, black women have been torn between their independent relation to the dominant culture and their people's relation to it. In complex ways, their self-perceptions retain a characteristically uneasy relation to the wrappings of gender. Is the black woman writer first a self, a solitary statue? Or is she first a woman? And if the latter, in relation to whom? No dilemma could more clearly expose the condition of any self as hostage to society, politics, and language.

NOTES

1. For my own views on autobiography as a genre, see Elizabeth Fox-Genovese, ed. and trans., *The Autobiography of Du Pont de Nemours* (Wilmington, Del.: Scholarly Resources Press, 1984), pp. 38–51. Among the many other recent works on autobiography, see James Olney, ed., *Autobiography: Essays Theoretical and Critical* (Princeton: Princeton University Press, 1980); Karl J. Weintraub, *The Value of the Individual: Self and Circumstance in Autobiography* (Chicago: University of Chicago Press, 1978); PhiPlippe Lejeune, *Le pacte Autobiographique* (Paris: Editions du Seuil, 1975); Janet Varner Gunn, *Autobiography: Toward a Poetics of Experience* (Philadelphia: University of Pennsylvania Press, 1982); Albert E. Stone, *Autobiographical Occasions and Original Acts* (Philadelphia: University of Pennsylvania Press, 1982); and, for a critical review of recent trends, Candace Lang, "Autobiography in the Aftermath of Romanticism," *Diacritics* (Winter 1982), 2–16.

2. The quintessential statement of the position remains Michel Foucault, "Qu'est-ce un auteur," *Bulletin de la Société Française de Philosophie* 63, no. 3 (1969), 75–104. For a third world feminist defense of deconstruction, see Gayatri Chakravorty Spivak, " 'Draupadi' by Mashaveta Devi," *Critical Inquiry* 8, no. 2 (Winter 1981), 381–402. For

a defense of the claims of gender and race, see also her "The Politics of Interpretations,"
Critical Inquiry 9, no. 1 (September 1982), 259–78.

3. Wole Soyinka, "The critic and society: Barthes, leftocracy and other mythologies,"
in *Black Literature and Literary Theory*, ed. Henry Louis Gates, Jr. (New York: Methuen, 1984), p. 55.

4. On the general problem of black women's autobiography see Regina Blackburn,
"In Search of the Black Female Self: African-American Women's Autobiographies and
Ethnicity," in Estelle C. Jelinek, ed., *Women's Autobiography: Essays in Criticism*
(Bloomington: Indiana University Press, 1980), pp. 133–48.

5. Mattie Griffiths, *Autobiography of a Female Slave* (New York: Redfield, 1857;
reprint Miami: Mnemosyne, 1969).

6. Robert Burns Stepto, "I Rose and Found My Voice: Narration, Authentication,
and Authorial Control in Four Slave Narratives," in Charles T. Davis and Henry Louis
Gates, eds., *The Slave's Narrative* (New York: Oxford University Press, 1985), pp. 225–
41, apparently reprinted from his *From Behind the Veil: A Study of Afro-American
Narrative* (Urbana: University of Illinois Press, 1979), pp. 3–31.

7. [Harriet Jacobs] Linda Brent, *Incidents in the Life of a Slave Girl. Written by
Herself.*, ed. Lydia Maria Child, new ed. Walter Teller (New York: Harcourt Brace
Jovanovich, 1973; orig. ed. 1861); Harriet E. Wilson, *Our Nig; or, Sketches from the
Life of a Free Black, in a Two-Story White House, North. Showing That Slavery's
Shadows Fall Even There. By "Our Nig."* ed. Henry Louis Gates (New York: Vintage
Books, 1983).

8. Gwendolyn Brooks, *Report From Part One* (Detroit, Mich.: Broadside Press,
1972), pp. 85–86. Brooks's autobiography should be read in conjunction with her autobiographical novel, *Maud Martha* (Boston: Atlantic Monthly Press, 1953). See Mary
Helen Washington, " 'Taming all that anger down': rage and silence in Gwendolyn
Brooks's *Maud Martha*," in Gates, ed., *Black Literature and Literary Theory*, pp. 249–
62. Barbara Christian, *Black Women Novelists: The Development of a Tradition, 1892–
1976* (Westport, Conn.: Greenwood Press, 1980), and her *Black Feminist Criticism:
Perspectives on Black Women Writers* (New York: Pergamon Press, 1985).

9. Claudia Tate, ed., *Black Women Writers at Work* (New York: Continuum, 1983),
p. 62.

10. Ibid., p. 63.

11. Ibid., p. 70.

12. Ibid., p. 64.

13. Selwyn R. Cudjoe, "Maya Angelou and the Autobiographical Statement," in Mari
Evans, ed., *Black Women Writers (1950–1980)* (Garden City, N.Y.: Doubleday, 1984),
p. 9.

14. The phrase is that of Harriet Wilson in *Our Nig*.

15. Brooks, *Report From Part One*; Nikki Giovanni, *Gemini: An Extended Autobiographical Statement on My First Twenty-Five Years of Being a Black Poet* (Indianapolis:
Bobbs Merrill, 1971).

16. Alfreda M. Duster, ed., *The Autobiography of Ida B. Wells* (Chicago: University
of Chicago Press, 1970); Era Bell Thompson, *American Daughter*, rev. ed. (Chicago:
University of Chicago Press, 1967).

17. See Christian, *Black Female Novelists* for a preliminary periodization. For a sharp
assessment of the relation between one black novelist and her readers, see Trudier
Harris, "On *The Color Purple*, Stereotypes, and Silence," *Black American Literature
Forum* 18, no. 4 (Winter 1984), 155–61.

18. The work on white women's writing, in sharp contrast to that on black women's
writing, has become extensive. Among many, see, Nina Baym, *Woman's Fiction: A
Guide to Novels by and about Women in America, 1820–1870* (Ithaca, N.Y.: Cornell

University Press, 1978); Mary Kelley, *Private Woman, Public Stage: Literary Domesticity in Nineteenth-Century America* (New York: Oxford University Press, 1984); Annette Kolodny, *The Land Before Her: Fantasy and Experience of the American Frontiers, 1630–1860* (Chapel Hill: University of North Carolina Press, 1984).

19. See in particular, Stanley Elkins, *Slavery. A Problem in American Institutional and Intellectual Life* (Chicago: University of Chicago Press, 1959). Elkins has not significantly revised his position in the two subsequent "revised" editions. Cf. Ann J. Lane, ed., *The Debate Over Slavery: Stanley Elkins and His Critics* (Urbana: University of Illinois Press, 1971). For alternate views of the effect of slavery on Afro-American men, see Vincent Harding, *There Is A River: The Black Struggle for Freedom in America* (New York: Harcourt Brace Jovanovich, 1981), and Eugene D. Genovese, *Roll, Jordan, Roll: The World the Slaves Made* (New York: Pantheon, 1974).

20. *Narrative of Sojourner Truth, A Bondswoman of Olden Time*, Olive Gilbert, comp. (New York: Arno Press, 1968; orig. ed., 1878), pp. 133–34. For a recent overview of women's position under slavery see Deborah G. White, *Ar'n't I A Woman: Female Slaves in the Plantation South* (New York: Norton, 1985).

21. Jean Fagan Yellin, "Texts and Contexts of Harriet Jacobs' *Incidents in the Life of a Slave Girl: Written by Herself*," in Charles Davis and Louis Henry Gates, eds., *The Slave's Narrative* (New York: Oxford University Press, 1985), pp. 262–82; and her "Written By Herself: Harriet Jacobs' Slave Narrative," *American Literature* 53, no. 3 (November 1981), 479–86. For Jacobs's own account of her experience and authorship, see her correspondence, University of Rochester Library, Post Family Papers. Dorothy Sterling has reprinted some of Jacobs's letters in her excellent anthology, *We Are Your Sisters: Black Women in the Nineteenth Century* (New York: Norton, 1984), pp. 73–84. On the general tradition of the slave narratives, see, among many, Marion Wilson Starling, *The Slave Narrative: Its Place in History* (Boston: G. K. Hall, 1981); John Sekora and Darwin T. Turner, eds., *The Art of Slave Narrative* (Macomb: Northern Illinois University Press, 1982); James Olney, " 'I Was Born': Slave Narratives, Their Status as Autobiography and as Literature," in Davis and Gates, eds., *The Slave's Narrative*, pp. 148–75; Houston A. Baker, Jr., "Autobiographical Acts and the Voice of the Southern Slave," *loc. cit.*, pp. 242–61; and Charles T. Davis, "The Slave Narrative: First Major Art Form in an Emerging Black Tradition," in his *Black Is the Color of the Cosmos: Essays on Afro-American Literature and Culture 1942–1981*, ed. Louis Henry Gates (New York: Garland Publishing, 1982), pp. 83–119. As a rule, the general treatments of slave narratives take little or no account of any female perception, in part because so few women either escaped or wrote narratives.

22. See, among many, Zora Neale Hurston's *Their Eyes Were Watching God* (Urbana: University of Illinois Press, 1978; orig. ed. 1937), p. 21: "Ah was wid dem white chillun so much till Ah didn't know Ah wuzn't white till Ah was round six years old."

23. See Louis Henry Gates's introduction to *Our Nig*. He offers a preliminary exploration of the role of white women in the novel, but does not discuss the problem of Wilson's attitude towards her readers. For a fuller discussion of the differences between women's roles in northern and southern households, see my *Southern Women, Black and White* (Chapel Hill: University of North Carolina Press, 1987).

24. Maya Angelou, *I Know Why the Caged Bird Sings* (New York: Random House, 1969), p. 86.

25. Zora Neale Hurston, *Dust Tracks on a Road: An Autobiography*, 2nd ed., ed. Robert Hemenway (Urbana: University of Illinois Press, 1984; orig. ed. 1942). On the facts of Hurston's life and the variants of the text, see Hemenway's introduction. See also his comprehensive study of her life and work, *Zora Neale Hurston. A Literary Biography* (Urbana: University of Illinois Press, 1977). For a composite picture of Hurston culled from her own writings, see Alice Walker, ed., *I Love Myself When I Am*

Laughing . . . And Then Again When I Am Looking Mean and Impressive: A Zora Neale Hurston Reader (Old Westbury, N.Y.: The Feminist Press, 1979). See also Alice Walker's essays on Hurston, "Zora Neale Hurston: A Cautionary Tale and a Partisan View," and "Looking for Zora," in her *In Search of Our Mothers' Gardens: Womanist Prose* (New York: Harcourt Brace Jovanovich, 1983); and Barbara Johnson, "Metaphor, metonymy and voice in *Their Eyes Were Watching God*," in Gates, ed., *Black Literature and Literary Theory*, pp. 205–20.

26. Zora Neale Hurston, *Mules and Men* (New York: Harper and Row, 1970; orig. ed. 1935). See also her *Tell My Horse* (Berkeley: Turtle Island, 1981; orig. ed., 1938).

27. Black women writers' use of African and Western myths deserves more attention than it has yet received. Angelou, for example, in *Gather Together In My Name* (New York: Random House, 1974), reworks the Persephone myth for her own purposes. Jacobs, in the account of her period of concealment and flight in *Incidents* draws on African mythology. Henry Louis Gates's concept of the "signifying monkey" opens the discussion, but does not pay special attention to the blending of cultures in Afro-American women's imaginations. See his "The "Blackness of Blackness': A Critique of the Sign and the Signifying Monkey," *Critical Inquiry* 9, no. 4 (June 1983), 685–724, and his book *The Signifying Monkey* (New York: Oxford University Press, 1985). For a sensitive discussion of Afro-American culture, see Lawrence W. Levine, *Black Culture and Black Consciousness: Afro-American Folk Thought from Slavery to Freedom* (New York: Oxford University Press, 1977).

A HATEFUL PASSION, A LOST LOVE

Hortense J. Spillers

> When I think of how essentially alone black
> women have been—alone because of our
> bodies, over which we have had so little
> control; alone because the damage done to
> our men has prevented their closeness and
> protection; and alone because we have had
> no one to tell us stories about ourselves; I
> realize that black women writers are an
> important and comforting prescence in my
> life. Only they know my story. It is absolutely
> necessary that they be permitted to discover
> and interpret the entire range and spectrum
> of the experience of black women and not be
> stymied by preconcieved conclusions. Because
> of these writers, there are more models of
> how it is possible for us to live, there are
> more choices for black women to make, and
> there is a larger space in the universe for us.[1]

Toni Morrison's *Sula* is a rebel idea, both for her creator[2] and for Morrison's
audience. To read *Sula* is to encounter a sentimental education so sharply
discontinuous from the dominant traditions of Afro-American literature in the
way that it compels and/or deadlocks the responses that the novel, for all its
brevity and quiet intrusion on the landscape of American fiction, is, to my
mind, the single most important irruption of black women's writing in our era.
I am not claiming for this novel any more than its due; *Sula* (1973) is not a
stylistic innovation. But in bringing to light dark impulses no longer contraband
in the black American female's cultural address, the novel inscribes a new
dimension of being, moving at last in contradistinction to the tide of virtue and
pathos that tends to overwhelm black female characterization in a monolith of
terms and possibilities. I regard Sula the character as a literal and figurative
breakthrough toward the assertion of what we may call, in relation to her literary
"relatives," new female being.

Without predecessors in the recent past of Afro-American literature, Sula is anticipated by a figure four decades removed from Morrison's symbol smasher: Janie Starks in Zora Neale Hurston's *Their Eyes Were Watching God* (1937). By intruding still a third figure—Vyry Ware of Margaret Walker's *Jubilee* (1966)—we lay hold of a pattern of contrast among three African-American female writers, who pose not only differences of character in their perception of female possibilities, but also a widely divergent vocabulary of feeling. This article traces the changes in black female characterization from *Sula* back toward the literary past, beginning with Margaret Walker's Vyry and Zora Neale Hurston's Janie, forward again to *Sula* and Morrison. It argues that the agents which these novels project are strikingly different, and that the differences take shape primarily around questions of moral and social value. And it explores the mediations through which all three writers translate sociomoral constructs into literary modes of discourse.

Margaret Walker's Vyry Ware belongs to, embodies, a corporate ideal. The black woman in her characterization exists for the race, in its behalf, and in maternal relationship to its profoundest needs and wishes. Sula, on the other hand, lives for Sula and has no wish to "mother" anyone, let alone the black race in some symbolic concession to a collective need. If Vyry is woman-for-the-other, then Sula is woman-for-self. Janie Starks represents a dialectical point between the antithesis, and the primary puzzle of *Their Eyes Were Watching God* is the contradiction of motives through which Janie Starks has her being; in other words, Janie might have been Sula, but the latter only through a resolution of negative impulses. These three characters, then, describe peak points in a cultural and historical configuration of literary issues. In *Sula's* case, the old love of the collective, for the collective, is lost, and passions are turned antagonistic, since, as the myth of the black woman goes, the latter is loving only insofar as she protects her children and forgives her man. The title of this article is a kind of shorthand for these longhanded notations.

The scheme of these observations, as I have already implied, is not strictly chronological. Hurston's affinities are much closer to Morrison's than Walker's, even though Hurston's *Their Eyes Were Watching God* was written nearly fifty years ago. The critical scheme I offer here is not precisely linear, because the literary movement I perceive, which theoretically might take in more women writers than my representative selections, does not progress neatly from year to year in an orderly advance of literary issues and strategies. My method aims at a dialectics of process, with these affinities and emphases tending to move in cycles rather than straight lines. I see no myth of descent operating here as in Harold Bloom's "anxiety of influence," exerted, in an oedipal-like formation, by great writers on their successors.[3] The idea-form which I trace here, articulated in three individual writers' metaphors and patterns of theme and structure, does not emerge within this community of writers in strict sequential order. Ironically, it is exactly the right *not* to accede to the simplifications and mystifications of a strictly historiographical time line that now promises the greatest freedom of discourse to black people, to black women, as critics, teachers, writers, and thinkers.

As the opening exercise in the cultural and literary perspective that this article wishes to consider, then, we turn immediately to Morrison's Sula, the "youngest" of three heroines. Few of the time-honored motifs of female behavioral description will suit her: not "seduction and betrayal," applied to a network of English and American fictions; not the category of "holy fool," as exemplified in various Baldwinian configurations of female character; not the patient long-suffering female, nor the female authenticated by male imagination. Compared with past heroines of black American fiction, Sula exists foremost in her own consciousness. To that extent, *Sula* and *Their Eyes Were Watching God* are studies in contrast to Walker and share the same fabric of values. The problem that Morrison poses in *Sula* is the degree to which her heroine (or antiheroine, depending on one's reading of the character) is self-betrayed. The audience does not have an easy time in responding to the agent, because the usual sentiments about black women have been excised, and what we confront instead is the entanglement of our own conflicting desires, our own contradictory motivations concerning issues of individual woman-freedom. Sula is both loved and hated by the reader, embraced and rejected simultaneously because her audience is forced to accept the corruption of absolutes and what has been left in their place—the complex, alienated, transitory gestures of a personality who has no framework of moral reference beyond or other than herself.

Insofar as Sula is not a loving human being, extending few of the traditional loyalties to those around her, she reverses the customary trend of "moral growth" and embodies, contrarily, a figure of genuine moral ambiguity about whom few comforting conclusions may be drawn. Through Sula's unalterable "badness," black and female are now made to appear as a *single* subject in its own right, fully aware of a plentitude of predicative possibilities, for good and ill.

In Sula's case, virtue is not the sole alternative to powerlessness, or even the primary one, or perhaps even an alternative at all. In the interest of complexity, Sula is Morrison's deliberate hypothesis. A conditional subjunctive replaces an indicative certainty: "In a way her strangeness, her naiveté, her craving for the other half of her equation was the consequence of an idle imagination. Had she paints, or clay, or knew the discipline of the dance, or strings; had she anything to engage her tremendous curiosity and her gift for metaphor, she might have exchanged the restlessness and preoccupation with whim for an activity that provided her with all she yearned for. And like any *artist with no art form* she became dangerous."[4]

In careful, exquisite terms Sula has been endowed with dimensions of other possibility. How they are frustrated occupies us for most of the novel, but what strikes me keenly about the passage is that Morrison imagines a character whose destiny is not coterminous with naturalistic or mystical boundaries. Indeed the possibility of art, of intellectual vocation for black female character, has been offered as a style of defense against the naked brutality of conditions. The efficacy of art cannot be isolated from its social and political means, but Sula is specifically circumscribed by the lack of an explicit tradition of imagination or aesthetic work, and not by the evil force of "white" society, or the absence of a man, or even the presence of a mean one.

Morrison, then, imagines a character whose failings are directly traceable to the absence of a discursive/imaginative project—some *thing* to do, some object-subject relationship which establishes the identity in time and space. We do not see Sula in relationship to an "oppressor," a "whitey," a male, a dominant and dominating being outside the self. No Manichean analysis demanding a polarity of interest—black/white, male/female, good/bad—will work here. Instead, Sula emerges as an embodiment of a metaphysical chaos in pursuit of an activity both proper and sufficient to herself. Whatever Sula has become, whatever she is, is a matter of her own choices, often ill-formed and ill-informed. Even her loneliness, she says to her best friend Nel, is her own—"My own lonely," she claims in typical Sula-bravado, as she lies dying. Despite our misgivings at Sula's insistence and at the very degree of alienation Morrison accords her, we are prepared to accept her negative, naysaying freedom as a necessary declaration of independence by the black female writer in her pursuit of a vocabulary of gesture—both verbal and motor—that leads us as well as the author away from the limited repertoire of powerless virtue and sentimental pathos. Sula is neither tragic nor pathetic; she does not amuse or accommodate. For black audiences, she is not consciousness of the black race personified, nor "tragic mulatto," nor, for white ones, is she "mammie," "Negress," "coon," or "maid." She is herself, and Morrison, quite rightly, seems little concerned if any of us, at this late date of Sula's appearance in the "house of fiction," minds her heroine or not.

We view Morrison's decision with interest because it departs dramatically from both the iconography of virtue and endurance and from the ideology of the infamous Ogre/Bitch complex, alternately poised as the dominant traits of black female personality when the black female personality exists at all in the vocabulary of public symbols.[5] Sula demands, I believe, that we not only see anew, but also *speak* anew in laying to rest the several manifestations of apartheid in its actual practice and in the formulation of the critical postulates that govern our various epistemologies.

That writers like Morrison, Toni Cade Bambara and Paule Marshall among them, participate in a tradition of black women writing in their own behalf, close to its moment of inception, lends their work thorough complexity. With the exception of a handful of autobiographical narratives from the nineteenth century, the black woman's realities are virtually suppressed until the period of the Harlem Renaissance and later. Essentially, the black woman as artist, as intellectual spokesperson for her own cultural apprenticeship, has not existed before, for anyone. At the source of her own symbol-making task, this community of writers confronts, therefore, a tradition of work that is quite recent, its continuities broken and sporadic.

It is not at all an exaggeration to say that the black woman's presence as character and movement in the American world has been *ascribed* a status of impoverishment or pathology, or, at best, an essence that droops down in the midst of things, as de Beauvoir describes female mystery in *The Second Sex*. Against this social knowledge, black women writers likely agree on a single point: whatever the portrayal of female character yields, it will be rendered from the point of view of one whose eyes are not alien to the humanity in front of them. What we can safely assume, then, is that black women write as partisans to a particular historical order—their own, the black and female one, with its hideous strictures against literacy and its subtle activities of censorship even now against words and deeds that would deny or defy the black woman myth. What we can assume with less confidence is that their partisanship, as in the rebellion of Sula, will yield a synonymity of conclusions.

The contrast between Sula and Margaret Walker's Vyry Ware is the difference between captive woman and free woman, but the distinction between them has as much to do with aspects of agency and characterization as it does with the kind of sensibility or sympathy that a writer requires in building one kind of character and not another. In other words, *what* we think of Sula and Vyry, for instance, has something to do with *how* we are taught to *see* and *value* them. In the terms of fiction that they each propose, *Jubilee*, *Their Eyes Were Watching God*, and *Sula* all represent varying degrees of plausibility, but the critical question is not whether the events they portray are plausible, or whether they confirm what we already believe, or think we do, but, rather, how each writer deploys a concept of character. Of the three, Toni Morrison looks forward to an era of dissensions: Sula's passions are hateful, as we have observed, and though we are not certain that the loss of conventional love brings her down, we are sure that she overthrows received moralities in a heedless quest for her own irreducible self. This radical intrusion of waywardness lends a different thematic emphasis to the woman's tale of generation, receding in Sula's awareness, and the result is a novel whose formal strategies are ambiguous and even discomforting in their uncertainties. Once we have examined an analogy of the archetype from which Sula deviates by turning to Margaret Walker's *Jubilee* and have explored Hurston's novel as a structural advance of the literary issues, we will return to *Sula* in a consideration of myth/countermyth as a discourse ordained by history.

In radical opposition to notions of discontinuity, confronting us as a fictional world of consecrated time and space, *Jubilee* worries one of the traditional notions of realism—the stirring to life of the common people[6]—to a modified definition. Walker completed her big novel in the mid sixties at the University of Iowa Creative Writers' Workshop. She tells the story of the novel, twenty years in the making, in *How I Wrote Jubilee*.[7] This novel of historical content has no immediate precedent in Afro-American literary tradition. To that extent, it bears little structural resemblance to Hurston's work before it, although both Hurston and Walker implement a search for roots, or to Morrison's work after it. *Jubilee*, therefore, assumes a special place in the canon.

From Walker's own point of view, the novel is historical, taking its models from the Russian writers of historical fiction, particularly Tolstoy. In its panoramic display, its massive configurations of characters and implied presences, its movement from a dense point of American history—the era of the Civil War—toward an inevitable, irreversible outcome—the emancipation of 10 million African-Americans—*Jubilee* is certainly historical. Even though it is a tale whose end is written on the brain, in the heart, so that there is not even a chance that we will be mistaken about closure, the novel unfolds as if the issues were new. We are sufficiently excited to keep turning the page of a twice-told tale accurately reiterating what we have come to believe is the truth about the "Peculiar Institution." But the high credibility of the text in this case leads us to wonder, eventually, what else is embedded in it that compels us to read our fate by its lights. My own interpretation of the novel is that it is not only historical, but also, and primarily, Historical. in other words, "Historical," in this sense, is a metaphor for the unfolding of the Divine Will. This angle on reality is defined by Paul Tillich as a theonomy. Human history is shot through with Divine Presence so that its being and time are consistent with a plan that elaborates and completes the will of God.[8] In this view of things, human doings are only illusions of a counterfeit autonomy; in Walker's novel agents (or characters) are moving and are moved under the aegis of a Higher and Hidden Authority.

For Vyry Ware, the heroine of *Jubilee*, and her family, honor, courage, endurance—in short, the heroic as transparent prophetic utterance—become the privileged center of human response. If Walker's characters are ultimately seen as one-dimensional, either good or bad, speaking in a public rhetoric that asumes the heroic or its opposite, then such portrayal is apt to a fiction whose value is subsumed in a theonomous frame of moral reference. From this angle of advocacy and preservation the writer does not penetrate the core of experience, but encircles it. The heroic intention has no interest in fluctuations or transformations or palpitations of conscience—these will pass away—but monumentality, or fixedness, becomes its striving. Destiny is disclosed to the hero or the heroine as an already-fixed and named event, and this steady reference point is the secret of permanence.

Set on a Georgia plantation before the Civil War, the novel is divided into three parts. The first recalls the infancy and youth of Vyry Ware, the central figure of the novel, and rehearses various modes of the domestic South in slavery. The second part recapitulates the war and its impact on the intimate life of families and individuals. One of the significant threads of the Peculiar Institution in objective time is closely imitated here—how the exigencies of war lead to the destruction of plantation hierarchy. In this vacuum of order a landscape of deracinated women and men dominates the countryside, and Walker's intensity of detail involves the reader in a scene of universal mobility—everything is moving, animate and inanimate, away from the centers of war toward peace, always imminent, in the shadows of Sherman's torch. Vyry and her first love Randall Ware are numbered among the casualties. They are separated as the years of war unhinge all former reality.

The third and final segment of the novel marks Vyry's maturity and the rebirth of a semblance of order in the South. The future is promising for the emancipated, and Vyry takes a new lover, Innis Brown, before the return of Randall Ware. This tying up the various threads of the narrative is undercut by a bitterly ironical perspective. The former enslaved will struggle as she or he has before now, with this difference: free by law, each remains a victim of arbitrary force, but such recognition is the reader's alone. This edge of perception reads into the novel an element of pathos so keenly defined that Vyry's fate verges on the tragic.

Variously encoded by signs associated with a magical/superstitious world order, echoes of maxims and common speech, *Jubilee* is immersed in the material. We are made to feel, in other words, the brutal pull of necessity—the captive's harsh relationship to this earth and its unrelenting requirements of labor—as they impel the captive consciousness toward a terrible knowledge of the tenuousness between life and death. The novel conjoins natural setting and social necessity in a dance of temporal unfolding; in fact, the institution of slavery described here is an elaboration of immanence so decisive in its hold on the human scene imposed upon it that Walker's humanity is actually "ventriloquized" through the medium of a third-person narrator. The narrative technique (with its overlay of mystical piety) is negotiated between omniscient and concealed narrators. Whatever the characters think, however they move and feel about their being, all is rendered through the eyes of another consciousness, not their own. We might say that the characters embody, then, historical symbols—a captive class and their captors—which have been encoded or transliterated as actors in a fiction. Walker's agents are types or valences, and the masks through which they speak might be assumed as well by any other name.

In attributing to Walker a theonomous view of human reality, I am also saying that her characters are larger than life; that they are overdrawn, that, in fact, their compelling agency and motivation are ahistorical, despite the novel's solid historical grounding. Walker's *lexis* operates under quite complicated laws, complicated because such vocabulary is no longer accessible, or even acceptable, to various mythoi of contemporary fiction. Walker is posing a subterranean structure of God terms, articulated in the novel through what we can identify as the *peripeteia*—that point of radical change in the direction that the forces of the novel are moving; in historical and secular terms this change is called emancipation. Historiographic method in accounting for the "long-range" and "immediate" causes of the Civil War and its aftermath does not name "God" as a factor in the liberation of black Americans,[9] and neither does Walker in any explicit way. But it seems clear to me that "God" is precisely what she means in all the grandeur and challenge of the Nominative, clear that the agency of Omnipresence—even more reverberative in its imprecise and ubiquitous *thereness*—is for Walker the source of one of the most decisive abruptions in our history.

Walker adopts a syntax and semantics whose meanings are recognizable in an explanation of affairs in human time. But these delegated efficacies register at a deeper level of import so that "nature," for instance, is nature and something more, and character itself acts in accordance with the same kind of mystical or "unrealistic" tendencies.

Walker's backdrop of natural representation has such forcefulness in the work that dialogue itself is undercut by its dominance, but her still life is counterposed by human doings that elaborate the malignancies of nature, that is, torture, beatings, mental cruelty, the ugly effects of nature embodied in the formal and institutional. The slaveholder and his class, in the abrogation of sympathy, lose their human form. The captors' descent into nature is seen as pernicious self-indulgence, ratified by institutional sanction, but it also violates a deeper structural motive, which Walker manipulates in the development of character. Though natural and social events run parallel, they are conjoined by special arrangement, and then there is a name for it—the act of magic or invocation that the enslaved opposes to the arbitrary willfulness of authority.

The evocation of a magical program defines the preeminent formalistic features of the opening segments of the novel. Prayers for the sick and dying and the special atmosphere that surrounds the deathwatch are treated from the outset with particular thematic prominence. In several instances mood is conveyed more by conventional notation—the number thirteen, boiling black pot, full moon, squinch owl, black crone—than any decisive nuance of thought or detail; or more precisely, fear is disbodied from internal agitations of feeling and becomes an attribute of things. "Midnight came and thirteen people waited for death. The black pot boiled, and the full moon rode the clouds high in the heavens and straight up over their heads. . . . It was not a night for people to sleep easy. Every now and then the squinch owl hollered and the crackling fire would glare and the black pot boil. . . ."[10]

The suspense that gathers about this scene is brought on by the active interaction of forces that move beyond and above the characters. An outburst would surprise. Sis. Hetta's death is expected here, and nothing more. The odd and insistent contiguity that Walker establishes among a variety of natural and cultural-material signs—"black pot boiled"; "full moon rode"—identifies the kind of magical/mystical grammar of terms to which I have referred.

"Black pot" and "full moon" may be recognized as elements that properly belong to the terrain of witchcraft, but we must understand that magic and witchcraft—two semiological "stops" usually associated with African-American rebellion and revolutionary fervor throughout the New World under the whip of slavery—are ritual terms of a shorthand which authors adopt to describe a system of beliefs and practices not entirely accessible to us now. In other words, Walker is pointing toward a larger spiritual and religious context through these notations, so that ordinary diurnal events in the novel are invested with extraordinary meaning. My own terms—theonomous meaning—would relate this extraordinary attribution to the Unseen, for which Protestant theology offers other clusters of anomalous phenomena, including "enthusiasm," "ecstasy," or the equivalent of Emile Durkheim's demon of oratorical power.[11] In specific instances of the novel, we see only pointers toward, or markers of, an entirely compelling structure of feelings and beliefs, of which "black pot," for instance, is a single sign. The risk I am taking here is to urge a synonymity between "God" and, for want of a better term, "magic." At least I am suggesting that Walker's vocabulary of God terms includes magic and the magical and the enslaved person's special relationship to natural forces.

Walker achieves this "extra" reading by creating a parallelism between natural and social/domestic issues that dominates the form of the novel. In its reinforcements, there is an absence of differentiation, or of the interplay between dominant and subdominant motifs. A nocturnal order pervades *Jubilee*— life under the confines of the slave community, where movement is constantly under surveillance; secret meetings; flights from the overseer's awful authority; illegal and informal pacts and alliances between slaves; and above all, the slave's terrible vulnerability to fluctuations of fate.

The scene of Vyry's capture after an attempted escape on the eve of the Civil War will provide a final example. After their union Vyry and Randall Ware, the free black man, have two children, Jim and Minna, and Ware makes plans for their liberation. His idea is that he or Vyry will return for the children later, but Vyry refuses to desert them. Her negotiation of a painful passage across the countryside toward the point of rendezvous groans with material burden. It has rained the day of their attempted escape, and mud is dense around the slave quarters by nightfall. Vyry travels with the two children—Jim toddling and the younger child Minna in her arms. The notion of struggle, both against the elements and the powerful other, is so forceful an aspect of tone that the passage itself painfully anticipates the fatefulness of Vyry's move; here are the nodal points:

> Every step Vyry and Jim took, they could feel the mud sucking their feet down and fighting them as they withdrew their feet from its elastic hold. . . . The baby still slept fitfully while Vyry pressed her way doggedly to the swamps. . . . At last they were in sight of the swamps. Feeling sorry for little Jim she decided to rest a few minutes before trying to wade the creek. . . . She sat down on an old log, meaning to rest only a few minutes. . . . A bad spasm clutched her stomach instinctively. She tensed her body with the sure intuition that she was not only being watched but that the watchful figures would soon surround her. Impassively she saw the patteroller and guards, together with Grimes [the overseer] emerge from the shadows and walk toward her. . . . (169–70)

This grim denial concludes with Vyry's capture and brutal punishment— "seventy-five lashes on her naked back." That Vyry has been robbed of selfhood on its most fundamental level is clear enough, but the passage further suggests that her movements replicate the paralysis of nightmare. One would move, but cannot, and awakens in spasms of terror. This direct articulation of night-mare content—puzzles and haltings, impediments and frights—dictates the crucial psychological boundaries of *Jubilee* and decides, accordingly, the aes-thetic rule.

The idea that emerges here is that Vyry's condition is the equivalent of nightmare, a nocturnal order of things that works its way into the resonances of the novel's structure. Her paralysis is symptomatic of a complex of fear and repression in the service of death. We could argue that the culture of slavery projected in the novel—its modalities of work and celebration, its civic functions and legal codes, its elaborate orders of brutality and mutilation—presents a spectacle of a *culture* in the service of death. Given this reality, the slave subject has no life, but only the stirrings of it. Vyry, trapped in a bad dream, cannot shake loose, and this terrible imposed impotence foreshadows the theme of liberation and a higher liberation as well, in which case the stalled movement is overcome in a gesture of revolutionary consciousness. For Vyry the freeing act is sparked by war whose intricate, formal causes are remote to her, though its mandates will require the reorganization of her human resources along new lines of stress. Above all, Vyry must move now without hesitation as the old order collapses around her.

For Vyry's class the postwar years stand as the revelation of the emotional stirrings they have felt all along. "Mine Eyes Have Seen the Glory of the Coming of the Lord" (the title of one of Walker's chapters) is as much a promise as it is an exercise in common meter, but the terms of the promise that Walker imitates are neither modern nor secular. They are eternal and self-generating, authored elsewhere, beyond the reach of human inquiry. Along this axis of time, with its accent on the eternal order of things, women and men in destiny move consistent with the stars of heaven.

This blending of a material culture located in the nineteenth century with a theme which appears timeless and is decisively embedded in a Christian metaphysic reveals the biographical inspiration behind Walker's work. *Jubilee* is, in effect, the tale translated of the author's female ancestors. This is a story of the foremothers, a celebration of their stunning faith and intractable powers of endurance. In that sense, it is not so much a study of characters as it is an interrogation into the African-American character in its poignant national destiny and through its female line of spiritual descent. A long and protracted praise piece, a transformed and elaborated prayer, *Jubilee* is Walker's invocation to the guiding spirit and genius of her people. Such a novel is not "experimental." In short, it does not introduce ambiguity or irony or uncertainty or perhaps even "individualism" as potentially thematic material because it is a detailed sketch of a *collective* survival. The waywardness of a Sula Peace, or even a Janie Stark's movement toward an individualistic liberation—a separate peace—is a trait of character development engendered by a radically different Weltanschauung.

Their Eyes Were Watching God enforces a similar notion of eternal order in the organic metaphorical structure through which Hurston manipulates her characters, but the complexities of motivation in the novel move the reader some distance from the limited range of responses evoked by *Jubilee*. Janie Starks, the heroine of the novel, defines a conglomerate of human and social interests so contradictory in its emphasis that a study of structural ambiguity in fiction might well include Janie Starks *and* her author. Perhaps "uncertainty" is a more useful word in this case than "ambiguity," since Hurston avoids the full elaboration or display of tensions that Janie herself appears to anticipate. In short, Janie Starks is a bundle of contradictions: raised by women, chiefly her grandmother, to seek security in a male and his properties, Janie, quite early in her career rejects Nanny's wisdom. In love with adventure, in love with the very idea of adventure, Janie is determined to know exactly what independence for the female means for her. This includes the critical quest of sexual self-determination. Janie's quite moving sense of integrity, however, is undercut in puzzling and peculiar ways.

Janie marries her first husband Logan Killicks because her grandmother wants her to do so, but Janie has little interest in a man who is not only not "glamorous" (as Joe Starks and Virgible "Teacake" Woods will be), but also not enlightened in his outlook on the world and the specifically amorous require-ments of female/male relationship. Killicks gets the brunt of a kind of social criticism in *Their Eyes Were Watching God* which mocks the rural person—hardworking, unsophisticated, "straight-arrow," earnest—and Hurston makes her point by having Killicks violate essentially Janie's "dream of the horizon." Janie will shortly desert Killicks for a man far more in keeping with her ideas concerning the romantic, concerning male gracefulness. Jody Starks, up from Georgia and headed for an adventure in real estate and town government, takes the place of Logan Killicks with an immediacy, which, in "real" life, would be somewhat disturbing, a bit indecent; but here the "interruption" is altogether lyrical, appropriate, and unmourned. Starks's appearance and intention are even "cinematic" in their decidedly cryptic and romantic tenor—Janie literally goes off "down the road" with the man.

Their destination is Eatonville, Florida, a town which Joe Starks will bring to life with his own lovely ego, shortly to turn arrogant and insulting as he attempts to impose on Janie his old-fashioned ideas about woman's place and possibilities. The closure on this marriage is not a happy one either, troubled by Starks's chauvinistic recriminations and Janie's own disenchantment. Starks dies of a kidney ailment, leaving Janie "Mrs. Mayor" of Eatonville and not particularly concerned, we are led to believe, to be attached again.

Janie's new love affair with Teacake is untrammeled by incompatibility be-tween the pair, though her friends express great concern that Teacake's social and financial status is not what it ought to be, let alone comparable to Jody Starks's. Janie is, however, at once traditionally romantic in her apparently male-centered yearnings and independent in her own imagination and the readiness to make her own choices. The convergence of these two emotional components is, in fact, not the diametrical opposition that contemporary femi-nists sometimes suppose; heterosexual love is neither inherently perverse nor necessarily dependence-engendering, except that the power equation between female and male tends to corrupt intimacies.[12] The trouble, then, with the relationship between Janie and Teacake is not its heterosexual ambience, but a curiously exaggerated submissiveness on Janie's part that certain other elements of the heroine's character contradict.

When, for instance, Janie follows Teacake to the Florida Everglades to become a migrant farm worker for several seasons, their love is solid and reliable, but the male in this instance is also perfectly capable, under Hurston's gaze, of exhibiting qualities of jealousy and possession so decisive that his occasional physical abuse of the female and his not-so-subtle manipulation of other females' sexual attraction to him seem condoned in the name of love. Hurston's pursuit of an alleged folk philosophy in this case—as in, all women enjoy an occasional violent outburst from their men because they know then that they are loved— is a concession to an obscene idea. One example will suffice. "Before the week was over he had whipped Janie. Not because her behavior justified his jealousy, but it relieved that awful fear inside him. Being able to whip her reassured him in possession. No brutal beating at all. He just slapped her around a bit to show he was boss. . . . It aroused a sort of envy in both men and women. The way he petted and pampered her as if those two or three slaps had nearly killed her made the women see visions and the helpless way she hung on him made men dream dreams. . . . "[13]

One might well wonder, and with a great deal of moral, if not poetic, justification if the scene above describes a *working posture* that Hurston herself might have adopted with various lovers. This scene is paradigmatic of the very quality of ambiguity/ambivalence that I earlier identified for this novel. The piece threatens to abandon primitive modes of consciousness and response from the beginning, but Hurston seems thwarted in bringing this incipience to fruition for reasons which might have to do with the way that the author understood certain popular demands brought to bear on her art. Hurston has detailed some of her notions of what Anglo-American audiences expected of the black writer and the black female writer of her time,[14] but it is not clear to me what African-American audiences expected of their chroniclers. The more difficult question, however, is what Hurston demanded of herself in imagining what was possible for the female, and it appears that beyond a certain point she could not, or would not plunge. *Their Eyes Were Watching God*, for all its quite impressive feminist possibilities, is an instance of "double consciousness," to employ W.E.B. Dubois's conceptualization in quite another sense and intention.[15] Looking two ways at once, it captivates Janie Starks in an entanglement of conflicting desires.

More concentrated in dramatic focus than *Jubilee*, Hurston's novel was written during the mid thirties; finished in seven weeks during the author's visit to Haiti, the novel is not simply compact. It is hurried, intense, and above all, haunted by an uneasy measure of control. One suspects that Hurston has not said everything she means, but means everything she says. Within a persistent scheme of metaphor, she seems held back from the awful scream that she has forced Janie to repress through unrelieved tides of change. We mistrust Janie's serenity, spoken to her friend Phoeby Watson in the close of the novel; complementarily, the reconciliation is barely acceptable in either structual or dramatic terms. Janie Starks, not unlike her creator, is gifted with a dimension of worldliness and ambition that puts her in touch with broader experience. This daughter of sharecroppers is not content to be heroic under submissive conditions (except with Teacake?); for her, then, nothing in the manners of small town Florida bears repeating. Its hateful, antisocial inclinations are symbolized by Janie's grandmother, whom she hates "and [has] hidden from herself all these years under the cloak of pity." "Here Nanny had taken the biggest thing God ever made, the horizon . . . and pinched it into such a little bit of a thing that she could tie it about her granddaughter's neck tight enough to choke her. She hated the old woman who had twisted her so in the name of love . . . " (76-77).

The grandmother not only represents a personal trauma for Janie (as the grandmother does in the author's autobiography),[16] but also terror and repression, intruding a vision of impoverishment within the race. Clustered around the symbolic and living grandmother are the anonymous detractors of experience who assume no dominating feature or motivation beyond the level of the mass. Hurston's rage is directed against this faceless brood with a moral ferociousness that verges on misogyny. This profound undercurrent is relieved, however, by a drift toward caricature. Exaggerating the fat of misshapen men and calling attention in public to their sexual impotence, gaining dimensions of comic monologue, and leaving no genuine clue for those who gaze at her, Janie has elements of a secret life which sustains her through the adventures of three husbands, a flood, justifiable homicide, trial, and vindication.

This psychological bent informing Janie's character is deflected by an anthropological strategy that all but ruins this study of a female soul. The pseudo-dialect of Southern patois gives Janie back to the folk ultimately, but this "return" contradicts other syntactical choices which Hurston superimposes on the structure through visions of Janie's interior life and Hurston's own narrative style. Janie implies new moral persuasions, while Hurston has her looking back, even returning, to the small town she desperately wishes to be free of. This dilemma of choices haunts the book from the very beginning and may, indeed, shed light on the "ancestral imperative."[17] That Janie does not break from her Southern past, symbolized in the "old talk," but grasps how she might do so is the central problematic feature of the novel, previously alluded to as an undercurrent of doubt running through Hurston's strategies.

Written long before *Jubilee, Their Eyes Were Watching God* anticipates the thematic emphases prominent in *Sula* to the extent that in both the latter novels only the adventurous, deracinated personality is heroic, and that in both, the roots of experience are poisonous. One would do well to avoid the plunge down to the roots, seeking, rather, to lose oneself in a larger world of chance and danger. That woman must break loose from the hold of biography as older generations impose it, even the broader movements of tribe, constitutes a controlling theme of Hurston's work.

Images of space and time, inaugurated in the opening pages of the novel, are sounded across it with oracular intensity, defining the dream of Janie Starks as a cosmic disembodiment that renders her experience unitary with the great fantastic ages. "Ships at a distance have every man's wish on board. For some they come in with the tide" (5). Consonant with this history of fantasy life, Janie is something of a solitary reaper, disillusioned, stoical, in her perception of fate and death. "So the beginning of this was a woman and she had come back from burying the dead. . . . The people all saw her because it was sundown. The sun was gone, but he had left his footprints in the sky. It was time to hear things and talk. . . " (5).

The novel is essentially informed by these ahistorical, specifically rustic, image clusters, giving the whole a topological consistency. Hurston, however, attempts to counterpoise this timeless current with elements of psychic specificity—Janie's growth toward an understanding of mutability and change and other aspects of internal movement. The novel's power of revelation, nonetheless, is rather persistently sabotaged at those times when Hurston intrudes metaphorical symbolism as a substitute for the hard precision of thought. Janie actually promises more than the author delivers. As a result, the novel is facile at times when it ought to be moving, captivated in stereotype when it should be dynamic.

The flood that devastates the Florida Everglades and the homes of the migrant farm workers of which Janie and Teacake are a part provides an example. The storm sequence is the novel's high point, its chief dramatic fulcrum, on which rests the motivation that will spur both Janie's self-defense against a rabid Teacake and her return to Eatonville and the Starks house. Waiting in their cabins for the storm to recede, Janie, Teacake, and their fellow laborers are senseless with wonder at its power, "They seemed to be staring at the dark, but their eyes were watching God" (131). What one wants in this sequence is a crack in the mental surface of character so acute that the flood cleaves the narrative precisely in half, pre- and postdiluvial responses so distinctly contrasting that the opening lines—"their souls asking if He meant to measure their puny might against His"—mature into the ineluctable event. The reader expects a convergence of outer scene and its inner correspondence, but Hurston appears to forego the fruition of this parallel rhythm, content on delineating the external behavior of the agents.

Nothing specific to the inner life of Janie appears again for several pages; the awe that greets the display of natural phenomena is replayed through the imagination of a third-person observer, dry feet and all, well above the action of furious winds. We miss the concentration on Janie's internal life which saves the entire first half of the narrative from the pathos of character buffeted by external circumstances. Janie never quite regains her former brilliance, and when we meet her considered judgments again, she has fled the 'Glades, after having had to shoot Teacake in self-defense (as a result of his violence, rabies-induced) and is seeking peace in the town where she has been "first lady." "Here was peace. She pulled in her horizon like a great fish-net. Pulled it from around the waist of the world and draped it over her shoulder. So much of life in its meshes! She called in her soul to come and see. . . (159).

One is not certain how these images of loss and labor should be read, nor why they strike with such finality, except that the lines make a good ending, this rolling in of fish nets and cleaning of meshes, but if we take Janie as a kind of adventurer, as a woman well familiar with the rites of burial and grief, then we read this closure as a eulogy for the living; Janie has been "buried" along with Teacake.

The fault with this scene is not that Janie has loved Teacake, but, rather, that the author has broken the potential pattern of revolt by having her resigned, as if she were ready for a geriatric retirement, to the town of frustrated love. We know that all novels do end, even if they end with "the," and so it is probably fitting for Janie to have a rest after the tragic events unleashed by the flood. But her decision to go back to Eatonville after the trial strikes me as a naive fictional pose. Or, more precisely, what she thinks about her life at that point seems inappropriate to the courageous defiance that she has often embodied all along. The logic of the novel tends to abrogate neat conclusions, and their indulgence in the end essentially mitigates the complex painful knowledge that Janie has gained about herself and the other.

The promise to seize upon the central dramatic moment of a woman's self-realization fizzles out in a litany of poetic platitudes about as opposite to Janie's dream of the horizon as the grandmother's obsessive fear of experience has been. We miss the knowledge or wisdom of revelation in the perfectly resolved ending—what is it that Janie knows now that she has come back from burying the dead of the sodden and bloated? Are the words merely decorative, or do they mobilize us toward a deeper mysterious sense? In a mode of fictive assumptions similar to Margaret Walker's, Zora Neale Hurston inherits a fabric of mystery without rethreading it. That is one kind of strategic decision. There are others.

Sula, by contrast, closes with less assurance. " 'All that time, all that time, I thought I was missing Jude.' And the loss pressed down on her chest and came up into her throat. 'We was girls together,' she said as though explaining something. 'O Lord, Sula,' she cried, 'girl, girl, girlgirlgirl' " (149).

Nel's lament not only closes *Sula*, but also reinforces the crucial dramatic questions which the novel has introduced—the very mystery of a Sula Peace and the extent to which the town of Medallion, Ohio, has been compelled by her, how they yearn for her, even to the point, oddly enough, of a collective rejection. Nel and Sula are more than girls together. They sustain the loss of innocence and its subsequent responsibilities with a degree of tormented passion seldom allowed even to lovers. More than anyone else in Medallion, they have been intimate witnesses of their mutual coming of age in a sequence of gestures that anticipates an ultimate disaffection between them, but the rhythm of its disclosure, determined early on by the reader as inexorable, is sporadic and intermittent enough in the sight of the two women that its fulfillment comes to both as a trauma of recognition. Nel Wright's "girl," repeated five times and run together in an explosion not only of the syntactical integrity of the line, but also of Nel's very heartbeat, is piercing and sudden remorse— remorse so long suspended, so elaborate in its deceptions and evasions that it could very well intimate the onset of a sickness-unto-death.

When Sula comes of age, she leaves Medallion for a decade in the wake, significantly, of Nel's marriage to Jude and her resignation to staid domestic life. Sula's return to Medallion, in a plague of robins, no less, would mark the restoration of an old friendship; Sula, instead, becomes Jude's lover for a brief time before abandoning him as she does other husbands of the town. Nel and Sula's "confrontation," on the deathbed of the latter, tells the reader and the best friend very little about what it is that makes Sula run. All that she admits is that she has "lived" and that if she and Nel had been such good friends, in fact, then her momentary "theft" of Jude might not have made any difference. Nel does not forgive Sula, but experiences, instead, a sense of emptiness and despair grounded, she later discovers after it doesn't matter anymore, in her own personal loss of Sula. She has not missed Jude, she finds out that afternoon, but her alter ego passionately embodied in the other woman. It turns out that the same degree of emotional ambivalence that haunts Nel plagues the female reader of this novel. What is it about this woman Sula that triggers such attraction and repulsion at once? We have no certain answers, just as Nel does not, but, rather, resign ourselves to a complex resonance of feeling, which suggests that Sula is both necessary and frightening as a character realization.

In the relationship between Nel and Sula, Morrison demonstrates the female's rites-of-passage in their peculiar richness and impoverishment; the fabric of paradoxes—betrayals and sympathies, silences and aggressions, advances and sudden retreats—transmitted from mother to daughter, female to female, by mimetic gesture. That women learn primarily from other women strategies of survival and "homicide" is not news to anyone; indeed, this vocabulary of reference constitutes the chief revisionist, albeit implicit, feature of the women's liberation effort. Because Morrison has no political axe to grind in this novel— in other words, she is not writing according to a formula that demands that her female agents demonstrate a simple, transparent love between women—she is free, therefore, to pursue the delicate tissue of intimate patterns of response between women. In doing so, she identifies those meanings of womanhood which statements of public policy are rhetorically bound to suppress.

One of the structural marvels of *Sula* is its capacity to telescope the process of generation and its consequent network of convoluted relationships. *Sula* is a woman's text par excellence, even subscribing in its behavior to Woolf's intimations that the woman's book, given the severe demands on her time, is spare.[18] The novel is less than two hundred pages of prose, but within its imaginative economy various equations of domestic power are explored. For instance, Sula's relationships to her mother Hannah and grandmother Eva Peace are portrayed in selective moments. In other words, Sula's destiny is located only in part by Nel, while the older Peace women in their indifference to decorous social behavior provide the soil in which her moral isolation is seeded and nurtured. Hannah and Eva have quite another story to tell apart from Sula's, much of it induced by Eva's abandonment by her husband BoyBoy and her awful defiance in response. The reader is not privy to various tales of transmission between Eva and Hannah, but we decide by inference that their collective wisdom leads Hannah herself to an authenticity of person not alterable by the iron-clad duties of motherhood, nor the sweet, submissive obligations of female love. In short, Hannah Peace is self-indulgent, full of disregard for the traditional repertoire of women's vanity-related gestures, and the reader tends to love her for it—the "sweet, low and guileless" flirting, no patting of the hair, or rushing to change clothes, or quickly applying makeup, but barefoot in summer, "in the winter her feet in a man's leather slippers with the backs flattened under her heels. . . . Her voice trailed, dipped and bowed; she gave a chord to the simplest words. Nobody, but nobody, could say 'hey sugar' like Hannah. . . " (36).

Just as Hannah's temperament is "light and playful," Morrison's prose glides over the surface of events with a careful allegiance to the riffs of folk utterance— deliberate, inclusive, very often on the verge of laughter—but the profound deception of this kind of plain talk, allegedly "unsophisticated," is the vigil it keeps in killing silence about what it suspects, even knows, but never expresses. This hidden agenda has a malicious side, which Sula inherits without moral revision and correction. Morrison's stylistic choice in this passage is a significant clue to a reading of Hannah's character, a freedom of movement, a liberty of responses, worked out in a local school of realism. Hannah Peace is certainly not a philosopher, not even in secret, but that she rationalizes her address to the other in an unfailing economy of nuances implies a potential for philosophical grace. Among the women of *Sula*, the light rhythyms usually conceal a deeper problem.

One of the more perplexing characters of recent American fiction, Eva Peace embodies a figure of both insatiable generosity and insatiable demanding. Like Hannah, Eva is seldom frustrated by the trammels of self-criticism, the terrible indecisiveness and scrupulosity released by doubt. Because Eva goes ahead without halting, ever, we could call her fault nothing less than innocence, and its imponderable cruelty informs her character with a kind of Old Testament logic. Eva behaves as though she were herself the sole instrument of divine inscrutable will. We are not exactly certain what oracular fever decides that she must immolate her son Plum.[19] Perhaps even his heroin addiction does not entirely explain it, but she literally rises to the task in moments of decisiveness, orchestrated in pity and judgment. Like an avenging deity who must sacrifice its creation in order to purify it, Eva swings and swoops on her terrible crutches from her son's room, about to prepare his fire. She holds him in her arms, recalling moments from his childhood before dousing him with kerosene:

> He opened his eyes and saw what he imagined was the great wing of an eagle pouring a wet lightness over him. Some kind of baptism, some kind of blessing, he thought. Everything is going to be all right, it said. Knowing that it was so he closed his eyes and sank back into the bright hole of sleep.
>
> Eva stepped back from the bed and let the crutches rest under her arms. She rolled a bit of newspaper into a tight stick about six inches long, lit it and threw it onto the bed where the kerosene-soaked Plum lay in smug delight. Quickly, as the *whoosh* of flames engulfed him, she shut the door and made her slow and painful journey back to the top of the house. . . .(40–41)

Not on any level is the reader offered easy access to this scene. Its enumerated, overworked pathos, weighed against the victim's painful ignorance not only of his imminent death, but also of the requirements of his manhood generates contradictory feelings between shock and relief. The reader resents the authorial manipulation that engenders such feelings. The act itself, so violently divergent from the normal course of maternal actions and expectations, marks a subclimax. Further, it foreshadows the network of destruction, both willful and fortuitous, that ensures Sula and Nel in an entanglement of pre-decided motivations. Eva, in effect, determines her own judgment, which Sula will seal without a hint of recourse to the deceptions or allegiances of kinship. Sula, who puts Eva in old age in an asylum, does not mistake her decision as a stroke of love or duty, nor does it echo any of the ambiguities of mercy.

Like Eva's, Sula's program of action as an adult woman is spontaneous and direct, but the reader in Sula's case does not temper her or his angle on Sula's behavior with compassion or second thought, as she or he tends to do in Eva's case. It could be argued, for instance, that Eva sacrifices Plum in order to save him, and however grotesque we probably adjudge her act, inspired by a moral order excluding contingency and doubt, no such excuse can be offered in Sula's behalf. We must also remember that Sula's nubile *singleness* and refusal of the acts and rites of maternity have implicitly corrupted her in our unconscious judgment and at a level of duplicity which our present " "sexual arrangements" protect and mandate.[20] We encounter the raw details of her individualism, not engaged by naturalistic piety or existential rage, as a paradigm of wanton vanity. Her moral shape, however, does not come unprecedented or autonomously derived. Merging Eva's arrogance on the one hand and Hannah's self-indulgence on the other, "with a twist that was all her own imagination, she lived out her days exploring her own thoughts and emotions, giving them full reign, feeling no obligation to please anybody unless their pleasure pleased her" (102).

Just as Hannah and Eva have been Sula's principal models, they have also determined certain issues which she will live out in her own career. It is probably not accidental that the question which haunts Hannah—have I been loved?—devolves on Sula with redoubtable fury. If it is true that love does not exist until it is named, then the answer to the enigma of Sula Peace is not any more forthcoming than if it were not so. Yet, certainly the enormous consequences of being loved or not are relevant by implication to the agents of the novel. Morrison does not elaborate, but the instances of the question's appearance—halting, uncertain, embarrassed, or inappropriate words on a character's tongue—conceal the single most important missing element in the women's encounter with each other. A revealing conversation between Eva and Hannah suggests that even for the adult female the intricacies and entanglements of mother love (or perhaps woman love without distinction) is a dangerous inquiry to engage. Hannah cannot even formulate the sentences that would say the magic words, but angles in on the problem with a childlike timidity, which she can neither fake nor conceal. "I know you fed us and all. I was talking 'bout something else. Like. Like. Playin' with us. Did you ever, you know, play with us?" (59).

This conversation may be compared with one that Sula overhears the summer of her twelfth year, between Hannah and a couple of friends. The three women confirm for each other the agonies of childrearing, but can never quite bring themselves around to admitting that love is contingent and human and all too often connected with notions of duty. Hannah tells one of the friends that her quality of love is sufficient. "You love [your child], like I love Sula. I just don't like her. That's the difference." And that's the "difference" that sends Sula "flying up the stairs," blankly "aware of a sting in her eye," until recalled by Nel's voice.

To pin the entire revelation of the source of Sula's later character development on this single episode would be a fallacy of overdetermination, but its strategic location in the text suggests that its function is crucial to the unfolding of events to come, to the way that Sula responds to them, and to the manner in which we interpret her responses. At least two other events unmistakably hark back to it. Chicken Little joins Sula and Nel later on the same afternoon in their play by the river. In the course of things Sula picked him up and "swung him outward and then around and around. His knickers ballooned and his shrieks of frightened joy startled the birds and the fat grasshoppers. When he slipped from her hands and sailed out over the water they could still hear his bubbly laughter. . . " (52).

Frozen in a moment of terror, neither girl can do more than stare at the "closed place in the water." Morrison aptly recreates the stark helplessness of two trapped people, gaining a dimension of horror because the people are children, drawn up short in a world of chance and danger. That they do nothing in particular, except recognize that Shadrack, the town's crack-brained veteran of World War I, has seen them and will not tell, consigns them both to a territory of their own most terrible judgment and isolation. In this case the adult conscience of each springs forth in the eyes of the other, leaving childhood abruptly in its wake. The killing edge is that the act itself must remain a secret. Unlike other acts of rites-of-passage, this one must *not* be communicated. At Chicken Little's funeral, Sula "simply cried" (55), and from his grave site she and Nel, fingers laced, trot up the road "on a summer day wondering what happened to butterflies in the winter" (57).

The interweave of lyricism and dramatic event is consistent with Morrison's strategies. Their juxtaposition does not appear to function ironically, but to present dual motifs in a progressive revelation that allows the reader to "swallow" dramatic occurrences whose rhetoric, on the face of it, is unacceptable. At the same time we get in right perspective Sula's *lack* of tension—a tension that distinguishes the character stunned by her own ignorance, or by malice in the order of things. Sula, by contrast, just goes along, "completely free of ambition, with no affection for money, property, or things, no greed, no desire to command attention or compliments—no ego. For that reason she felt no compulsion to verify herself—be consistent with herself" (103). That Sula apparently wants nothing, is curiously free of mimetic desire and its consequent pull toward willfulness, keep pity in check and release unease in its absence.

Sula's lack of egoism—which appears an incorrect assessment on the narrator's part—renders her an antipassionate spectator of the human scene, even beholding her mother's death by fire in calculated coolness. Weeks after Chicken's burial Hannah is in the backyard of the Peace household, lighting a fire in which she accidentally catches herself and burns to death. Eva recalls afterward that "she had seen Sula standing on the back porch just looking." When her friends insist that she is more than likely mistaken since Sula was "probably struck dumb" by the awful spectacle, Eva remains quietly convinced "that Sula had watched Hannah burn not because she was paralyzed, but because she was interested. . . " (67).

This moment of Sula's interestedness, and we tend to give Eva the benefit of the doubt in this case, must be contrasted to her response to Chicken's drowning, precluding us from remaining impartial judges of her behavior, even as we understand its sources in the earlier event. Drawn into a cycle of negation, Sula at twelve is Sula at twenty, and the instruments of perception which the reader uses to decipher her character do not alter over the whole terrain of the work. From this point on, any course of action that she takes is already presumed by negating choices. Whether she steals Nel's husband or a million dollars matters less to the reader than to the other characters, since we clearly grasp the structure of her function as that of a radical amorality and consequently of a radical freedom. We would like to love Sula, or damn her, inasmuch as the myth of the black American woman allows only Manichean responses, but it is impossible to do either. We can only behold in an absolute suspension of final judgment.

Morrison induces this ambiguous reading through an economy of means, none of which relate to the classic *bête noire* of black experience—the powerful predominance of white and the endless litany of hateful responses associated with it. That Sula is not bound by the customary alliances to naturalism or historical determinism at least tells us what imperatives she does not pursue. Still, deciding what traditions do inspire her character is not made easier.

I would suggest that Hurston's Janie Starks presents a clear precedent. Though not conforming at every point, I think the two characters lend themselves to a comparative formula. In both cases, the writer wishes to examine the particular details and propositions of liberty under constricted conditions in a low mimetic mode of realism, that is, an instance of realism in which the characters are not decisively superior in moral or social condition to the reader.[21] Both Janie and Sula are provided an arena of action within certain limits. In the former case, the character's dreams are usually too encompassing to be accommodated within the space that circumscribes her. The stuff of her dreams, then, remains disembodied, ethereal, out of time, nor are her dreams fully differentiated, inasmuch as all we know about them is their metaphorical conformity to certain natural or romantic configurations. It is probably accurate to say that the crucial absence for Janie has been an intellectual chance, or the absence of a syntax distinctive enough in its analytical requirements to realign a particular order of events to its own demands. In other words, Janie is stuck in the limitations of dialect, while her creator is free to make use of a range of linguistic resources to achieve her vision.

The principle of absence that remains inchoate for Janie is articulate for Sula in terms whose intellectual implications are unmistakable—Sula lacks the shaping vision of art, and the absence is as telling in the formation of her character as the lack of money or an appropriately ordered space might be for the heroines, for example, of Henry James's *Portrait of a Lady* or *Wings of the Dove*; in both of James's works the heroines are provided with *money*, a term that James's narrator assigns great weight in deciding what strategies enable women to do battle with the world, though the equation between gold and freedom is ironically burdened here. In Woolf's conception of personal and creative freedom for the woman, *money*, *space*, and *time* figure prominently.

It is notable that Janie and Sula, within the social modalities that determine them, are actually quite well off. Their suffering, therefore, transcends the visceral and concrete, moving progressively toward the domain of symbols. In sharp contrast to Walker's Vyry, the latter-day heroines approach the threshold of speaking and acting *for self*, or the organization of one's resources with preeminent reference to the highest form of self-regard, the urge to speak one's own words urgently. Hurston and Morrison after her are both in the process of abandoning the vision of the corporate good as a mode of heroic suffering. Precisely what will take its place defines the dilemma of *Sula* and its protagonist. The dilemma itself highlights problems of figuration for black female character whose future, whose terms of existence, are not entirely known at the moment.

The character of Sula impresses the reader as a problem in interpretation because, for one thing, the objective myth of the black American woman, at least from the black woman's point of view, is drawn in valorized images that intrude against the text, or compete with it like a jealous goddess. That this privileged other narrative is counterbalanced by its opposite, equally exaggerated and distorted, simply reinforces the heroics to the extent that the black woman herself imagines only one heroine—and that is herself. *Sula* attempts a correction of this uninterrupted superiority on the one hand and unrelieved pathology on the other; the reader's dilemma arises in having to choose. The duplicitous reader embraces the heroics with no intent of disproof or unbelief, while the brave one recognizes that the negating countermyth would try to establish a dialectical movement between the subperspectives, gaining a totally altered perspective in the process.[22] In other words, Sula, Vyry, and Janie need not be seen as the terms of an either/or proposition. The three characters here may be identified as subperspectives, or *angles onto* a larger seeing. The struggle that we bring with us to *Sula*, indeed, the implicit proposition upon which the text is based, is the imperative that requires our coming to terms with the very complexities that a juggling of perspectives demands.

Sula is not the "other" as one kind of reading would suggest, or perhaps as we might wish, but a figure of the rejected and vain part of the self—ourselves— who in its thorough corruption and selfishness cannot utter, believe in, nor prepare for, love. I am not entirely sure that Sula speaks for us on the lower frequencies—though she could very well. The importance of this text is that she speaks at all.

In a conversation with Robert Stepto, Toni Morrison confirms certain critical conjectures that are made here concerning the character of Sula. "[She] was hard, for me; very difficult to make up that kind of character. Not difficult to think it up, but difficult to describe a woman who could be used as a classic type of evil force. Other people could use her that way. And at the same time, I didn't want to make her freakish or repulsive or unattractive. I was interested at that time in a very old, worn-out idea, which was to do something with good and evil, but putting it in different terms. . . . "[23]

As Morrison goes on to discuss the idea, Sula and Nel are to her mind an alterity of agents—"two sides of the same person, or two sides of one extra-ordinary character."[24] Morrison does not attribute the birth of her idea to any particular cultural or historical event and certainly not to the most recent wave of American feminism, but it does seem fairly clear that a Sula Peace is *for black American literature*, if not for the incredibly rich potential of black American female personality, a radical alternative to Vyry Ware and less so, to placid Janie Crawford Starks. "This was really part of the difficulty—I didn't know anyone like her. I never knew a woman like that at any rate. But I knew women who looked like that, who looked like they *could* be like that. And then you remember women who were a little bit different in [one's] town, you know."[25]

If we identify Sula as a kind of countermythology, we are saying that she is no longer bound by a rigid pattern of predictions, predilections, and antici-pations. Even though she is a character in a novel, her strategic place as *potential being* might argue that *subversion* itself—law breaking—is an aspect of liber-ation that women must confront from its various angles, in its different guises. Sula's outlawry may not be the best kind, but that she has the will toward rebellion itself *is* the stunning idea. This project in liberation, paradoxically, has no particular dimension in time, yet it is for all time.

NOTES

1. Mary Helen Washington, ed. *Black-Eyed Susans: Classic Stories by and about Black Women* (New York: Anchor Books, 1975). From the introduction, xxxii.

2. "Intimate Things in Place: A Conversation with Toni Morrison," in *Chant of Saints: A Gathering of Afro-American Literature, Art and Scholarship*, ed. Michael S. Harper and Robert B. Stepto (Urbana: University of Illinois Press, 1979), pp. 213–30.

3. Harold Bloom's by-now familiar revision on the Freudian oedipal myth in relation to the theme of literary successions and fortunes is not applicable to the community of black American women writers, even as a necessary critical fable. Bloom speaks for a powerful and an *assumed* patriarchal tradition, posited by a dominative culture, in the transmission of a political, as well as literary, wealth; in the case of black women's writing (and women's writing without modification) the myth of wealth as an aspect of literary "inheritance" tends to be sporadic. See Bloom, *The Anxiety of Influence: A Theory of Poetry* (New York: Oxford University Press, 1973), and *A Map of Misreading* (New York: Oxford University Press, 1975).

4. Toni Morrison, *Sula* (New York: Bantam Books, 1975), p. 105, emphases mine. All references are from this edition, and page numbers are supplied in parentheses in the text.

5. Bell Hooks [Gloria Watkins], *Ain't I A Woman: Black Women and Feminism* (Boston: South End Press, 1981). The particular role of Daniel Moynihan's *Report* is put in perspective here with what Hooks calls "the continuing devaluation of black womanhood," pp. 51–87.

It is with crucial deliberation that the editors of a recent feminist collection of scholarship call their volume *All the Women Are White, All the Blacks Are Men, But Some of Us Are Brave* (Old Westbury, N.Y.: Feminist Press, 1982). Editors Gloria T. Hull, Patricia Bell Scott, and Barbara Smith realize that public discourse—certainly its most radical critical statements included—lapses into a cul-de-sac when it approaches this community of women and their writers.

6. Erich Auerbach, "Fortunata," in *Mimesis: The Representation of Reality in Western Literature*, trans. Willard Trask (New York: Doubleday Anchor Books, 1957). In tracing the shift in stylistic convention and emotional resonance from the literature of classical antiquity to the modern period, Auerbach provides a definition of the change which I would consider crucial to any consideration of the issue of "realism," "the birth of a spiritual movement in the depths of the common people, from within the everyday occurrences of contemporary life, which thus assumes an importance it could never have assumed in antique literature" (p. 37).

7. Margaret Walker, *How I Wrote Jubilee* (Chicago: Third World Press, 1972). *Jubilee* was submitted as Walker's Ph.D. dissertation to the University of Iowa Creative Writer's Workshop. The source material for the novel is based on the life story of the author's great-grandmother, told to her by her grandmother in the best tradition of oral his/herstory. The specificities of this transmitted tale from one generation to another was researched by Walker over nearly two decades, and it anticipates another odyssey of search in Alex Haley's *Roots*, a detailed study of an African-American genealogy. Walker later on actually brought suit against Haley for the supposed plagiarizing of a theme that Walker considers special, if not unique, to her own work.

8. Paul Tillich, *A History of Christian Thought: From Its Judaic and Hellinistic Origins to Existentialism*, ed. Carl E. Braaten (New York: Touchstone, 1972). My own use of Tillich's "theonomy" is vastly simplified and lifted out of the context that the theologian establishes between the idea and its relationship to the Christian European eras of sacred theology. But I hope that we might summarize a complicated idea here without seriously violating the original.

9. The student of Americana will immediately recognize that "God" is manifest cause to worldly effect within a certain configuration of cultural values; Perry Miller's classic work on early New England communities renders a detailed analysis of the view; cf. "God's Controversy With New England," in *The New England Mind: The Seventeenth Century* (Boston: Beacon Press, 1961), pp. 463–92.

10. Margaret Walker, *Jubilee* (Boston: Houghton Mifflin, 1966), pp. 3–4 All references are from this edition, and page numbers are supplied in parentheses in the text.

11. Emile Durkheim, *The Elementary forms of Religious Life*, trans. Joseph Ward Swain (New York: Free Press, 1965).

12. Robert Hemenway, *Zora Neale Hurston: A Literary Biography* (Urbana: University of Illinois Press, 1977). This important work on Hurston's life provides an exhaustive account of the writer's various relationships. Hurston herself was a lover of males, but never sustained the liaisons quite long enough for us to see any pattern in this chapter of her biography except as short-lived serial monogamies.

13. Zora Neale Hurston, *Their Eyes Were Watching God* (New York: Fawcett Premier Books, 1969), p, 121. All references are to this edition and page numbers are supplied in parentheses in the text.

14. Zora Neale Hurston, "What White Publishers Won't Print," in *I Love Myself When I am Laughing . . . and Then Again When I am Looking Mean and Impressive*, ed. Alice Walker (Old Westbury, N.Y.: Feminist Press, 1979), pp. 169–73. In discussing why white American publishers of her time would only publish the "morbid" about the lives of black Americans, Hurston suggests what is both frightening and familiar to contemplate. "It is assumed that all non-Anglo-Saxons are uncomplicated sterotypes. Everybody knows all about them. They are lay figures mounted in the museum where all may take them in at a glance. They are made of bent wires without insides at all. So how could anybody write a book about the non-existent?" (p. 170). But we might also consider whether or not the obscene didn't happen—if black people themselves did not come to see their lives as a very fixed, monolithic, immobile quality of human experience? Alice Walker in the dedication to this volume (p. 2) points out that if Hurston were a "colorist," as some of her critics have claimed, then she "was not blind and . . . saw that black men (and black women) have been, and are, colorist to an embarrasing degree."

15. W.E.B. DuBois, *The Souls of Black Folk: Essays and Sketches* (New York: Fawcett Publications, 1967). Dubois's classic reading of the African-American predicament is posed in the opening chapter of this germinal piece. He writes, "one ever feels his twoness,—an American, a Negro; two souls, two thoughts, two unreconciled strivings; two warring ideals in one dark body, whose dogged strength alone keeps it from being torn asunder" (p. 17).

16. Zora Neale Hurston, "My Folks," *Dust Tracks On A Road*, introduction by Larry Neal (Philadelphia: J.P. Lippincott, 1971), pp. 12–32.

17. The term "ancestral imperative" does not originate in Albert Murray, but his use of it is dialectical and expansive. The best demonstration of Murray's argument is his *South to a Very Old Place* (New York: McGraw-Hill, 1971).

18. Virginia Woolf, *A Room of One's Own* (New York: Harcourt, Brace and World, 1957), pp. 61–81.

19. Professor Nellie McKay recently reminded me that African-American women during the era of slavery often killed their offspring in order to forestall their enslavement. Read against McKay's interpretation, Eva Peace's "intervention" is historically grounded at the same time that it does not lose its awful aspects. The convergence of historical motivation, individual willfulness, and the mother's violation of blood rites would create one of the profounder bases of tension across the work.

20. See, for example, the description of these arrangements in Dorothy Dinnerstein,

The Mermaid and the Minotaur: Sexual Arrangements and the Human Malaise (New York: Harper Colophon Books, 1976).

21. The terms are taken from Northrop Frye, "Historical Criticism: Theory of Modes," in *Anatomy of Criticism: Four Essays* (Princeton: Princeton University Press, 1971), pp. 36–67.

22. Kenneth Burke, "The Four Master Tropes," in *A Grammar of Motives*, appendix D (New York: Prentice-Hall, 1945), pp. 503–17. Burke's refinement of a notion of dialectics in art is significant both as an image and concept of radical revision. His "perspective of perspectives"—the principle of the "modified noun"— locates an ideal against which we might try to imagine the future of Afro-American letters and our meditation concerning them.

23. Harper and Stepto, p. 215.

24. Ibid., p. 216.

25. Ibid., p. 217.

MODERNISM OF THE "SCATTERED REMNANT"
Race and Politics in H.D.'s Development

Susan Stanford Friedman

> Your country *is* desolate, your cities are
> burned with fire: your land, strangers devour
> it in your presence.... Except the Lord of
> hosts had left unto us a very small remnant,
> we should have been as Sodom
> and... Gomorrah.... And it shall come to
> pass in that day that the remnant of
> Israel... shall return.... For though thy
> people Israel be as the sand of the sea, *yet* a
> remnant of them shall return.
>
> > *Isaiah* 1: 7, 9; 10: 20–22

> If you are consoled or integrated, you help
> console and integrate the scattered remnant. I
> don't think society can be reconstructed from
> outside. I have said if there is comfort, it is
> solitary. When the ego or centre of our
> amorphous, scattered personality crystallizes
> out, then and then only, are we of use to
> ourselves and other people. I have said it is
> *sauve qui peut*, even for the best of us. In
> saving myself, one creates a shell, not the
> isolated, highly individual spiral-shell I spoke
> of, but a minute coral-shell, one of a million,
> or a single wax-cell of the honey-comb.
>
> > H.D., *The Sword Went Out to Sea* (*Synthesis of
> > a Dream*) (41)

> The DREAM [*The Sword*] is, as I said before,
> fantasy-cum-reality. But the five-year "reality"
> of bombs, fly-bombs and V2 was by far the less
> stable, or "real" than the world of
> imagination.... It [the novel] stands or falls or
> fades on its own merit or its own
> "message"—the "Message" being simply, that
> the world was, perhaps is and possibly will be
> "crashing to extinction," if those in authority,
> no matter where or who, don't stop smashing

up things with fly-bombs, V2 and the
ubiquitous (possibly) so-called "atom." They
could do something with the atom—better
than smashing cherry-orchards . . . that is all I
am trying to put over in the DREAM.

H.D., Letter to Richard Aldington, 6 June 1950?

Although H.D. conceived of *The Sword Went Out to Sea (Synthesis of a Dream)* (1946–1947) as a pacifist statement against Hiroshima, she never directly promoted political causes or social movements in her writing. As a poet, novelist, and essayist, H.D. abandoned the overtly political direction she had charted around 1913 in "The Suffragist," an early feminist conversion narrative that ends with her post-Jamesian innocent American following a British feminist to a political meeting. In spite of her strong anti-fascist convictions, the alliance between writers and activism in the thirties held no attractions for H.D. Although her work in the forties and fifties encodes a critique of patriarchy and violence, H.D. did not believe that genuine social change could effectively originate in mass movements. Like Anaïs Nin, she feared that political organizations reproduce on a dangerously large scale the unresolved violence within the individual. Deeply influenced by psychoanalysis, H.D. believed that lasting change begins within the individual psyche, within the personal, even the solitary.[1]

While the once common view of H.D. as the escapist dryad too delicate for modern life has largely been dismissed by the new wave of reading and writing about her, the charge of political escapism on her part may take the place of the earlier critical view.[2] In *Herself Defined: The Poet H.D. and Her World*, Barbara Guest characterizes H.D.'s politics as an unquestioning, old-fashioned conservatism common to many late nineteenth-century upper-middle class Americans. "To take it further," she concludes, "H.D. avoided politics of any kind" (116). No one has yet associated H.D.'s politics with the views of many of the male modernists she knew well—Ezra Pound's anti-Semitic fascism, T. S. Eliot's reverant Toryism, W. B. Yeats's cultural elitism, D. H. Lawrence's flirtations with racism and fascism, or Wyndham Lewis's general bigotry. It is possible, however, that people will come to regard H.D.'s politics as a gentler version of the generally reactionary direction of these men.[3]

H.D.'s focus on the single cell of the honeycomb, the minute coral of the shell community as an alternative to mass movements, is not as conservative, naive, or as apolitical as it might at first seem, for several reasons. First, the relationship between politics and art is much too complex to be resolved by a reductionistic determination of an artist's role in political movements. William Faulkner was not alone in producing novels more progressive than his political pronouncements on race; nor was Richard Wright alone in finding the demands of his political party a tyranny for his art. Second, the dismissal of the profound feminism of H.D.'s poetic mythmaking and *Künstlerromane* from a consideration of her politics is based on a definition of politics that marginalizes the issue of gender. It reenacts the trivializing of women that her epics and novels themselves attack. The concept of "politics" itself needs revision so that it includes the concerns of women.

Third, the politics of both women and men in the modernist movement needs serious reexamination to determine the possible impact of gender in the differing political visions expressed in their work. While modernism did produce the overtly political, aesthetic activism of women like Käthe Kollwitz, Rebecca West, Nancy Cunard, and Muriel Rukeyser, the exclusion of women in general from the public political process also led the alienation from politics as it has conventionally been defined. H.D.'s distrust of political activism may be part of a larger gender-based pattern that includes writers like Virginia Woolf, Gertrude Stein, Dorothy Richardson, May Sinclair, Zora Neale Hurston, Djuna Barnes, and Jean Rhys, as well as Anaïs Nin. Different in degree, extent, and explicitness, these women nonetheless expressed a progressive politics originating in an exploration of the power structures underlying the personal. The private domain of the individual self in relationship to others, the scene of woman's very confinement, served as the point of political origins.[4] How far each woman took her political analysis as expressed in her life and work— particularly how much she made connections between gender and issues of race, class, religion, sexual preference, and state power—is a matter of individual variation.

This essay argues that a conventional definition of political engagement as public activism has obscured the significant role of politics in the development of H.D.'s post World War I modernism. More specifically, it argues that H.D.'s personal experience with the Harlem Renaissance played a key role in deepening and broadening her early feminism into a fully progressive modernism based in an identification with all the people who exist as "the scattered remnant" at the fringes of culture. Rather than activism providing an agenda for her life and art, H.D.'s writing itself constituted her action against the dominant culture. Based in the personal, her texts craft a honeycomb, a coral shell, that reaches out toward a broader community of the exiled. Her choice of the Biblical phrase "the scattered remnant" to identify her companions evokes Isaiah's promise of redemption for the "scattered remnant" of exiled Jews and by extension all those in spiritual diaspora from the madness of the mainstream.

The Biographical Record

As an expatriate American who did not visit the U.S. between 1921 and 1936, H.D. appears to have missed the Harlem Renaissance, as well as the periodic disruptions against class and race privilege that disturbed the political and social surface of American life. World War I had served as the culminating disintegrating force tearing apart the political and moral rigidities of the nineteenth century, including the unquestioned racism of a Jim Crow apartheid throughout many parts of the United States. The return of black soldiers from a less overtly racist Europe played a major role in the revival of a civil rights movement and the initiation of a cultural renaissance centered in Harlem and constituting the Afro-American expression of modernism. For blacks, the creative cross-currents of the Harlem Renaissance provided a validating mileau in which they could define, despair of, and celebrate their history and identity in their own language, music, art, and dance. For interested whites, in contrast, Harlem's explosive energies provided a fascinating window into Otherness—all too often defined and exploited as exotic and primitive, but nonetheless introducing them to the outrages of discrimination. In particular, the Harlem Renaissance drew many progressive white artists and intellectuals like a magnet and profoundly influenced the form and content of their own modernist work.[5]

Although H.D. did not directly take part in the fashionable exodus of white intellectuals to the salons, nightclubs, and ballrooms of Harlem, she was well acquainted with those who did. First, she knew both Carl Van Vechten and Nancy Cunard, key bridge figures between the black and white avant-garde of the twenties and thirties. As a white man, Van Vechten used his wealth and influence to introduce not only the works of Stein to the American literary world, but also those of many black writers, musicians, and artists to white audiences. His controversial best seller, *Nigger Heaven* (1925), was a novel that many believed sensationalized black life at the same time that it exposed patterns of discrimination in New York (Huggins, 98–126). H.D. was probably referring to this novel when she wrote from London to her American friend Viola Jordan, "I have been reading a good deal on the 'darky' problem lately. Do you care for Van Vechten?" (February 24, 1926).

H.D. probably knew Van Vechten personally as well as through his writing because both knew Stein and her circle in Paris.[6] Robert McAlmon, the editor of an avant-garde press that published Stein, was H.D.'s close friend and Winifred Bryher's husband. After the birth of her daughter and the final dissolution of her marriage to Richard Aldington in 1919, H.D. lived and traveled with Bryher for many years. Held together by love and loyalty to each other, these vastly different women charted intellectual and creative pathways through the currents of the avant-garde that are virtually inseparable. H.D. read widely in Bryher's vast library, which included many of the little magazines of modernism, a steady supply of newspapers and magazines from the States, and all the latest books.

Through McAlmon, H.D. and Bryher became friends in the twenties with Cunard, an avant-garde British writer who scandalized aristocratic society with her black lover and political causes. Cunard considered Van Vechten to be "the spirit of vulgarity," the epitome of whites who "go slumming" in Harlem "out of curiosity and jealousy and don't-know-why" (Ford, 118–20).[7] But like Van Vechten, Cunard was an important bridge figure between the black and white cultural centers of Harlem, London, and Paris. After visiting Harlem in 1931 and 1932, Cunard published her monumental anthology *Negro* (1934), an eight-hundred page collection of black and white writers about Afro-American culture.

Cunard was in some ways an uncanny combination, but less inhibited version of Bryher and H.D., which may explain why H.D. and Bryher had such ambivalent feelings about Cunard over the years. Daughters of England's two most powerful shipping magnates, Bryher and Cunard both rebelled against their families' great wealth and used what money they controlled to sponsor the arts and promote progressive political causes. Possessing startling beauty, which made them the muses of many men, H.D. and Cunard both fought to forge their own voices as women in their writing. But Cunard was more flamboyant in her rebellions than either the more puritanical Bryher or the intensely private H.D. Bryher wrote to H.D. that she didn't "approve of" Cunard (April 1924). In spite of her own rebelliousness, Bryher detested bohemianism, drinking, and sexual promiscuity, all of which she associated with Cunard. To Bryher and H.D., Cunard represented a kind of public sexual and political engagement that both fascinated and repelled them. However, neither Bryher's disapproval nor her divorce in 1927 from Cunard's close friend McAlmon stopped their association. Cunard became a confidante of Norman Douglas, a member of Bryher's intimate circle. Bryher was fully sympathetic with Cunard's efforts to promote equality for blacks and supported her Scottsboro defense organization in the spring of 1933. Having read about the case in the *New Masses*, to which she probably subscribed, Bryher had sent in her protest form, as she told her second husband Kenneth Macpherson in a letter dated January 14, 1933.[8]

Less well known in the history of the Harlem Renaissance, Macpherson and his friend Robert Herring nonetheless played key roles in initiating H.D. and Bryher to its art. Beginning in 1926, Macpherson and H.D. became lovers, an affair that Bryher agreed to screen by marrying Macpherson in 1927. As H.D. wittily described their *ménage* to Havelock Ellis, "The Macphersons are almost

MYSELF, we seem to be a composite beast with three faces" (1928?). A Scottish artist and writer, Macpherson established with Bryher the POOL film company and co-edited *Close-Up*, the first film journal to treat cinema as a serious art form. Herring was a British writer and intimate friend, whom Bryher later named the editor of *Life and Letters Today* after her purchase of the avant-garde review. Like Cunard, Macpherson and Herring were part of the white crowd for whom "the Negro was in vogue" (Huggins, 84–136). They regularly visited Harlem on their trips to the States with Bryher and brought back to Europe all the latest black writing and music. While Bryher hated the Harlem parties as much as she had detested the Parisian café scene, Macpherson and Herring immersed themselves in Afro-American culture, writing home to H.D. about how much she would enjoy the ferment and excitement of this world. More substantively, Herring made the connection directly between their avant-garde film work in the expressionist short *Wing-Beat* and Jean Toomer's *Cane*, when he wrote to H.D.: "Have you read *Cane*? I've been so excited. It's so *Wing-Beat*, and the, it is in prose rather what Hughes is in verse" (1931?).

Herring, who had many personal friends in Harlem, introduced the internationally acclaimed singer and actor Paul Robeson and his wife Eslanda Goode Robeson into H.D.'s circle in the late twenties after the Robesons moved to London. H.D. heard Robeson sing spirituals on record and in person. She either knew about or attended his performances of Eugene O'Neill's *Emperor Jones* and *All God's Chillun Got Wings*; the London production of Jerome Kern's *Showboat* (1928), an American musical on the explosive subject of miscegenation; and *Othello* at London's Savoy Theatre (1930), which outraged or thrilled viewers depending on their feelings about race. By 1929, Macpherson began work on his first (and only) full-length film. Starring the Robesons and H.D., *Borderline* provided Robeson with his first chance to act on the screen. Released in 1930 to the acclaim of important directors like W.B. Pabst and the confusion of many conventional viewers, *Borderline* is a modernist silent film focusing on the sexual and racial entanglements of a white couple and black couple in the Swiss Alps. The white man initiates an affair with the black woman, a love that nearly destroys the dignity of the black man, unhinges the white woman entirely, and ends in rage and violence. H.D. wrote the pamphlet *Borderline* that was released with the film as an extended statement of its thematic and technical innovations.[9]

The film provided the basis for an ongoing friendship with the Robesons that survived the personal turmoil in their lives. The Robesons stayed at Bryher's hotel during the filming of *Borderline* and were later guests at Kenwin, her Bauhaus villa built in 1931. In spite of the Robesons' separation in 1930, Essie's condescending book *Paul Robeson: Negro*, and their reunion in 1932 (Gilliam,

57–64), they remained in touch. Herring in particular continued well into the thirties to see Paul regularly, and Bryher arranged and paid for some psycho-analysis for Paul Robeson, Jr., whom Essie took to Vienna in 1931.[10]

These friendships were complicated by the sexual ambiguities and shifting relationships, in which race played a definite part. By temperament a bisexual like H.D., Macpherson's immersion in the Harlem Renaissance led to a series of black lovers after 1928. H.D. was devastated by Macpherson's first serious affair with a black café singer and again by a young black lover who contracted tuberculosis. During the early thirties, Bryher and H.D. often commiserated with each other about Macpherson's tubercular "black boy," Borzoi as they called him, although they were clearly resigned to Macpherson's changing sexual allegiance. Bryher continued to pay all the bills and in June of 1933 tried to arrange for Anna Freud to psychoanalyze him. As late as 1934, H.D. assured Bryher that he no longer disturbed her: "I am happy about Kex [Macpherson] and his 'cho. baby' " (19 November). Bryher responded with a report of her attempts to help: "We are all now, self, Dog [Macpherson], Smide [Walter Schmideberg, Macpherson's analyst] and friends of Schmide trying to fix up Borzoi but the color business is most difficult, there is practically nothing between a pauper ward where they are guaranteed to die within 3 months and about eight guineas a week private. However we still work" (November 21, 1934).

Robeson himself may have been the object of Macpherson's attraction for black men. Macpherson's fascination with Robeson's beauty as a body to film is evident in his stills, sketches, and montage for *Borderline*. The film may well have provided a sublimated outlet for the erotic attraction to blacks that was soon to break across his affair with H.D. Herring, a homosexual, was also deeply attached to Robeson, and his impatience with Essie's continual inter-ruptions of his conversations with Paul may reflect an attraction that he did not admit even to his confident, H.D. To complicate things even further, Macpherson may well have fallen for Cunard, as H.D.'s husband Aldington had done a few years before. At one point in 1933, Macpherson was seeing so much of Cunard while he was staying in H.D.'s empty London flat that Bryher wrote him, "Be careful about Nancy and her negroes—it wouldn't be fair to get Kat [H.D.] kicked out of Sloane, or with a bad reputation there. I couldn't bear another scandal for at least 3 months" (March 16, 1933).

H.D. herself was clearly attracted to Robeson, although there is no evidence to suggest that they had an affair. Robeson was just the kind of man who would have appealed to her. Embodying a Platonic ideal, Robeson was scholar, athlete, and artist. The two "Nude Studies" of Robeson by photographer Nicolas Murray seem modeled on the classical sculpture that H.D. loved (Susan Robeson, 43–45). He had All-American awards for football in 1917 and 1918, a Phi Beta

Kappa degree from Rutgers University, and a law degree from Columbia University. Although Robeson was more distinguished and famous than H.D.'s friends, his combination of qualities is reminiscent of Aldington himself and the other men, like Sir High Dowding, who stood in for Aldington later in her life.[11]

Highly coded, erotic undertones are present in a short story and two poems H.D. wrote about Robeson. "Two Americans," written in 1930, is an evocative prose sketch centering on an intense moment of intimacy between her own persona and the Robeson figure at a private party. "Red Roses for Bronze," published in 1931, is a poem offering sculpture as tribute to the "bronze god" she loves, but with whom she refuses a casual affair. When Bryher wrote her that Macpherson didn't like "Two Americans," H.D.'s response reveals the undercurrents of interracial jealousy among the friends: "Thank you for sticking up for Two Americans. Nobody seems to like it. I felt it did a lot for what it was trying to do. Kex [Macpherson] is jealous, always was—thought I wrote Red Roses for Bronze for P. Robeson" (October 31, 1934). Robeson was still much on her mind in the last poem she wrote, *Hermetic Definition* (1961). The poem's archetypal lover is directly modeled on a black Haitian journalist, Lionel Durand, whom she identifies with Rafer Johnson, the black decathlon star of the 1960 Olympics. He, in turn, sets her thinking of the "living bronze" she loved in "Red Roses for Bronze," "the tall god standing where the race is run"—that is, Robeson himself (*Hermetic Definition*, 14–15; *Collected Poems*, 211–15).

On its face, the biographical record suggests that H.D. and her white friends might fit the pattern of so many liberal whites whose disgust for discrimination and sympathy for blacks ran very deep, but whose friendship and fascination were often tainted by covert forms of racism. Black artists paid a price for white attraction to black folk forms—the price of all patronage: the threat of continued Otherness, dependence, powerlessness, and appropriation. Although personal friends like Langston Hughes defended Van Vechten, *Nigger Heaven* was attacked by many black intellectuals as an exploitation and distortion of black culture. According to some, whites were merely celebrating the very stereotype of black culture originally created by racists—primitivism, sensuality, emotionalism, intuition, unschooled artistry, child-like simplicity. More invidious than outright bigotry, this projection of the sexual and irrational onto blacks continued to deny full humanity and autonomy to black artists. Mrs. R. Osgood Mason, the white patron of Hughes and Hurston, epitomizes the tendency of many liberal whites to enforce the continued infantilization of black artists. In exchange for her patronage, she expected to shape and control what and when "her" black artists produced. Both Hughes and Hurston had to break away from the patronizing forms of the deadly security and interest she provided in order to establish their integrity as human beings and artists (Huggins, 118, 129–33; Walker, 83–92).

Although black artists generally found European culture freer of racism than American society, Robeson himself may have been hinting at paternalism in his highly guarded apologia, *Here I Stand*. He describes how "gratifying" it was to accept the "friendly welcome" he received in London from the "upper-class people who patronized the arts" (32). During the late twenties and early thirties, he moved freely in the aristocratic circles of England, where he was treated "as a gentleman and a scholar" (32). But as he became acquainted with African people, history, and language in London, he left the aritocratic circles largely behind and began to travel among "the common people" in the British Isles. Collecting their songs, he felt really at home and did not miss the "great country houses where I had often been welcomed as guest, having tea and exchanging smiles with Lord and Lady This-and-that," where he increasingly found a disturbing sympathy with fascism (48–52).

Bryher was violently anti-fascist and impatient with the British aristocracy. Her father, a self-made millionaire of poor and probably Jewish origins, may have been England's second richest man, but he was in no position to place his family at the center of Britain's upper-class society. Bryher's refugee work to help Jews escape Germany was well underway when Robeson himself became appalled with Nazi anti-Semitism (Gilliam, 71; Bryher, 275–77). Nonetheless, Bryher's patronage of the Robesons may have partially fit into the category of the patronizing associations he increasingly abandoned. Certainly the racism of Bryher's and H.D.'s private references to the "chocolate baby" suggest the possibility of covert racism in dealings with the Robesons. Essie Robeson's return of Bryher's loan in 1934 suggests that the Robesons wanted no hint of financial obligation. In her typically blunt way, Bryher wrote to H.D.: "Essie wrote me to return money borrowed in Switzerland years ago, I guess she wants dirt [gossip]" (October 30, 1934).

Given the sexual and racial entanglements of the people in H.D.'s circle, it is even more tempting to suppose that she and her friends were drawn into the sexual politics of interracial erotics. The interracial sexuality of the Harlem Renaissance was no doubt not immune from the patterns identified more recently by such writers as Alice Walker in *Meridian*, Eldridge Cleaver in *Soul on Ice*, and Michelle Wallace in *Black Macho*.[12] Some black men and white women defiantly broke through the sexual taboos erected by the institutions of racism and sexism. At its best, some couples may have achieved, at least for a time, a transcendence of racial division in their private relationships. But at its worst, the psychic scars of racism resulted in white women's and black men's use and abuse of each other: the white woman expiating her racial guilt in a manipulative or masochistic relationship with a black man; the black man asserting the manhood denied him by white men by possessing the white man's woman.

The publicity surrounding their lives put Cunard and Robeson at the center of much speculation about interracial sexuality. At the very time of his friendship with H.D.'s circle, Robeson had numerous affairs with white women, one of whom he nearly married (Gilliam, 57–65). Cunard lived with a black composer, Henry Crowder (Gilliam, 71). But the scandal sheets in England and America printed the worst about both. Cunard was attacked for her "Negrophilism," her passion for racial justice that the scandal mongers believed covered a passion for the forbidden black man. "Any interest manifested by a white person [in black causes]," Cunard retorted, "is immediately transformed into a sex 'scandal' " (Ford, 121–22). White men like Van Vechten had a greater freedom to travel to Harlem, but a white woman who took an openly political stand for racial justice was viewed as a whore and traitor to her race. The particular scandal to which Cunard alluded was the accusation by the press that during her visit to Harlem in 1931, she had adjoining rooms with Robeson at a hotel in Harlem. White and black papers on the East Coast continually reported that she was "chasing and being chased by lustful Negro men." Officials detained her at Ellis Island before deportation on grounds of "moral turpitude" (Ford, 143). The London press printed equally vicious accounts and quoted her mother's private description of Cunard as a "nigger lover." Cunard's own pamphlet denouncing the racism of her Virginia-born mother undoubtedly fueled the racist flames. Entitled "Black Man and White Ladyship" (1932), this essay is an astonishing manifesto of personal politics, a public declaration of her private hatred for her mother's class and race prejudice and her own right to love and live with whom she pleased.

These are undoubtedly the kind of scandals Bryher hoped to avoid in 1933 when she begged Macpherson to be discreet in using H.D.'s empty flat with "Nancy and her negroes." Did she half-believe the presses' accusation of Cunard's racial promiscuity? Cunard did not, after all, win her libel suits against the British Press until 1934. Even closer to home, did Bryher and H.D. regard Macpherson's succession of black lovers and Herring's possibly erotic feelings as a homosexual version of the sexual "negrophilism" of which Cunard was accused? In any case, H.D. had fearfully guarded her privacy ever since the dissolution of her marriage and the affair with Cecil Gray that had resulted in the birth of Perdita. Cunard's insistence on fighting racial injustice through public disclosure of private relationships would have horrified and terrified H.D. Cunard's particular brand of personal politics must have been a strikingly negative model. Within the privacy of her own fantasy, however, H.D.'s certain jealousy of Macpherson's black lovers and her own attraction for Robeson could have easily drawn her into the vortex of interracial conflict and eroticism.

The Literary Record

Although Bryher's wealth and the interracial erotics in H.D.'s circle constituted the conditions of white paternalism, the Harlem Renaissance did not
function for H.D. as a fashionable excursion into the dangerously exotic and
erotic world of Otherness. Instead, her connections with the people and art of
Afro-America provided an experience that helped her to define a modernism
of the margins, a modernism based on an identification with those left out of
the cultural mainstream. In a series of texts written between 1927 and 1930,
when her connection with the Harlem Renaissance was at its height, H.D.
explored the issue of race as a way of identifying the bonds between her own
and other's experience of being different in a hostile world. In each case, her
development of a politics of race emerged directly out of personal relationship,
out of the inner, subjective world where H.D.'s politics always began.

The first of these texts is *HER*, the *roman à clef* she wrote in 1927 about
the intertwined crises of sexuality and vocation that she experienced between
1905 and 1910. The focus of the novel is the troubled Hermione, nicknamed
Her, who has just failed out of college and feels torn between her love for the
unconventional poet George Lowndes (Pound) and the even more unconventional fey mystic, Fayne Rabb (Frances Gregg). Race by no means appears
central to the unfolding narrative of her engagement to George, her decision
to escape his determination to make her his muse, her commitment to Fayne,
and Fayne's betrayal of lesbian love in her affair with George. But nonetheless,
Hermione's relationship with Mandy, the family's black cook, helps to clarify
Hermione's basic alienation from her family and foreshadows the major transformations later in the novel.[13] A narrative that focuses on a young white girl
who loves the family's black servant dangerously evokes the conventional stereotyped script so scathingly attacked in Alice Childress's hilarious *Just One of
the Family*.[14] What is interesting about the issue of race in *HER* is the degree
to which H.D. avoids that familiar pattern.

Early in the novel, Hermione comes into the kitchen to give Mandy a letter
after spending a disastrous afternoon mentally and physically wandering in
circles in the nearby woods. Her despair is significant: "I am Hermione Gart,
a failure," she thinks (4). In her confusion, she is without words and feels that
"she could put no name to the things she apprehended" (13). "Words beat and
formed unformulated syllables" in her brain (25). Her exchange with Mandy
both symbolically and linguistically suggests that she will one day find the
words, the formula, to break out of her isolation.

Mandy is pitting cherries, perhaps an evocative image of the ripening sexuality of the young Hermione at the opening of this *Bildungsroman*. Fleeing all

exchanges with her family, Hermione wants to find some "excuse to stay" in the kitchen with Mandy. "Plunge hands into the wide deep corn-coloured bowl and help Mandy," she thinks (26). Helping leads to talking, which she has been too distraught to do in any conventional sense. Talking leads to being drawn into Mandy's language: "Her fell into the rhythm of Mandy's speech, the moment she began to speak to Mandy" (26). Mandy has not only a powerful language, the words Hermione lacks, but she also has "her formula," a sense of herself and the world that guides her through each day. Mandy's power of perception reassures the young woman trapped in the mad circling of her own mind. H.D. emphasizes the unspoken bond between the two by joining black and white in the cherry bowl as if they were part of the same body: "Her slipped a white hand into the deep bowl, black arm lifted from the deep bowl" (27).

This identification of the white girl with the black woman foreshadows the lesbian fusion of selves Hermione later achieves with Fayne. H.D.'s use of the nickname "Her" in the subject position in the early kitchen scene anticipates the word play to follow in Hermione's recognition that her love for Fayne has given her a sense of identity: "I know her. I know her. Her. I am Her. She is Her. Knowing her, I know Her" (158). H.D.'s description of the two women bending toward each other to kiss echoes the ambiguous and condensed syntax used earlier to connect the white and black arms: "Her face bent forward, face bent toward Her" (163). Identification with the black woman paves the way for her later experience of difference, the lesbian love that brings with it a validation of her self and her writing.

H.D.'s lyric celebration of the bond between white and black rests within an ironic context that suggests an attempt to avoid the white tendency to sentimentalize the black-mammy-with-the-heart-of-gold. The moment of fusion Hermione and Mandy experience follows an ironic verbal exchange in which the white girl twice chides the black woman, reprimands that can occur only because of her own white privilege. H.D. underlines that structure of mistress and servant by having Hermione say "Mandy, I don't see how you keep the flies out" and then think "Reprimand Mandy, find some excuse to stay here" (26). This thought, born of class and race privilege, foreshadows a more ironic reprimand on the subject of discrimination itself. Mandy insists that her husband has picked the wrong cherries because "A black man is a black man. You don't get no black man rightly to pick cherries." Hermione's liberal perspective dictates white correction of the black woman's "racism:" " 'A gardener is a gardener, a black gardener is as good as a white gardener. There's no need *discriminating.*' Mandy would appreciate that last affectation. '*Dis*-criminating,' she went on with it, let it sink into Mandy's appreciative consciousness (there was no one for appreciating the fine distinctions of the English language like their Mandy)" (26–27). As they argue on about discrimination, the words become "abstract," a "Platonic" play of language with "finesse, aplomb, subtlety" (27). The "real" content of their exchange is increasingly the wordless bond between them.

It is possible to read this exchange as patronizing on H.D.'s part—a valorizing of the educated white girl who knows more about discrimination than uneducated blacks themselves. Such a reading, however, does not take into account the subtle irony and humor that permeates the texture of *HER*, a level of self-qualification that parallels *Portrait of the Artist as a Young Man*, a *Künstlerroman* that H.D.'s novel echoes and answers. *HER*'s narrative presents Hermione's halting search to break the conventional life-scripts of a young girl of her class and race. To do so, she must separate from the conventionalities of her family. Her relationship with Mandy is the first medium of rebellion in the novel, as incomplete as H.D. shows Hermione's understanding to be. Hermione defines her difference from her conventionally feminine sister-in-law Minnie by contrasting their opposite responses to Mandy. Minnie wants to turn Mandy into an ornament by dressing her up in a white cap and constantly correcting her work (36–37), while Hermione carries on a violent interior monologue against her hated sister-in-law's treatment of Mandy. Hermione's identification with Mandy against her family foreshadows the rebellion that will soon erupt against the confinement of upper-middle class femininity.

H.D.'s subsequent literary efforts to absorb the insights of the Harlem Renaissance also came directly out of her personal relationships, this time with the Robesons. Building on the empathetic approach of *HER*, these texts present a series of identifications across racial lines that avoid the pitfalls of interracial erotics and foreshadow her feminist modernism of the forties and fifties. Her public document, *Borderline*, which reveals no personal relationship whatsoever, nonetheless lays out the basis of identification in stark terms. The movie's title, she explains, was chosen deliberately as a metaphor for a state of mind characteristic of "the lost generation" after the war. The setting, "some indefinite mid-European mountain district" is "borderline"; the two couples, white and black, are each "borderline" in their own way. The whites, Astrid and Thorne:

> are borderline social cases, not out of life, not in life; the woman is a sensitive neurotic, the man, a handsome, degenerate dipsomaniac. . . . Astrid, the white-cerebral is and is not outcast, is and is not a social alien, is and is not a normal human being, she is borderline. These two are specifically chosen to offset another borderline couple of more dominant integrity. These last, Pete and his sweetheart Adah, have a less intensive problem, but border; they dwell on the cosmic racial borderline. They are black people among white people. (5–6)

"Borderline" is a geographic, psychological, and racial metaphor that creates a group of white and black people who exist at the margins, not in the mainstream of culture. As in *HER*, H.D.'s emphasis is not on discrimination and therefore on difference, but on identification and the common experience of alienated whites and blacks. The problem of Pete and Adah, she stresses, is "not dealt with as the everlasting black-white Problem with a capital" (6). Louis Martz correctly uses H.D.'s borderline metaphor to characterize the partial alienation evident in her earliest Imagist poetry as well as her post-war work (H.D., *Collected Poems*, xi–xii). But it is significant that this striking metaphor of alienation first appears in her work in a text and film about interracial relationships—as if contemplating the situation of "black people among white people" helped her to articulate her own "borderline" existence. This identification comes without obscuring the real difference between whites and blacks, but rather through her attempt as a white woman to imaginatively put herself in the place of the Other. As she writes of a scene in the movie: "In the little café through which Pete stalks and his mistress turns, gazing with great eyes at a vague conglomeration of whites, we have something of the nightmare that we would imagine a sensitive negro might have, on facing a room full of antagonistic presences" (32), H.D. stresses that Macpherson's handling of perspective and montage have been designed to give the audience an experience of this "nightmare."

Borderline identifies the artist of "modernity" with those on the spiritual "borderlines" of culture. In praising Macpherson's work as director, H.D. defines her own modernism, one that charts a pathway between pure political activism and pure abstraction. Macpherson, she writes, exhibits the ideal balance of extremes: "He is not at all allied with the ultra-modern abstract school of rhomboid and curve and cross-beam of tooth pick or coal shovel"(6)—a contentless abstraction. But "he is, in no way whatever, concerned personally with the black-white political problem. As an artist, he sees beauty. . . . he seems to say again and again, 'I'm not busy with party politics' " (9). Nonetheless, she finds in Macpherson's modernism a political result achieved precisely because he focuses on the personal, the individual in the context of race:

> Nevertheless, in his judicious, remote manner, he has achieved more for that much mooted and hooted Problem (with a capital) than if he went about to gain sympathy. He says, "here is a man, he is black," he says, "here is a woman also of partial African abstraction." He says, not "here is a black man, here is a mulatto woman," but "here is a *man*, here is a *woman*." He says, "look, sympathize with them and love them," not because they are black but because they are man, because they are woman. This race presentation will be no palliative for a decadent palette. (9)

While using a minority experience of marginality as a paradigm of the spiritual affliction of many post-war wanderers, H.D. is careful not to collapse the distinction between racial oppression and other forms of alienation. She writes that although the movie does not focus on discrimination, "It remains however a motive to be counted on; though the threads are woven in and through the fabric, white into black and black into white, Pete and Adah must inevitably remain 'borderline,' whether by their own choice and psychic affiliation or through sheer crude brute causes" (6). As an exploration of racism, the film is brutally honest about white privilege, a fact H.D. stresses in her interpretation of the character Astrid. As she imaginatively projected herself into the black psyche, so she also acted out the part of the racist white woman—literally in the film; figuratively in the pamphlet. Furious with Thorne's love of the black woman, Astrid "screams 'it has all happened because these people are *black*' " (33). H.D. describes Astrid's "intemperate fury" and draws a frighteningly negative portrait of the woman she acted, whose "borderline" characteristics were so like her own: "Astrid, the woman, terribly incarnated and wracked with the most banal of feminine vices, jealousy. . . . Astrid rises in abstraction of fiend-rage and claws the air shouting, 'nigger-lover!' " (34, 38). It is certainly possible that H.D. projected into this character her own rage and jealousy at the black lovers for whom Macpherson had left her. If so, it is all the more remarkable that she could confront and condemn the racist form a betrayed white woman's anger could take.

H.D.'s sense of triumph in making *Borderline* may well have included an element of victory in crossing the borderline into the taboo afflicting the white cultural tradition: her own and others' racism. In October 1930, she wrote to Macpherson: "You have no idea, in retrospect, how wonderful it all seems, not only the making but the showing [of *Borderline*]. I feel we did a very brave thing, it would never be like that again, we would know and could gauge on our reactions and the actions of others. I feel it was a sort of 'the veil of the temple was rent in twain.' "

Borderline scarcely hints at the feelings H.D. had for Robeson himself, nor are biographical undertones at all evident. H.D.'s privately printed "Two Americans," however, is a frankly autobiographical sketch of an evening party in Vaud with herself, the Robesons, Macpherson, Bryher, and Herring. The names are the masks H.D. used in a number of her *roman à clef* from the period: the expatriate poet Raymonde Ransom (H.D.), Gareth (Bryher), Daniel (Macpherson), and the new figures, Saul Howard (Paul Robeson), Paula Howard (Essie Robeson), and Benny Mathews (Herring). The origins of this post-Jamesian sketch were self-consciously political, as H.D. defined the concept for herself. On May 13, 1930, H.D. wrote to Bryher: "Have been reading the Negro scandal too. Horrible, like all the others in time and plot. Virgin, black savage. Time something was done . . . am dragging a suggestion of that into my TWO AMERICANS as much as is compatible with my Deep Forest Dodona outlook." The "scandal" may have been the storm of abuse on Fleet Street after the publication of Cunard's "Black Man and White Ladyship," or more likely the kind of lynching cases to which H.D. referred in *Borderline* (34).[15] H.D.'s self-directed irony is telling. Given her persona as a "dendrophilic" dryad (*HER*, 63), a Cunard-type diatribe wouldn't "do." But H.D. clearly saw her type of psychological exploration in "Two Americans" as her attempt to "do something" about the racist formula: black-man-rapes-helpless-white-woman-and-deserves-to-be-lynched-to-protect-white-womanhood-and-keep-the-black-man-in-his-place. The intent, if not the technique, is didactic, political. Like *Borderline*, "Two Americans" is not "party politics," but its function is broadly political.[16]

As an answer to the formulaic plot of black man-white woman relations, "Two Americans" unfolds as a moment of intimacy between two complex human beings whose similarities are never allowed to obscure their differences. This intimacy is not based in erotic attraction, but rather in Raymonde's growing identification with Saul as an American and an artist. As the story opens, Raymonde is only aware of the great distance between herself and Saul: "their faces remained faces yet for all that, those faces had turned now forever into static symbols, they were mask on contrasting mask, the one white, the other as it happened, black. The two Americans faced each other in a crowded little living-room" (93). She begins to break through the racial mask in realizing that they are both exiled Americans, in Europe because in America they cannot practice their art. She, as a woman, found the greater freedom of a foreigner to break through a conventional feminine destiny. He, as a black, found greater freedom to sing and celebrate the music of his people. The racial masks whites and blacks wear in each other's company drop momentarily when Saul says to Raymonde that "Daniel is a lovely fellow" (93). Saul's praise for her lover, whom so many people dislike, leads Raymonde to describe how Daniel restored some of her faith in herself and art after the devastations of the Great War. This moment of truthful intimacy falls back into the conventional play of white and black masks when others interrupt: "The present day features struggled to re-adjust, to become one again with the eternal symbol. . . . She quickly tightened that mask, screwed, as it were, the flexible edges tighter" (96–97). The moment vanishes, but its residue of reflection produces healing identification.

Raymonde realizes that both have been "at war" with forces beyond their control. "That very so-Great War" had destroyed her personal life and certain sense of artistic direction; "for him, he had been always at war. They met in a field of honour, herself entirely defeated, himself yet to be acclaimed for some King-ship the world is not ready to recognize" (93–94). His "war" with racism, however, has not destroyed his power to sing:

> where he was complete, she was strikingly deficient. She was deficient, even, you might say, crippled in some psychic song-wing; his song flowed toward all

the world, effortless, full of benign power, without intellectual gap or cross-
purpose of hyper-critical consciousness to blight it. There was no swerving from
the beginning, the root, the entire deep in-rooted power of his gigantic Being.
(94)

"Crippled in some psychic song-wing," Raymonde is at least momentarily
healed by her exchange with Saul. Her lover Daniel is jealous. "I see," Daniel
tells Raymonde, "the man had an incredible fascination for you. . . . I can see
how you reach out to him" (107–108). But Raymonde knows that Daniel has
totally missed the point. Instead, what has happened in her brief conversation
with Saul is that she has regained a sense of her own power by identifying with
his. She recalls first seeing him in a play by Terence Deal [O'Neill], in which
he had said " 'I ain't no longer any poor white's chattel.' So he had worked out
a sort of circular state-gesture that, as he had demonstrated it, had shown her
all time, all slaves, all whites, all hunted and war-ridden creatures" (97).[17] In
the climax of the story, when Raymonde is reflecting on Saul's meaning for
her, she imaginatively puts herself in his place on stage: "Raymonde, self-
conscious, lost self; she revolved again; 'this is the way he said he moved when
the imaginary host of whites rises, off stage, in Deal's play.' She made the
circular gesture . . . Herself, seemed to have grown to some disproportion,
seemed to stand equal to him. If she could let go things fantastically in-grown,
she might yet be Saul Howard's equal" (110). As her series of meditations ends,
Raymonde sees herself "standing on the thin edge of something," now having
the power to call down the living divinity to earth, to hear the "messages," to
see "what is written" (112–113). Identification with Saul, the uncrowned king,
restores her sense of self and artistic direction.

Raymond's identification with Saul as a powerful symbol of resistance is made
possible by their personal exchange, not by a conventionally political morality.
But H.D.'s personal politics do not fall into the pitfall of denying the significance
of racial difference. Like the ironic suggestion of Hermione's white privilege
in *HER*, "Two Americans" exposes the covert racism of many progressive white
intellectuals and the psychic scars it leaves on the Howards. Before Benny
introduced Saul to his friends, they watched him sing "Ol' Man River" in *Show
Boat* and decided that he was "a light mulatto, as Gareth put it, 'one of those
Harvard niggers who talk English.' They had dismissed Saul Howard as a high-
brow sort of over-educated negro, who was descending out of some superior
idea of fashionable race-loyalty, to singing spirituals of the moment" (107).[18]
Raymonde is the first to break out of that racist dismissal in identifying with
him as an American exiled in Europe. The others follow suit in the course of
meeting Saul personally. Their stereotype disproven, "they were so many somewhat rain-drenched butterflies, opening wings in his presence" (100).

But the Howards pay a price for being black in a white world, as H.D.

sensitively suggests. Saul's very power as a black artist depersonalizes him, makes him into an "eternal symbol, a public presence." Swayed by the "in-rooted power of his gigantic Being," Raymonde thinks, "He was really no person at all. . . . For her, the 'voice' was speaking. It spoke to the world, every gramophone window displayed Saul Howard's record. The voice spoke on everyone's wireless" (94). The seeming effortlessness and simplicity of his artist-ry on stage made it appear that he didn't "have to think things out" (97). But as their moment of intimacy makes clear, there is a person beneath the persona. "Nevertheless," Raymonde thinks, "with an astonishing analytical power, he did think. That was the odd thing about Saul Howard, he did think. He had a mind, a steadfast sort of burning, a thing that glowed like a whole red sunset or like a coal-mine, it was steady, a steady sort of warmth and heat, yet all the time intellectual" (98).[19]

Paula's price as a black woman is not the result of fame, but of her status as her husband's appendage, as her name "Paul-a" suggests. While no one in H.D.'s circle much liked Essie Robeson, H.D. defends her in "Two Americans." Although she dotes on her husband (she "must watch each twitch of muscle, must tabulate each little gesture," [100]), Saul wouldn't "in the least be where he is, acclaimed by everybody on everybody's wireless and in all the gramo-phone shops, if it weren't for Paula" (99). "The tragedy of Paula," Raymonde thinks, is that on her own, Paula "would be so far more interesting than most of their white friends." But by Saul's side, "she showed up horribly her defi-ciencies" (102). As Saul's wife, she must both manage his career and serve as his ornament, which led her into an imitation of Paris chic and a rejection of things black: "Paula was Paris, was striking, yet, all the time, she made it very clear that she was not to be confounded with that tribe who had given jazz to Europe. . . . [she] thought more as white folks, consistently, being more than half white" (98, 101). Whether or not H.D.'s portrait of Essie Robeson is ac-curate, "Two Americans" attempts to portray sympathetically the pressure on black women to meet white standards of beauty and femininity.[20]

H.D.'s "answer" to the conventional script of black man-white woman re-lations is to present a delicate moment of intimacy and identification that is distinctly not erotic. In "Red Roses for Bronze," H.D. allowed herself to ap-proach the erotic undertones of her feelings for Robeson by utterly disguising his identity and mythologizing their exchange. The speaker of the poem is a sculptor who finds solace for her aborted love in sculpting a bronze statue that she offers as tribute to her archetypal Lover. Where *Borderline* and "Two Americans" directly addressed the historical issues of race relations, the poem encodes these subjects, taking the moment out of historical time as H.D.'s lyrics always do. The only hint of race in the poem is the repetition of "bronze," a color H.D. had used to describe Mandy in *HER*, and a brief description of the Lover's hair: "your dark hair/ catches the light/ in serpent curves" (*Collected Poems*, 213). Such coding is characteristic of all H.D.'s poems about the men and women she knew and loved. Disguise made frank exposure possible. To reveal, she concealed. But the taboo against interracial love and desire probably intensified the need for disguise.

What is interesting about the poem is the way H.D. rewrites the conventional script of such a forbidden love so as to avoid the cycle of the white woman's expiation of racial guilt, possession of blackness, and ultimate masochistic fantasy. H.D. avoids this cycle by her reversal of the Pygmalion tradition. Pygmalion, the sculptor whose desire for the woman he carves brings her to life, possesses and controls what he creates. H.D.'s sculptor, in contrast, carves the Lover in order to "sate my wretched fingers in ecstatic work" (211). To fashion his face in bronze will bring her peace, will free her from the passion that cannot be fulfilled in life. Her emotions are strong, erotic, even violent. But H.D. subverts the implicit rape fantasies of both the conventional Pygmalion myth and the black man-white woman script. "Sensing underneath the garment seam,/ ripple, flash and gleam/ of indrawn muscle," the speaker doesn't imagine herself raped, but instead feels "that I must turn and tear and rip/ the fine cloth/ from moulded thigh and hip/ force you to grasp my soul's sincerity,/ and single out/ me,/ me/ something to challenge,/ handle differently" (212–13). Having toyed with the image of the woman-artist raping the Lover, H.D. turns the force of desire into a demand that the Lover step outside conventional erotics to see her as autonomous, unique. Recognizing that this kind of equal exchange will not happen, she refuses to join the crowd of (white) women who worship at his feet. Instead, she sublimates her desire, "jealousy, and hate" into the completion of her bronze statue. Consolation comes only in the thought that her tribute to "the tall god," her "red roses for bronze," will outlast the wilted flowers offered by his other lovers. "Red Roses for Bronze" is a poem in which H.D. explored her attraction for Robeson, her sense of companionship with him as an artist, and her refusal to participate in the masochistic cycle of interracial erotics.

Conclusions

H.D.'s open identification with, even disguised desire for, Robeson played an important role in the formation of her personal politics and modernism. In the black experience defined through the Harlem Renaissance and epitomized by Robeson, she found an eloquent mirror for her own marginality, her sense of spiritual exile and alienation. Her literary articulations of racial borderlines helped her to formulate the nature of her own borderline existence as a woman in a male literary tradition, as a bisexual woman in a heterosexual world, as an American exiled in Europe, as a pacifist shattered by war.

Race served this function in the origins of H.D.'s modernism at least partly because of her insistence on a politics that begins with the personal, with human relationships. Mandy in *HER*, Saul Howard in "Two Americans," and Pete in "Borderline" do not owe their existence to an abstract political conviction, to a white liberal's adoption of an oppressed people's cause. Instead, H.D.'s attempt to oppose and transcend racism through identification came directly out of personal experience. This focus on politics as it permeates the inner life is partially responsible for the degree to which H.D. avoided the exploitative objectification of blacks that characterized the fascination of so many wealthy white liberals involved in the Harlem Renaissance.

Identification with Otherness rather than a perpetuation of it was equally responsible for the sensitivity with which H.D. approached the subject of race. This process continued right through the thirties, even after the Robesons and Macpherson passed out of H.D.'s life. Her involvement with psychoanalysis carried with it a profound identification with Jews. She broke off her correspondence with Pound in 1933 because of his anti-Semitism, and to some extent aided Bryher with her massive efforts to gain papers and jobs for some hundred religious and political refugees. During the war, H.D. began researching her Moravian history, only to discover that this mystical sect had undergone centuries of persecution. To escape, her family had come to the New World, where their cooperative and peaceful relationships with the Indians were a startling contrast to other colonies. *The Gift*, H.D.'s autobiographical account of her Moravian heritage completed just before she began *Trilogy*, reflects extensive research on these Indians and a spiritual identification with the Indian leader who was buried in her family's cemetary in Bethlehem.[21]

H.D.'s deeply personal identification with marginalized groups did not begin with the Harlem Renaissance. It was already encoded in *Sea Garden* (1916), in which her distaste for the "sheltered garden" and her celebration of wild, scraggly, stunted sea roses were images of escape into a modernist green world beyond the confines of Victorian respectability and femininity. World War I remained for her the key event initiating her own Diaspora—"perhaps dispersion is the key-word. We were dispersed and scattered after War I," she wrote in *Notes on Recent Writing* (10). But the Harlem Renaissance deeply reinforced H.D.'s identification with the different and dispersed. Working through issues of race played a significant role in the development of her political syncretism, a modernism of the margins rather than the reactionary center. H.D.'s particular modernism developed out of her identification with all the others who have been "dispersed and scattered" by the forces of history: blacks, Jews, Indians, homosexuals and lesbians, women, even artists. "There is a legend," she recalled in relation to her own work in *Notes on Recent Writing*, "of a wandering Jew, of a hidden Church, or an unrecognized Divinity or of a reviled Humanity" (16). These constitute the "scattered remnant" with whom H.D. identified, with whom she would build her coral-shell community.

NOTES

I would like to thank Perdita Schaffner, H.D.'s literary executor; David Schoonover, Curator of the American Literature Collection at Beinecke Rare Book and Manuscript Library; and the Morris Library of Southern Illinois University for their generous permission in allowing me to quote from manuscript materials. I am also indebted to Michael King, Nellie McKay, Rachel Blau DuPlessis, Michael Hinden, Jane Marcus, and Wendy McCown for their suggestions.

Winifred Bryher's letters to H.D. and Kenneth Macpherson. Beinecke Rare Book and Manuscript Library, Yale University (hereafter Beinecke).

References to Hilda Doolittle's published and unpublished works include the following:

H.D. *Borderline—A Pool Film with Paul Robeson*. London: Mercury Press, 1930.
——. *Collected Poems, 1912–1944*. Ed. Louis Martz. New York: New Directions, 1984.
——. *End to Torment*. Ed. Norman Holmes Pearson and Michael King. New York: New Directions, 1979.
——. *The Gift*. New York: New Directions, 1982. Manuscript, Beinecke.
——. *The Hedgehog*. London: Brendin, 1936.
——. *Hermetic Definition*. New York: New Directions, 1972.
——. *HERmione*. New York: New Directions, 1981.
——. Letters to Bryher, Havelock Ellis, Viola Jordan, Robert McAlmon, Kenneth Macpherson. Beinecke.
——. Letters to Richard Aldingon. Morris Library, Southern Illinois University.
——. *Notes on Recent Writing* (1949). Unpublished manuscripts, Beinecke.
——. "The Suffragist." Unpublished manuscript, Beinecke.
——. *The Sword Went Out to Sea (Synthesis of a Dream)* (1946–1947). Unpublished manuscript, Beinecke.
——. "Two Americans" (1930). In *The Usual Star*. Dijon: Imprimerie Darantiere, 1934.

1. In *Diary* 11 (1934–1939), ed. Gunther Stulmann (New York: Harvest, Brace and World, 1967), Nin writes, "I don't believe man can be changed by outer systems. It has to come from within" (310). See also pp. 144–45, 152–55, 292–93, 309. H.D. probably knew Nin, for she wrote to Aldington, "Please remember me to Nin when you write" (February 15, late 1940s–early 1950s?).

2. For discussions of escapism, see Douglas Bush, *Mythology and the Romantic Tradition in English Poetry* (Cambridge, Mass.: Harvard University Press, 1937), pp. 497–506; E. B. Greenwood, "H.D. and the Problem of Escapism," *Essays in Criticism* 31 (1971), 365–76; Susan Stanford Friedman, "Who Buried H.D.? A Poet, The Critics and 'The Literary Tradition,' " *College English* 36 (March 1975), 801–14; Ian Hamilton, "At the Right Place at the Right Time," *Bookworld* (February 19, 1984), 3–4; R. Z. Sheppard, "The Astronomer's Daughter," *Time* (January 16, 1984), 71; Alfred Kazin,

"A Nymph of the New," *New York Review of Books* 31 (March 1984), 15–16. Kazin misses entirely the significance H.D. gives to Nazism in *Tribute to Freud* (16).

3. For a general discussion of politics and (male) modernists, see John R. Harrison, *The Reactionaries* (London: Victor Gollancz, 1966). E. M. Forster, whose novels record the break-up of the British class system and the Empire, is an important exception. In the U.S., another important exception is Eugene O'Neill, whose innovative plays often express a perspective based in his engagement with leftist, particularly anarchist, intellectuals and activists. See Winnifred L. Frazer, *E.G. and E.G.O.: Emma Goldman and The Iceman Cometh* (Gainsville: University Presses of Florida, 1974).

4. For feminist theoretical discussions of the role of the personal in definitions of the political, see Kate Millett, *Sexual Politics* (New York: Avon, 1969) and Sheila Rowbotham, *Woman's Consciousness, Man's World* (London: Penguin, 1973). Other feminist critics have already begun to revise the analysis of politics in women writers. See especially Jane Marcus, "Laughing at Leviticus: *Nightwood* as Woman's Circus Epic," in Mary Lynn Broe, ed., *Silence and Power: Djuna Barnes, A Revaluation* (Carbondale: University of Southern Illinois Press, 1986), and Marcus, ed. *New Feminist Essays on Virginia Woolf* (Lincoln: University of Nebraska Press, 1980), especially pp. xiii–xv, 1–30.

5. See Nathan Irvin Huggins, *Harlem Renaissance* (London: Oxford University Press, 1971); Jervis Anderson, *This Was Harlem: A Cultural Portrait* (New York: Farrar Straus, 1982); and David L. Lewis, *When Harlem Was In Vogue* (New York: Knopf, 1981). For discussions of the war's impact on improving women's status, see Sandra M. Gilbert, "Soldier's Heart: Literary Men, Literary Women, and the Great War," *Signs* 8 (Spring 1983), 422–50. Huggins argues that Toomer's *Cane* is the only seriously avant-garde work of the Harlem Renaissance. I would argue instead that the concept of the avant-garde has been too narrowly defined. Writers like Hughes and Hurston experimented with black English, music, and myth, linguistic and formal innovations that should be seen as Afro-American forms of the general modernist disruption of language, mythic systems, and conventional genre boundaries. See especially, Langston Hughes, *Montage of a Dream Deferred* (New York: Holt, 1951); Zora Neale Hurston, *Their Eyes Were Watching God* (Urbana: University of Illinois Press, 1978; orig. ed. 1937); and Cyrena N. Pondrom, "Hurston's *Their Eyes Were Watching God*: Powerful Black Expression of a Universal Myth," unpublished essay.

6. See Carl Van Vechten, *Nigger Heaven* (New York: Knopf, 1926). Van Vechten's 1938 photograph of Bryher (at Beinecke Library) suggests that the association continued for some time.

7. Hugh Ford, ed. *Nancy Cunard: Brave Poet, Indomitable Rebel, 1896–1965* (Philadelphia: Chilton, 1968), pp. 118–20.

8. See also Barbara Guest, *Herself Defined: The Poet H.D. and Her World* (New York: Doubleday, 1984), pp. 159–66; Noel Riley Fitch, *Sylvia Beach and the Lost Generation: A History of Literary Paris in the Twenties and Thirties* (New York: Norton, 1983), pp. 136–37, 298; Nancy Cunard, *Grand Man: Memories of Norman Douglas* (London: Secker and Warburg, 1954), pp. 16, 65–67, 283; and Winifred Bryher, *The Heart to Artemis: A Writer's Memoirs* (New York: Harcourt, Brace and World, 1962), pp. 202 ff. Anne Friedberg has also suggested to me that the large bracelets H.D. wore in *Wing-Beat* indirectly alluded to Cunard, whose African bracelets were her trademark. As late as 1950, H.D. was sending regular news of Cunard to McAlmon, who in turn sent H.D. Afro-American periodicals. H.D. also explained why she and Bryher did not see Cunard during the war: "we were simply swamped with people from the country and bombed-out friends; we couldn't cope with 'politics' " (February 24, 1949). The public nature of Cunard's political advocacies also did not appeal to Robert Herring, who wrote that Cunard's party for the Scottsboro defense was a "fiasco." "Quivering,"

she called for a vote he wrote H.D. disapprovingly, " 'WHO are the friends of the Negro?' " (Letter to H.D., April 1933). H.D.'s response also must have been critical because Herring next wrote, "She is too tied up with destruction. Her own draws her to that of others, and she gets some psychic recompense and reinforcement from each increasing the others. You were so right about her—that terrible combination of distinction and doom," perhaps a combination H.D. herself was seeking to avoid in refusing public activism (May 6–7, 1933).

9. For discussions of the film, see Guest, pp. 196–201; Dorothy Butler Gilliam, *Paul Robeson: All American* (Washington, D. C.: New Republic, 1976), p. 61; Susan Robeson, *The Whole World In His Hands: A Pictorial Biography of Paul Robeson* (Secaucus N.J.: Citadel Press, 1981), p. 64; Freedomways, eds. *Paul Robeson: The Great Forerunner* (New York: Dodd, Mead, 1965), p. 73; Bryher, *The Heart to Artemis*, pp. 261–62; Anne Friedberg, "Approaching *Borderline*," *Millenium Film Journal* (Fall–Winter 1980–1981), 130–39; and Adalaide Morris, "The Concept of Projection: H.D.'s Visionary Powers," *Contemporary Literature* 25 (Winter 1984), 411–36. The film itself is kept at the George Eastman House (Rochester, New York) and has been shown several times in recent years. The Museum of Modern Art (New York) has fragments from both *Wing-Beat* and *Foothills* (1928); the originals are lost.

10. See Gilliam, p. 62. In a letter to H.D., Bryher reported that she was paying the London analyst Mary Chadwick for Paul, Jr. (May 11, 1932). The letters of H.D., Bryher, Herring, and Macpherson contain frequent references to the Robesons until 1935.

11. For H.D.'s superposition of different men onto each other and the projection of a composite figure into her art, see Rachel Blau DuPlessis, "Romantic Thralldom in H.D.," *Contemporary Literature* 20 (Summer 1979), 178–203; Albert Gelpi, "Hilda in Egypt," *The Southern Review* 18 (Spring 1982), 233–50; and Susan Stanford Friedman, *Psyche Reborn: The Emergence of H.D.* (Bloomington: Indiana University Press, 1981), pp. 37–38, 147–48.

12. Alice Walker, *Meridian* (New York: Harcourt Brace Jovanovich, 1976); Alice Walker, *In Search of Our Mothers' Gardens: Womanist Prose* (New York: Harcourt Brace Jovanovich, 1983), pp. 83–118; Eldridge Cleaver, *Soul on Ice* (New York: Delta, 1968), pp. 155–210; Michelle Wallace, *Black Macho and the Myth of the Super Woman* (New York: Dial Press, 1978).

13. For extended analysis of *Her*'s bisexual narrative, see Susan Stanford Friedman and Rachel Blau DuPlessis, " 'I Had Two Loves Separate': The Sexualities of H.D.'s *Her*," *Montemora* 8 (1981), 3–30.

14. Alice Childress, *Like One of the Family* (New York: Independence Publishers, n. d.).

15. *The New York Times*, to which Bryher subscribed, lengthily reported on mob violence in Sherman, Texas (May 10, 1930, 1: 8). A mob burned down the Grayson County Court House, which contained George Hughes, a black man locked in a vault and accused of raping a white woman.

16. H. D. also wrote to Viola Jordan about the political origins of *The Hedgehog* (1936), ostensibly a children's tale. In 1925, she was asked to do a " 'peace' and 'war-orphan' book," but she was told her manuscript was "too mystical." She dropped the project until 1935.

17. Terrence Deal is most certainly Eugene O'Neill, who wrote two plays in the twenties based on Afro-American experience and white racism: *The Emperor Jones* (1920) and *All God's Chillun Got Wings* (1924). Although not about race, his experiments with masks in *The Great God Brown* (1925) may have influenced the elaborate metaphors of white and black masks in "Two Americans." Michael Hinden has suggested to me that Raymonde's memory of Saul on stage is probably a free adaptation of Scene V in *The Emperor Jones*, in which Robeson acted to rave reviews in September 1925, in

London. In this scene, Jones is alone in a clearing, standing on top of a stump that becomes in the mime of the play an auction block surrounded by Southern planters before the Civil War. Much like H.D.'s adaptation, the scene recounts Jones's trans-formation from paralyzed terror to powerful rebellion: "What you all doin', white folks? What's all dis? What you all lookin' at me fo'? What you doin' wid me, anyhow? (*Suddenly convulsed with raging hatred and fear.*) Is dis a auction? Is you sellin' me like dey uster befo' de war? (*Jerking out his revolver just as the AUCTIONEER knocks him down to one of the planters—glaring from him to the purchaser.*) And *you* sells me? And *you* buys me? I shows you I'se a free nigger, damn yo' souls! (*He fires at the AUCTIONEER and at the PLANTER . . .*). Eugene O'Neill, *The Emperor Jones* (1920) in Sylvan Barnet et al., eds. *Types of Drama: Plays and Essays* (Boston: Little, Brown and Co., 1972), p. 41.

18. H.D. may have deliberately echoed Herring's letter, in which he reported that Essie had a petrol shampoo for hair straightening, fainted, and arrived two hours late to meet Bryher, who was "very high-hat about these uppity negroes" (1930?). Herring's many references to blacks throughout the period show considerable disdain for whites whose trips to Harlem are "like looking at monkeys" (1933?). Herring's repeated sen-sitivity to white exploitation of Harlem artists in letters to H.D. supports the view that her exposure of racism in "Two Americans" was deliberate.

19. H.D.'s portrait of Robeson trapped in his public persona reflects several letters Herring wrote to her on this account. In 1933, when Herring was seeing a great deal of Robeson, he wrote about occasional glimpses beneath Robeson's "grave and majestic" surface. For example, "the night I went to say good-bye, he was pre-occupied, and I had once before said he always made one take him so seriously and he said he wished I wouldn't, everyone took him seriously and wouldn't let him play. So when I found him pre-occupied, I said, 'Don't be so reverend, Paul,' and he said extremely sadly, 'I think I always am rather reverend with myself, Buddy' " (May 6–7, 1933). See Paul Robeson, *Here I Stand* (Boston: Beacon Press, 1958); Philip S. Foner, ed. *Paul Robeson Speaks: Writings, Speeches, Interviews, 1918–1974* (New York: Brunner, 1978).

20. H.D.'s description of Essie Robeson is strikingly like the photo in Gilliam and Gilliam's own interpretation of her character.

21. Not published in the highly edited New Directions version of *The Gift* (1982) are H.D.'s "Notes," ninety-four pages which include an extensive account of the contact between the Moravians and various Indian tribes, as well as her assertion that their mutual influence emerged from a bond built on recognition of mutual bondage. For H.D.'s anger with Pound's anti-Semitism, see her letters to Viola Jordan (May 1, 1941 and April 23, 1945) and *End to Torment*, p. 34.

CONTRIBUTORS

NINA AUERBACH
is author of *Communities of Women: An Idea in Fiction; Woman and the Demon: The Life of a Victorian Myth*; and *Romantic Imprisonment: Women and Other Glorified Outcasts*. She is presently writing a study of the Victorian actress Ellen Terry.

NINA BAYM is Professor of English and Director of the School of Humanities at the University of Illinois, Urbana-Champaign. She is the author of *Novels, Readers, and Reviewers: Responses to Fiction in Antebellum America; Woman's Fiction: A Guide to Novels by and about Women in America, 1820–1870*; and *The Shape of Hawthorne's Career*. Of particular interest to readers of this collection is her "Melodramas of Beset Manhood: How Theories of American Fiction Exclude Women Authors," published in the *American Quarterly*. She is also editor of the *Norton Anthology of American Literature*.

SHARI BENSTOCK is Associate Professor of English at the University of Miami. She is the co-author of *Who's He When He's at Home: A James Joyce Directory*, author of *Women of the Left Bank: Paris, 1900–1940*; editor of *The Private Self: Theory and Practice in Women's Autobiographical Writings* (forthcoming). She is the former editor of *Tulsa Studies in Women's Literature*. Author of "From Letters to Literature: *La Carte Postale* in the Epistolary *Genre*," (in *Genre*, fall 1985), she is currently working in genre theory.

JOSEPHINE DONOVAN is the author of *Feminist Theory: The Intellectual Traditions of American Feminism; New England Local Color Literature: A Woman's Tradition; Sarah Orne Jewett*, and the editor of *Feminist Literary Criticism: Explorations in Theory*.

ELIZABETH FOX-GENOVESE is Professor of History and Director of the Women's Studies Program at Emory University. She is the co-author of *The Origins of Physiocracy*; author of *Fruits of Merchant Capital*; and she has edited and translated *The Autobiography of P. S. DuPont de Nemours*. She is author of *Southern Women, Black and White* (forthcoming).

SUSAN STANFORD FRIEDMAN is Professor of English and Women's Studies at the University of Wisconsin, Madison. She is author of *Psyche Reborn: The Emergence of H. D.* and co-author of *A Woman's Guide to Therapy*. She is currently completing a study of H. D.'s prose writings and is editing a volume of letters between Bryher and H.D., 1933–1934, about Freud. Her essay, "Gender and Genre Anxiety: Elizabeth Barrett Browning and H. D. as Epic Poets," was published in *Tulsa Studies in Women's Literature* 5,2 (1986).

JUDITH KEGAN GARDINER teaches courses in English literature and Women's Studies at the University of Illinois at Chicago. She has published a book and essays on English Renaissance literature, contemporary women writers, and feminist theory. She is also author of *The Hero as her Author's Daughter: Jean Rhys, Christina Stead, Doris Lessing* (forthcoming).

JANE MARCUS is Professor of English and Women's Studies at the City College of New York. She has edited three collections of essays on Virginia Woolf, and *The Young Rebecca West*. She is also the author of *Virginia Woolf and the Languages of Patriarchy*.

JUDITH NEWTON is author of *Women, Power, and Subversion: Social Strategies in Women's Fiction, 1780–1860* and *Sex and Class in Women's History*, and co-editor of *Feminist Criticism and Social Change: Sex, Class, and Race in Literature and Culture*. Her current work in progress includes *Victorian Women/Victorian Men: Gender, Sexuality and Class in the 1840s*.

LILLIAN S. ROBINSON is an Affiliated Scholar at Stanford University's Center for Research on Women. She is the author of *Sex, Class, and Culture* (reprinted this year by Methuen) and co-author of *Feminist Scholarship: Kindling in the Groves of Academe*, and *Monstrous Regiment* (forthcoming). Her essay, "Treason Our Text: Feminist Challenges to the Literary Canon," was published in *Tulsa Studies in Women's Literature* 2, 1 (1983) and has been reprinted in Elaine Showalter, ed., *The New Feminist Criticism*, and is scheduled for reprinting in Adams and Poole, eds., *Literary Theory Since 1965* (forthcoming). Its companion piece, "Their Canon, Our Arsenal," is published in the Stanford CROW Working Papers (No. 21, 1985).

ELAINE SHOWALTER is Professor of English at Princeton University. Her publications include *A Literature of Their Own: Women Novelists from Brontë to Lessing* and *The Female Malady: Women, Madness, and Culture*. She is editor of *Writing and Sexual Difference* and an anthology, *The New Feminist Criticism: Essays on Women, Literature, and Theory*. She has contributed numerous essays to books on Victorian literature, women writers, and feminist criticism.

HORTENSE J. SPILLERS is Associate Professor of English at Haverford College. She is the author of *Chosen Place, Timeless People: Some Figurations on the New World* and *Conjuring: Black Women, Fiction, and Literary Tradition*. She has published various articles on black women writers.

CATHARINE R. STIMPSON is Dean of the Graduate School and Director of the Institute for Research on Women at Rutgers University, New Brunswick. She is currently editor of a book series for University of Chicago Press and was the founding editor of *Signs: Journal of Women in Culture and Society*. She is the author of a novel, *Class Notes*; the editor of six books; and has published more than 75 monographs, short stories, essays, and reviews. She now serves as Chair of the New York State Council for the Humanities; of the *Ms. Magazine* Board of Scholars; and of the National Council for Research on Women. Her book on Gertrude Stein and cultural change is under contract to the University of Chicago Press.

PAULA A. TREICHLER is Assistant Professor in the College of Medicine and the Institute for Communications Research, University of Illinois at Urbana-Champaign. She is co-author of *A Feminist Dictionary: In Our Own Words* and co-editor of *For Alma Mater: Theory and Practice in Feminist Scholarship.* She co-edits the interdisciplinary research publication, *Women and Language.* The essay in this collection is part of a larger work on language and women's writing that includes published essays on Kate Chopin and Dorothy Parker.

INDEX